C000070333

MICROSOFT OFFICE · Microsoft® Office · USER SPECIALIST

APPROVED COURSEWARE

Step by by Step Courseware

Microsoft® **Word** 2000

Microsoft Office Application

Core Skills Student Guide

/Active**Education**™

PUBLISHED BY
Microsoft Press
A Division of Microsoft Corporation
One Microsoft Way
Redmond, Washington 98052-6399

Copyright © 2000 by ActiveEducation, Inc.

Library of Congress Cataloging-in-Publication Data
Microsoft Word 2000 Step by Step Courseware Core Skills Student Guide / ActiveEducation.
        p. cm.
    Includes index.
    ISBN 0-7356-0699-4 (4 color) -- ISBN 0-7356-0978-0 (1 color)
    1. Microsoft Word.   2. Word processing. I. ActiveEducation (Firm)
Z52.5.M52 M496   2000
652.5'5369--dc21   99-044098

Printed and bound in the United States of America.

1 2 3 4 5 6 7 8 9   WCWC   5 4 3 2 1 0

Distributed in Canada by Penguin Books Canada Limited.

A CIP catalogue record for this book is available from the British Library.

Microsoft Press books are available through booksellers and distributors worldwide. For further information about international editions, contact your local Microsoft Corporation office or contact Microsoft Press International directly at fax (425)
936-7329. Visit our Web site at mspress.microsoft.com.

For ActiveEducation:
Managing Editor: Ron Pronk
Series Editor: Kate Dawson
Project Editor: Carrice L. Cudworth
Writers: Ron Pronk, Lori Bottom
Production/Layout: Nicole C. French, Craig K. Wise,
 Linda Savell, Tracey Varnell
Technical Editor: Jennifer Jordan
Proofreader: Nicole C. French
Indexer: Lisa Probasco

For Microsoft Press:
Project Editors: Jenny Moss Benson,
 Kristen Weatherby
Acquisitions Editor: Susanne M. Forderer

Contents

Course Overview

Welcome to the *Step by Step Courseware* series for Microsoft Office 2000 and Microsoft Windows 2000 Professional. This series facilitates classroom learning, letting you develop competence and confidence in using an Office application or operating system software. In completing courses taught with *Step by Step Courseware*, you learn to use the software productively and discover how to make the software work for you. This series addresses core-level and expert-level skills in Microsoft Word 2000, Microsoft Excel 2000, Microsoft Access 2000, Microsoft Outlook 2000, Microsoft FrontPage 2000, and Microsoft Windows 2000 Professional.

The *Step by Step Courseware* series provides:

- A time-tested, integrated approach to learning.
- Task-based, results-oriented learning strategies.
- Exercises based on business scenarios.
- Complete preparation for Microsoft Office User Specialist (MOUS) certification.
- Attractive student guides with full-featured lessons.
- Lessons with accurate, logical, and sequential instructions.
- Comprehensive coverage of skills from the basic to the expert level.
- Review of core-level skills provided in expert-level guides.
- A CD-ROM with practice files.

A Task-Based Approach Using Business Scenarios

The *Step by Step Courseware* series builds on the strengths of the time-tested approach that Microsoft developed and refined for its Step by Step series. Even though the Step by Step series was created for self-paced training, instructors have long used it in the classroom. For the first time, this popular series has been adapted specifically for the classroom environment. By studying with a task-based approach, you learn more than just the features of the software. You learn how to accomplish real-world tasks so that you can immediately increase your productivity using the software application.

The lessons are based on tasks that you might encounter in the everyday work world. This approach allows you to quickly see the relevance of the training. The task-based focus is woven throughout the series, including lesson organization within each unit, lesson titles, and scenarios chosen for practice files.

An Integrated Approach to Training

The *Step by Step Courseware* series distinguishes itself from other series on the market with its consistent delivery and completely integrated approach to learning across a variety of print and online training media. With the addition of the *Step by Step Courseware* series, which supports classroom instruction, the *Step by Step* training suite now provides a flexible and unified training solution.

Print-Based Self-Training in the Step by Step Training Suite

The proven print-based series of stand-alone *Step by Step* books has consistently been the resource that customers choose for developing software skills on their own.

Online Training in the Step by Step Training Suite

For those who prefer online training, the *Step by Step Interactive* products offer highly interactive online training in a simulated work environment, complete with graphics, sound, video, and animation delivered to a single station (self-contained installation), local area network (LAN), or intranet. *Step by Step Interactive* has a network administration module that allows a training manager to track the progress and quiz results for students using the training. For more information, see *mspress.microsoft.com*.

Preparation for Microsoft Office User Specialist (MOUS) Certification

This series has been certified as approved courseware for the Microsoft Office User Specialist certification program. Students who have completed this training are prepared to take the related MOUS exam. By passing the exam for a particular Office application, students demonstrate proficiency in that application to their employers or prospective employers. Exams are offered at participating test centers. For more information, see *www.mous.net*.

A Sound Instructional Foundation

All products in the *Step by Step Courseware* series apply the same instructional strategies, closely adhering to adult instructional techniques and reliable adult learning principles. Lessons in the *Step by Step Courseware* series are presented in a logical, easy-to-follow format, helping you find information quickly and learn as efficiently as possible. To facilitate the learning process, each lesson follows a consistent structure.

Designed for Optimal Learning

The following "Lesson Features" section shows how the colorful and highly visual series design makes it easy for you to see what to read and what to do when practicing new skills.

Lessons break training into easily assimilated sessions. Each lesson is self-contained, and lessons can be completed in sequences other than the one presented in the table of contents. Sample files for the lessons don't depend on completion of other lessons. Sample files within a lesson assume only that you are working sequentially through a complete lesson.

The *Step by Step Courseware* series features:

- **Lesson objectives.** Objectives clearly state the instructional goals for each lesson so that you understand what skills you will master. Each lesson objective is covered in its own section, and each section or topic in the lesson is covered in a consistent way. Lesson objectives preview the lesson structure, helping you grasp key information and prepare for learning skills.

- **Informational text for each topic.** For each objective, the lesson provides easy-to-read, technique-focused information.

- **Hands-on practice.** Numbered steps give detailed, step-by-step instructions to help you learn skills. The steps also show results and screen images to match what you should see on your computer screen. The accompanying CD contains sample files used for each lesson.

- **Full-color illustrations in color student guides.** Illustrated screen images give visual feedback as you work through exercises. The images reinforce key concepts, provide visual clues about the steps, and give you something to check your progress against.

- **MOUS icon.** Each section or sidebar that covers a MOUS certification objective has a MOUS icon in the margin at the beginning of the section. The number of the certification objective is also listed.

- **Tips.** Helpful hints and alternate ways to accomplish tasks are located throughout the lesson text.

- **Important.** If there is something to watch out for or something to avoid, this information is added to the lesson and indicated with this heading.

- **Sidebars.** Sidebars contain parenthetical topics or additional information that you might find interesting.

- **Margin notes.** Margin notes provide additional related or background information that adds value to the lesson.

- **Button images in the margin.** When the text instructs you to click a particular button, an image of the button and its label appear in the margin.

- **Lesson Glossary.** Terms with which you might not be familiar are defined in the glossary. Terms in the glossary appear in boldface type within the lesson and are defined upon their first use within lessons.

- **Quick Quiz.** You can use the short-answer Quick Quiz questions to test or reinforce your understanding of key topics within the lesson.

Lesson Features

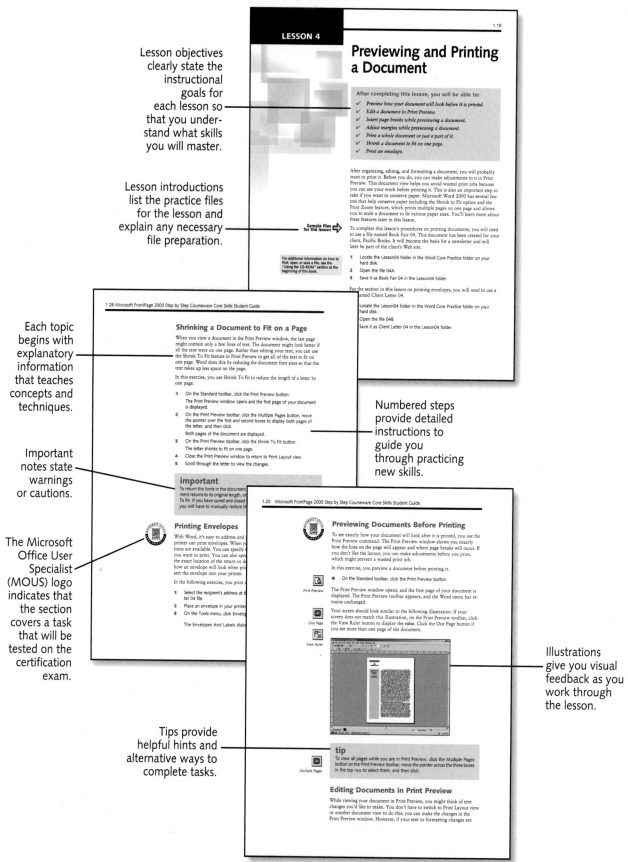

Lesson objectives clearly state the instructional goals for each lesson so that you under-stand what skills you will master.

Lesson introductions list the practice files for the lesson and explain any necessary file preparation.

Each topic begins with explanatory information that teaches concepts and techniques.

Important notes state warnings or cautions.

The Microsoft Office User Specialist (MOUS) logo indicates that the section covers a task that will be tested on the certification exam.

Tips provide helpful hints and alternative ways to complete tasks.

Numbered steps provide detailed instructions to guide you through practicing new skills.

Illustrations give you visual feedback as you work through the lesson.

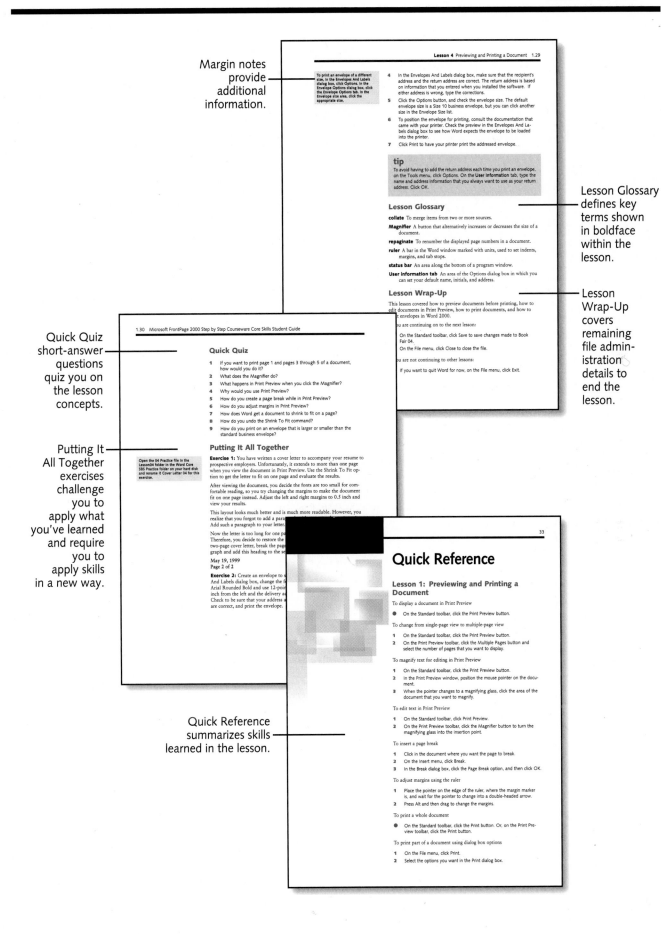

Margin notes provide additional information.

Lesson Glossary defines key terms shown in boldface within the lesson.

Lesson Wrap-Up covers remaining file administration details to end the lesson.

Quick Quiz short-answer questions quiz you on the lesson concepts.

Putting It All Together exercises challenge you to apply what you've learned and require you to apply skills in a new way.

Quick Reference summarizes skills learned in the lesson.

Lesson 4 Previewing and Printing a Document 1.29

To print an envelope of a different size, in the Envelopes And Labels dialog box, click Options. In the Envelope Options dialog box, click the Envelope Options tab. In the Envelope size area, click the appropriate size.

4   In the Envelopes And Labels dialog box, make sure that the recipient's address and the return address are correct. The return address is based on information that you entered when you installed the software. If either address is wrong, type the corrections.

5   Click the Options button, and check the envelope size. The default envelope size is a Size 10 business envelope, but you can click another size in the Envelope Size list.

6   To position the envelope for printing, consult the documentation that came with your printer. Check the preview in the Envelopes And Labels dialog box to see how Word expects the envelope to be loaded into the printer.

7   Click Print to have your printer print the addressed envelope.

tip
To avoid having to add the return address each time you print an envelope, on the Tools menu, click Options. On the **User Information** tab, type the name and address information that you always want to use as your return address. Click OK.

Lesson Glossary

collate To merge items from two or more sources.

Magnifier A button that alternatively increases or decreases the size of a document.

repaginate To renumber the displayed page numbers in a document.

ruler A bar in the Word window marked with units, used to set indents, margins, and tab stops.

status bar An area along the bottom of a program window.

User information tab An area of the Options dialog box in which you can set your default name, initials, and address.

Lesson Wrap-Up

This lesson covered how to preview documents before printing, how to edit documents in Print Preview, how to print documents, and how to print envelopes in Word 2000.

If you are continuing on to the next lesson:

On the Standard toolbar, click Save to save changes made to Book Fair 04.

On the File menu, click Close to close the file.

If you are not continuing to other lessons:

If you want to quit Word for now, on the File menu, click Exit.

1.30   Microsoft FrontPage 2000 Step by Step Courseware Core Skills Student Guide

Quick Quiz

1   If you want to print page 1 and pages 3 through 5 of a document, how would you do it?

2   What does the Magnifier do?

3   What happens in Print Preview when you click the Magnifier?

4   Why would you use Print Preview?

5   How do you create a page break while in Print Preview?

6   How do you adjust margins in Print Preview?

7   How does Word get a document to shrink to fit on a page?

8   How do you undo the Shrink To Fit command?

9   How do you print on an envelope that is larger or smaller than the standard business envelope?

Putting It All Together

Open the 04 Practice file in the Lesson04 folder in the Word Core SBS Practice folder on your hard disk and rename it Cover Letter 04 for this exercise.

Exercise 1: You have written a cover letter to accompany your resume to prospective employers. Unfortunately, it extends to more than one page when you view the document in Print Preview. Use the Shrink To Fit option to get the letter to fit on one page and evaluate the results.

After viewing the document, you decide the fonts are too small for comfortable reading, so you try changing the margins to make the document fit on one page instead. Adjust the left and right margins to 0.5 inch and view your results.

This layout looks much better and is much more readable. However, you realize that you forgot to add a para[...] Add such a paragraph to your letter[...]

Now the letter is too long for one pa[...] Therefore, you decide to restore the [...] two-page cover letter, break the pag[...] graph and add this heading to the se[...]

May 19, 1999
Page 2 of 2

Exercise 2: Create an envelope to [...] And Labels dialog box, change the f[...] Arial Rounded Bold and use 12-poin[...] inch from the left and the delivery a[...] Check to be sure that your address a[...] are correct, and print the envelope.

33

Quick Reference

Lesson 1: Previewing and Printing a Document

To display a document in Print Preview

●   On the Standard toolbar, click the Print Preview button.

To change from single-page view to multiple-page view

1   On the Standard toolbar, click the Print Preview button.

2   On the Print Preview toolbar, click the Multiple Pages button and select the number of pages that you want to display.

To magnify text for editing in Print Preview

1   On the Standard toolbar, click the Print Preview button.

2   In the Print Preview window, position the mouse pointer on the document.

3   When the pointer changes to a magnifying glass, click the area of the document that you want to magnify.

To edit text in Print Preview

1   On the Standard toolbar, click Print Preview.

2   On the Print Preview toolbar, click the Magnifier button to turn the magnifying glass into the insertion point.

To insert a page break

1   Click in the document where you want the page to break.

2   On the Insert menu, click Break.

3   In the Break dialog box, click the Page Break option, and then click OK.

To adjust margins using the ruler

1   Place the pointer on the edge of the ruler, where the margin marker is, and wait for the pointer to change into a double-headed arrow.

2   Press Alt and then drag to change the margins.

To print a whole document

●   On the Standard toolbar, click the Print button. Or, on the Print Preview toolbar, click the Print button.

To print part of a document using dialog box options

1   On the File menu, click Print.

2   Select the options you want in the Print dialog box.

■ **Putting It All Together exercises.** These exercises give you another opportunity to practice skills that you learned in the lesson. Completing these exercises helps you to verify whether you understand the lesson, to reinforce your learning, and to retain what you have learned by applying what you have learned in a different way.

■ **Quick Reference.** A complete summary of steps for tasks taught in each lesson is available in the back of the guide. This is often the feature that people find most useful when they return to their workplaces. The expert-level guides include the references from the core-level guides so that you can review or refresh basic and advanced skills on your own whenever necessary.

■ **Index.** Student guides are completely indexed. All glossary terms and application features appear in the index.

Suggestions for Improvements

Microsoft welcomes your feedback on the *Step by Step Courseware* series. Your comments and suggestions will help us to improve future versions of this product. Please send your feedback to SBSCfdbk@microsoft.com.

Support requests for Microsoft products should not be directed to this alias. Please see "Using the CD-ROM" for information on support contacts.

Conventions and Features Used in This Book

This book uses special fonts, symbols, and heading conventions to highlight important information or to call your attention to special steps. For more information about the features available in each lesson, refer to the "Course Overview" section on page vii.

Convention	Meaning
Sample files for the lesson	This icon identifies the section that lists the files that the lesson will use and explains any file preparation that you need to take care of before starting the lesson.
If your hard disk uses a letter other than C, substitute the appropriate drive letter in place of C.	Notes in the margin area are pointers to information provided elsewhere in the workbook or provide brief notes related to the text or procedures.
2000 New!	This icon indicates a new or greatly improved feature in this version of the software product and includes a short description of what is new.
W2000.3.17	This icon indicates that the section where this icon appears covers a Microsoft Office User Specialist (MOUS) exam objective. The number below the icon is the MOUS objective number. For a complete list of the MOUS objectives, see the "MOUS Objectives" section on page xix.
tip	Tips provide helpful hints or alternative procedures related to particular tasks.
important	Importants provide warnings or cautions that are critical to exercises.
Save	When a toolbar button is referenced in the lesson, the button's picture and label are shown in the margin.
Alt+Tab	A plus sign (+) between two key names means that you must press those keys at the same time. For example, "Press Alt+Tab" means that you hold down the Alt key while you press Tab.
Boldface type	This formatting indicates text that you need to type Or It indicates a glossary entry that is defined at the end of the lesson.

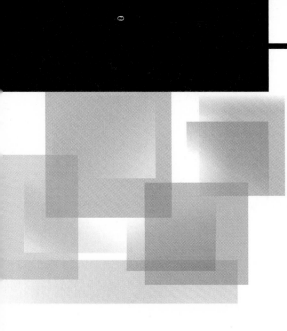

Using the CD-ROM

The CD-ROM included with this student guide contains the practice files that you'll use as you perform the exercises in the book. By using the practice files, you won't waste time creating the samples used in the lessons, and you can concentrate on learning how to use Microsoft Word 2000. With the files and the step-by-step instructions in the lessons, you'll also learn by doing, which is an easy and effective way to acquire and remember new skills.

The CD-ROM also includes a Microsoft Word file called Testbank.doc, which provides multiple-choice and true/false questions that you can use to test your knowledge following the completion of each lesson or the completion of the *Microsoft Word 2000 Step by Step Courseware Core Skills* course.

System Requirements

Your computer system must meet the following minimum requirements for you to install the practice files from the CD-ROM and to run Microsoft Word 2000.

> **important**
>
> The Word 2000 software is not provided on the companion CD-ROM at the back of this book. This course assumes that you have already purchased and installed Word 2000.

- A personal computer running Microsoft Word 2000 on a Pentium 75-megahertz (MHz) or higher processor with the Microsoft Windows 95 or later operating system with 24 MB of RAM, or the Microsoft Windows NT Workstation version 4.0 operating system with Service Pack 3 and 40 MB of RAM.

- At least 2 MB of available disk space (after installing Word 2000 or Microsoft Office 2000).

- A CD-ROM drive.

- A monitor with VGA or higher resolution (Super VGA recommended; 15-inch monitor or larger recommended).

- A Microsoft mouse, a Microsoft IntelliMouse, or other compatible pointing device.

If You Need to Install
or Uninstall the Practice Files

Your instructor might already have installed the practice files before you arrive in class. However, your instructor might ask you to install the practice files on your own at the start of class. Also, if you want to work through any of the exercises in this book on your own at home or at your place of business after class, you will need to first install the practice files.

To install the practice files:

1   Insert the CD-ROM in the CD-ROM drive of your computer.

A menu screen appears.

important

If the menu screen does not appear, start Windows Explorer. In the left pane, locate the icon for your CD-ROM, and click this icon. In the right pane, double-click the file StartCD.

2   Click Install Practice Files, and follow the instructions on the screen.

The recommended options are preselected for you.

3   After the files have been installed, click Exit.

A folder called Word Core Practice has been created on your hard disk, the practice files have been placed in that folder, and a shortcut to the Microsoft Press Web site has been added to your desktop.

4   Remove the CD-ROM from the CD-ROM drive.

Use the following steps when you want to delete the lesson practice files from your hard disk. Your instructor might ask you to perform these steps at the end of class. Also, you should perform these steps if you have worked through the exercises at home or at your place of business and want to work through the exercises again. Deleting the practice files and then reinstalling them ensures that all files and folders are in their original condition if you decide to work through the exercises again.

To uninstall the practice files:

1   On the Windows taskbar, click the Start button, point to Settings, and then click Control Panel.

2   Double-click the Add/Remove icon.

3   Click Word Core Practice in the list, and click Add/Remove. (If your computer has Windows 2000 Professional installed, click the Remove or the Change/Remove button.)

4   Click Yes when the confirmation dialog box appears.

Using the Practice Files

Each lesson in this book explains when and how to use any practice files for that lesson. The lessons are built around scenarios that simulate a real work environment, so you can easily apply the skills you learn to your own work. The scenarios in the lessons use the context of the fictitious Impact Public Relations, a public relations firm, and its client, Lakewood Mountains Resort, a hotel and convention center located in the mountains of California.

By default, Word 2000 places the Standard and Formatting toolbars on the same row below the menu bar to save space. To match the lessons and exercises in this book, the Standard and Formatting toolbars should be separated onto two rows before the start of this course. To separate the Standard and Formatting toolbars:

● Position the mouse pointer over the move handle at the beginning of the Formatting toolbar until it turns into the move pointer (a four-headed arrow), and drag the toolbar down until it appears on its own row.

The following is a list of all files and folders used in the lessons.

File Name	Description
Lesson02 - folder	Folder used in Lesson 2
Brochure 02	File used in Lesson 2
SkillCheck Lesson 02	File used in Putting It All Together
Lesson03 - folder	Folder used in Lesson 3
IPR January 00 Flyer 03	File used in Lesson 3
Lesson04 - folder	Folder used in Lesson 4
Brochure 04	File used in Lesson 4
Invitation 04	File used in Putting It All Together
Logo 04	File used in Lesson 4
Memorandum 04	File used in Lesson 4
Lesson05 - folder	Folder used in Lesson 5
Salary Survey 05	File used in Lesson 5
Lesson06 - folder	Folder used in Lesson 6
Letter 06	File used in Lesson 6
Logo 06	File used in Lesson 6
Lesson07 - folder	Folder used in Lesson 7
Brochure 07	File used in Lesson 7
Ruffles Article 07	File used in Putting It All Together
Lesson08 - folder	Folder used in Lesson 8
Tailspin Toys 08	File used in Lesson 8
Balloon	Graphic used in Lesson 8
Lesson09 - folder	Folder used in Lesson 9
Brochure 09	File used in Lesson 9
Industries Services 09	File used in Putting It All Together
Lesson10 - folder	Folder used in Lesson 10
Salary Survey 10	File used in Lesson 10
Lesson11 - folder	Folder used in Lesson 11
Brochure 11	File used in Lesson 11
Web Practice 11	File used in Putting It All Together

Replying to Install Messages

When you work through some lessons, you might see a message indicating that the feature that you are trying to use is not installed. If you see this message, insert the Microsoft Word 2000 CD or Microsoft Office 2000 CD 1 in your CD-ROM drive, and click Yes to install the feature.

Locating and Opening Files

After you (or your instructor) have installed the practice files, all the files you need for this course will be stored in a folder named Word Core Practice located on your hard disk. To navigate to this folder from within Word and open a file:

Open

1   On the Standard toolbar, click the Open button.

2   In the Open dialog box, click the Look In down arrow, and click the icon for your hard disk.

3   Double-click the Word Core Practice folder.

4   Double-click the file that you want to open.

All the files for the lessons appear within the Word Core Practice folder.

On the first page of each lesson, look for the margin icon *Sample files for the lesson*. This icon points to the paragraph that explains which files you will need to work through the lesson exercises.

If You Need Help with the Practice Files

If you have any problems regarding the use of this book's CD-ROM, you should first consult your instructor. If you are using the CD-ROM at home or at your place of business and need additional help with the practice files, see the Microsoft Press Support Web site at *mspress.microsoft.com/support*.

important

Please note that support for the Word 2000 software product itself is not offered through the above Web site. For help using Word 2000, rather than this Microsoft Press book, you can visit *www.microsoft.com/support* or call Word 2000 Technical Support at (425) 635-7070 on weekdays between 6 A.M. and 6 P.M. Pacific Standard Time. Microsoft Product Support does not provide support for this course.

MOUS Objectives

Core Skills

Objective	Activity	Page
W2000.1.1	Use the Undo, Redo, and Repeat command	2.9
W2000.1.2	Apply font formats (Bold, Italic, and Underline)	4.2
W2000.1.3	Use the SPELLING feature	7.4
W2000.1.4	Use the THESAURUS feature	7.8
W2000.1.5	Use the GRAMMAR feature	7.6
W2000.1.6	Insert page breaks	5.5
W2000.1.7	Highlight text in document	7.17
W2000.1.8	Insert and move text	2.7
W2000.1.9	Cut, Copy, Paste, and Paste Special using the Office Clipboard	4.7, 4.9, 4.11, 4.12
W2000.1.10	Copy formats using the Format Painter	6.11
W2000.1.11	Select and change font and font size	4.2
W2000.1.12	Find and replace text	7.10, 7.12
W2000.1.13	Apply character effects (superscript, subscript, strikethrough, small caps, and outline)	4.4
W2000.1.14	Insert date and time	7.18
W2000.1.15	Insert symbols	7.20
W2000.1.16	Create and apply frequently used text with AutoCorrect	7.14
W2000.2.1	Align text in paragraphs (Center, Left, Right, and Justified)	4.5
W2000.2.2	Add bullets and numbering	6.5, 6.6
W2000.2.3	Set character, line, and paragraph spacing options	5.6
W2000.2.4	Apply borders and shading to paragraphs	4.16, 4.19
W2000.2.5	Use indentation options (Left, Right, First Line, and Hanging Indent)	5.9
W2000.2.6	Use TABS command (Center, Decimal, Left, and Right)	5.10, 5.12
W2000.2.7	Create an outline style numbered list	6.7
W2000.2.8	Set tabs with leaders	5.12
W2000.3.1	Print a document	4.21
W2000.3.2	Use print preview	4.20
W2000.3.3	Use Web Page Preview	
W2000.3.4	Navigate through a document	2.3
W2000.3.5	Insert page numbers	5.16
W2000.3.6	Set page orientation	5.20

Objective	Activity	Page
W2000.3.7	Set margins	5.2, 5.3
W2000.3.8	Use GoTo to locate specific elements in a document	7.11
W2000.3.9	Create and modify page numbers	5.16
W2000.3.10	Create and modify headers and footers	5.17, 5.18
W2000.3.11	Align text vertically	5.5
W2000.3.12	Create and use newspaper columns	9.2
W2000.3.13	Revise column structure	9.6, 9.7
W2000.3.14	Prepare and print envelopes and labels	6.16, 6.18
W2000.3.15	Apply styles	4.14
W2000.3.16	Create sections with formatting that differs from other sections	4.4, 4.14
W2000.3.17	Use Click & Type	1.9
W2000.4.1	Use Save	1.10
W2000.4.2	Locate and open an existing document	2.2
W2000.4.3	Use Save As (different name, location, or format)	2.12, 2.13
W2000.4.4	Create a folder	2.11
W2000.4.5	Create a new document using a Wizard	3.7
W2000.4.6	Save as Web Page	11.9
W2000.4.7	Use templates to create a new document	3.2
W2000.4.8	Create hyperlinks	11.2
W2000.4.9	Use the Office Assistant	1.12
W2000.4.10	Send a Word document via e-mail	11.6
W2000.5.1	Create and format tables	10.2
W2000.5.2	Add borders and shading to tables	10.13, 10.14
W2000.5.3	Revise tables (insert and delete rows and columns, change cell formats)	10.2, 10.10
W2000.5.4	Modify table structure (merge cells, change height and width)	10.8, 10.12
W2000.5.5	Rotate text in a table	10.17
W2000.6.1	Use the drawing toolbar	8.13
W2000.6.2	Insert graphics into a document (WordArt, ClipArt, and Images)	8.1, 8.3, 8.8

Taking a Microsoft Office User Specialist Certification Test

The Microsoft Office User Specialist (MOUS) program is the only Microsoft-approved certification program designed to measure and validate your skills with the Microsoft Office suite of desktop productivity applications: Microsoft Word, Microsoft Excel, Microsoft PowerPoint, Microsoft Access, and Microsoft Outlook.

By becoming certified, you demonstrate to employers that you have achieved a predictable level of skills in the use of a particular Office application. Certification is often required by employers either as a condition of employment or as a condition of advancement within the company or other organization. The certification examinations are sponsored by Microsoft but administered through Nivo International.

For each Microsoft Office 2000 application, two levels of MOUS tests are currently or will soon be available: core and expert. For a core-level test, you demonstrate your ability to use an application knowledgeably and without assistance in a day-to-day work environment. For an expert-level test, you demonstrate that you have a thorough knowledge of the application and can effectively apply all or most of the features of the application to solve problems and complete tasks found in business.

Preparing to Take an Exam

Unless you're a very experienced user, you'll need to use a test preparation course to prepare to complete the test correctly and within the time allowed. The *Step by Step Courseware* training program is designed to prepare you for either core-level or expert-level knowledge of a particular Microsoft Office application. By the end of this course, you should have a strong knowledge of all exam topics, and with some additional review and practice on your own, you should feel confident in your ability to pass the appropriate exam.

After you decide which exam to take, review the list of objectives for the exam. This list can be found in the "MOUS Objectives" section at the front of the appropriate *Step by Step Courseware* student guide; the list of MOUS objectives for this book begins on page xvii. You can also easily identify tasks that are included in the objective list by locating the MOUS logo in the margin of the lessons in this book.

For an expert-level test, you'll need to be able to demonstrate any of the skills from the core-level objective list, too. Expect some of these core-level tasks to appear on the expert-level test. In the *Step by Step Courseware Expert Skills Student Guide*, you'll find the core skills included in the "Quick Reference" section at the back of the book.

You can also familiarize yourself with a live MOUS certification test by downloading and installing a practice MOUS certification test from *www.mous.net*.

To take the MOUS test, first see *www.mous.net* to locate your nearest testing center. Then call the testing center directly to schedule your test. The amount of advance notice you should provide will vary for different testing centers, and it typically depends on the number of computers available at the testing center, the number of other testers who have already been scheduled for the day on which you want to take the test, and the number of times per week that the testing center offers MOUS testing. In general, you should call to schedule your test at least two weeks prior to the date on which you want to take the test.

When you arrive at the testing center, you might be asked for proof of identity. A driver's license or passport is an acceptable form of identification. If you do not have either of these items of documentation, call your testing center and ask what alternative forms of identification will be accepted. If you are retaking a test, bring your MOUS identification number, which will have been given to you when you previously took the test. If you have not prepaid or if your organization has not already arranged to make payment for you, you will need to pay the test-taking fee when you arrive. The current test-taking fee is $50 (U.S.).

Test Format

All MOUS certification tests are live, performance-based tests. There are no multiple-choice, true/false, or short answer questions. Instructions are general: you are told the basic tasks to perform on the computer, but you aren't given any help in figuring out how to perform them. You are not permitted to use reference material other than the application's Help system.

As you complete the tasks stated in a particular test question, the testing software monitors your actions. An example question might be:

> Open the file named LMR Guests and select the word *Welcome* in the first paragraph. Change the font to 12 point, and apply bold formatting. Select the words *at your convenience* in the second paragraph, move them to the end of the first paragraph using drag and drop, and then center the first paragraph.

The sample tests available from *www.mous.net* give you a clear idea of the type of questions that you will be asked on the actual test.

When the test administrator seats you at a computer, you'll see an online form that you use to enter information about yourself (name, address, and other information required to process your exam results). While you complete the form, the software will generate the test from a master test bank and then prompt you to continue. The first test question will appear in a window. Read the question carefully, and then perform all the tasks stated in the test question. When you have finished completing all tasks for a question, click the Next Question button.

You have 45 to 60 minutes to complete all questions, depending on the test that you are taking. The testing software assesses your results as soon as you complete the test, and the results of the test can be printed by the test administrator so that you will have a record of any tasks that you performed incorrectly. A passing grade is 75 percent or higher. If you pass, you will receive a certificate in the mail within two to four weeks. If you do not pass, you can study and practice the skills that you missed and then schedule to retake the test at a later date.

Tips for Successfully Completing the Test

The following tips and suggestions are the result of feedback received by many individuals who have taken one or more MOUS tests:

- Make sure that you are thoroughly prepared. If you have extensively used the application for which you are being tested, you might feel confident that you are prepared for the test. However, the test might include questions that involve tasks that you rarely or never perform when you use the application at your place of business, at school, or at home. You must be knowledgeable in *all* the MOUS objectives for the test that you will take.

- Read each exam question carefully. An exam question might include several tasks that you are to perform. A partially correct response to a test question is counted as an incorrect response. In the example question on the previous page, you might apply bold formatting and move the words *at your convenience* to the correct location, but forget to center the first paragraph. This would count as an incorrect response and would result in a lower test score.

- You are allowed to use the application's Help system, but relying on the Help system too much will slow you down and possibly prevent you from completing the test within the allotted time. Use the Help system only when necessary.

- Keep track of your time. The test does not display the amount of time that you have left, so you need to keep track of the time yourself by monitoring your start time and the required end time on your watch or a clock in the testing center (if there is one). The test program displays the number of items that you have completed along with the total number of test items (for example, "35 of 40 items have been completed"). Use this information to gauge your pace.

- If you skip a question, you cannot return to it later. You should skip a question only if you are certain that you cannot complete the tasks correctly.

- Don't worry if the testing software crashes while you are taking the exam. The test software is set up to handle this situation. Find your test administrator and tell him or her what happened. The administrator will work through the steps required to restart the test. When the test restarts, it will allow you to continue where you left off. You will have the same amount of time remaining to complete the test as you did when the software crashed.

■   As soon as you are finished reading a question and you click in the application window, a condensed version of the instruction is displayed in a corner of the screen. If you are unsure whether you have completed all tasks stated in the test question, click the Instructions button on the test information bar at the bottom of the screen and then reread the question. Close the instruction window when you are finished. Do this as often as necessary to ensure you have read the question correctly and that you have completed all the tasks stated in the question.

If You Do Not Pass the Test

If you do not pass, you can use the assessment printout as a guide to practice the items that you missed. There is no limit to the number of times that you can retake a test; however, you must pay the fee each time that you take the test. When you retake the test, expect to see some of the same test items on the subsequent test; the test software randomly generates the test items from a master test bank before you begin the test. Also expect to see several questions that did not appear on the previous test.

LESSON 1

Getting Started with Word

After completing this lesson, you will be able to:

✔ *Start Word.*
✔ *Explore the Word window.*
✔ *Use menus.*
✔ *Use personalized menus.*
✔ *Enter text in a document.*
✔ *Insert text by using Click And Type.*
✔ *Save a document.*
✔ *Close a document and quit Word.*
✔ *Use the Office Assistant.*

Just a few years ago correspondance was created with paper and pencils, pens or typewriters. Gone are the days of correction fluid, crossed-out words, and wads of crumpled papers scattered around your garbage can. Today most personal and professional correspondence is created using computers. In fact, just about everyone who has used a computer has used a word-processing program.

With the help of Microsoft Word, you can quickly and easily create memos, faxes, reports, letters, charts, and newsletters. You can also add graphics to documents, use other Microsoft Office 2000 programs to import data into a Word document, and more. Not only is Word a convenient time-saver, but Word also allows you to check spelling and edit documents before printing. No longer do reports, letters, and other documents have to be completely retyped just because of an error or two. Word makes editing quick and leaves you with a very clean, professional-looking document (and saves you from emptying your garbage can so often).

In this lesson, you will learn how to start and quit Word and how to identify the various components in the Word window, such as the menu bar and **toolbar**. You'll use menus to perform various actions, you'll practice entering text into a document, and then you'll save a document. You'll also practice using the Office Assistant.

To complete the procedures in this lesson, you will create your own practice files.

A toolbar is a group of buttons used to carry out commands. For example, the Drawing toolbar contains buttons that you can use to draw and format pictures.

Sample files for the lesson

Starting Word

You start Word by clicking the Start button, which is at the left end of the Microsoft Windows **taskbar**. After you start Word, it appears in its own **window** with a new, blank **document** open. A window is an area of the screen that is used to display a program or document. Every window has common components, including scroll bars and toolbars. You'll learn more about the components of the Word window later in this lesson. A document is a self-contained piece of work created by using a program.

In other words, the Word window and each open document are displayed in separate windows. You can use Word to open multiple documents (therefore multiple document windows) at a time, you can resize a document window, and you can also **minimize** a document window. When you minimize a document window, the document window is reduced to a button on the Windows taskbar. The document is still open; you just can't see it.

The Word window contains graphical components to help you use the application, including menus, toolbars, and buttons. Becoming familiar with the components in the Word window will save you time when you begin creating and editing documents.

In this exercise, you use the Start button to open Word.

> The taskbar is the strip along the bottom of the screen. You use the mouse pointer to open applications on the taskbar.

1   Click the Start button at the left end of the Windows taskbar, which is located along the bottom of the screen.

The Start menu appears.

2   On the Start menu, point to Programs.

The Programs submenu appears.

3   On the Programs submenu, click Microsoft Word.

Word 2000 starts.

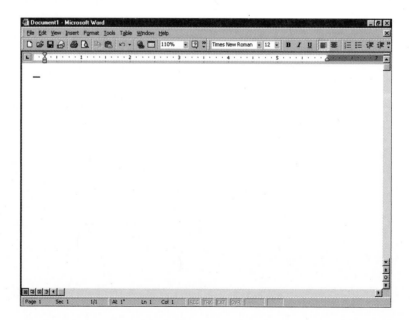

A desktop shortcut is represented by an icon with a curved arrow in the left corner. You can create a shortcut by right-clicking the desired button-icon and clicking Create Shortcut. The shortcut icon can be moved to the desktop by dragging the icon to the desktop.

tip

Rather than clicking the Start button, pointing to Programs, and clicking the program that you want to use, you can save time by creating a desktop shortcut. You simply double-click a shortcut icon to start its associated program. To create a desktop shortcut to Word, click the Start button, point to Programs, point to Microsoft Word, and hold down the Ctrl key while you drag the Microsoft Word icon to the desktop. Double-click the Word shortcut icon to open Word 2000.

Exploring the Word Window

Many components in the Word window are similar to those in other Windows programs. The following illustration displays the elements in the Word window, and a description of each element follows the figure.

Notice in this illustration that the Standard and Formatting toolbars are on separate lines to allow you to view them clearly.

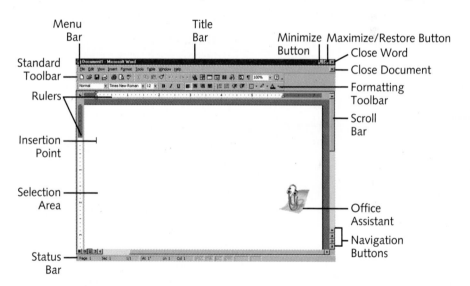

Office Assistant A feature that provides tips on how to accomplish tasks and suggests new features to try. By default, the Office Assistant appears as an animated paper clip, but it can take other shapes, too. (For more information about the Office Assistant, read the section "Using the Office Assistant," later in this lesson.)

Title bar The area of a window or dialog box that displays the name of the current dialog box or application and the name of the current document. It is located along the top of the window.

Menu bar The area that lists the names of the menus available in Word. A **menu** is a collection of related commands from which you can make a selection. The menu bar is located just below the title bar.

A button contains either a word, phrase, or an icon. An icon is a small picture that appears on the screen and represents a program or document.

Standard toolbar A toolbar that provides quick access to the editing functions you use frequently. For example, on the Standard toolbar, the **button** that you use to save a document contains an **icon** of a floppy disk. The Standard toolbar is located just below the menu bar.

By default, Word 2000 places the Standard and Formatting toolbars on the same row below the menu bar to save window space.

When the Standard and Formatting toolbars share one row, you can't see all the buttons, but you can access other buttons by clicking the More Buttons down arrow at the end of the toolbar.

More Buttons

You can position the Standard and Formatting toolbars on two separate rows. Position the mouse pointer over the move handle at the left end of the Formatting toolbar until it turns into the move pointer (a four-headed arrow), and drag the toolbar down a bit until it appears on its own row. (The vertical drag handle is a light gray vertical line that appears at the left side of each toolbar.)

Minimize

Maximize

Restore

×

Close

Formatting toolbar A toolbar that provides quick access to the formatting functions that you use frequently. The names of buttons are displayed in **ScreenTips** when you position the **mouse pointer** over the buttons.

Insertion point A blinking vertical line in the document window that indicates where the next **character** (any single letter, number, space, tab, page break, paragraph mark, or symbol that can be entered in a document) typed from the keyboard will appear.

Selection area The area between the left edge of the window and the left edge of a line of text. You position the mouse pointer in the selection area to select an entire line of text. The pointer changes to a right-pointing arrow when it is positioned in the selection area.

Ruler An on-screen scale marked with inches or other units of measure, which changes the indentation of paragraphs, resets a page margin (an area of blank space between the edge of the paper and the text), and adjusts the width of columns. The ruler is located below the toolbars.

Scroll bars Bars that are used for moving the view of the document. The vertical scroll bar is located along the right side of the window, and the horizontal scroll bar is located along the lower portion of the window, just above the status bar.

Navigation buttons Buttons that are used for moving the view in a long document. These buttons are located on the vertical scroll bar.

Status bar A bar that displays explanations of currently selected text at the bottom edge of the program window.

Minimize button A button that reduces a window to a button on the Windows taskbar. It appears as a button with a horizontal line and is located in the top-right corner of the window.

Maximize/Restore button A button that switches back and forth, or **toggles** (alternately turns an option on or off each time that the option is selected) between displaying a window in its maximum size and restoring a window to its previous size. It is located in the top-right corner of the window.

Close button A button that closes the current window or application. It is located in the top-right corner of the window.

ScreenTip A help item that shows the name of a button or screen element when you restthe mouse pointer on a toolbar button or screen element.

In this exercise, you display ScreenTips for a few buttons and screen elements to become more familiar with Word.

New Blank Document

1 Position the mouse pointer over the New Blank Document button for a few seconds, but don't click.

A small yellow ScreenTip appears, displaying the words *New Blank Document*.

Save

2 Position the mouse pointer over the Save button on the Standard toolbar.

A small yellow ScreenTip appears, displaying the word *Save*.

Previous Page

3 Position the mouse pointer on the lower portion of the vertical scroll bar, over the Previous Page button.

A ScreenTip appears when you position the pointer over the Previous Page button.

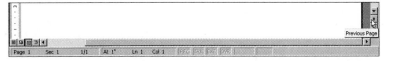

Next Page

4 Position the mouse pointer on the lower portion of the vertical scroll bar, over the Next Page button.

A ScreenTip appears when you position the pointer over the button.

OVR

Overtype

5 On the status bar, position the mouse pointer over the Overtype button.

A small yellow ScreenTip is shown, displaying the word *Overtype*.

In Overtype mode, existing text is deleted and replaced by the text you type. You can learn more about the Overtype button in Lesson 2, "Editing a Document."

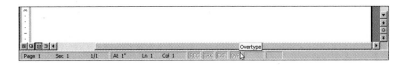

Using Menus

Menus display commands that you can click to perform an action in the active window or object. When you display the menu, you see various commands. To display a menu, on the menu bar, click the name of the menu. Then click a command displayed on the menu to perform that command. On some menus, you might find that certain selections appear in a light, almost unreadable shade. The lighter shade indicates that those commands are not applicable to the current operation and, therefore, are not available at that time. Those same selections will be displayed in a normal shade as soon as they become relevant to the operation being performed.

> You can easily find most of the tools and commands that you need on the Word menus and the Standard and Formatting toolbars.

When you first display a menu, you will see a short menu that displays the commands that are most frequently used by Word users. When you display a menu, various menu commands might show right-pointing arrows after the command. Hold the mouse pointer over the command with a right-pointing arrow to display the **cascading menu**.

> A cascading menu (or *submenu*) is a list of commands that appears as a result of pointing to a command on the main menu that has an arrow to the right of it. The submenu's commands are related to the command from which they are linked.

In this exercise, you display a menu.

1   On the menu bar, click View.

The View menu appears. Notice that the menu command Toolbars has an arrow to the right of it.

2   Point to Toolbars, but don't click.

The Toolbars cascading menu appears.

3   Click anywhere outside the menu.

The menu closes.

Using Personalized Menus

Word 2000 has a new feature that personalizes your menus. When you click a menu name on the menu bar, the menu is displayed, but not in its entirety. A short menu appears because those are the most popular commands used by most Microsoft users. Finding a menu command on a short menu is much easier and quicker than finding a menu command on an expanded menu.

> **2000**
> **New!**
>
> If a menu has been expanded, Word displays this command on the short menu. If you stop using the command over time, Word returns the command to the expanded menu.

Two downward pointing arrows are displayed on the bottom of the menu, alerting you that more menu commands are currently hidden. You click the double arrows to open the entire menu. After you select a command on the menu, and open the menu again, Word displays your selection on the menu, so you don't have to open the menu in its entirety to select that command again. Over time, Word adapts to your usage, and the commands that appear on the short menu are the commands that *you* most frequently use.

In this exercise, you personalize the Edit menu.

1   Click Edit on the menu bar to view the Edit menu.

The Edit menu appears.

> You can also view the expanded menu by holding the mouse pointer over the double arrows and waiting a few seconds for the expanded menu to appear.

2   Click the arrows at the bottom of the Edit menu to view the expanded menu.

The expanded Edit menu appears.

3   Click Go To.

The Go To **dialog box** appears.

> A dialog box is a screen element that appears when you need to communicate with a program. A dialog box provides a way for you to make decisions and select options.

4   Click the Close button in the Go To dialog box.

5   On the menu bar, click Edit again.

Notice that Go To is now displayed on the Edit menu. Word has personalized the Edit menu for you.

> You can turn off the personalized menus feature so that all commands appear all the time on the menus. On the Tools menu, click Customize, and then click the Options tab. Clear the Menus Show Recently Used Commands First check box, and click the Close button.

Entering Text

You begin creating a document by simply typing text. When you enter text into a document, you don't have to press Enter at the end of each line. Word's **word wrap** automatically wraps text from one line to the next each time the insertion point reaches the right margin. Word wrap breaks lines of text so that they stay within margin boundaries; you don't have to enter hard returns. You press Enter only when you want to begin a new paragraph or insert a blank line. Word uses left and right page margins of 1.25 inches and top and bottom margins of 1 inch by default; however, you can reset the page margins. You'll learn more about resetting margins in Lesson 5, "Changing the Layout of a Document."

Notice in the first illustration that the first three letters of the word *Public* are on the first line. In the second illustration, when the rest of the word has been typed, Word wraps the word to the second line.

Impact Public Relations was established in 1990 to provide a forum for professional Pub

To place the insertion point at the end of an existing line of text, click after the text that has been entered.

Impact Public Relations was established in 1990 to provide a forum for professional Public

As you type text, the insertion point moves, indicating the location for the next character. If you make a mistake, press Backspace to delete characters to the left of the insertion point or press Delete to delete characters to the right of the insertion point.

In this exercise, you enter text in a document to see how Word's word wrap feature works.

1   Type **Founded in 1990** into the blank document currently displayed in the window. (The blank document was displayed when you started Word.)

2   Type a comma, and press the Spacebar.

3   Continue typing the following:

Did you notice a red or green wavy line under your text? Don't worry. Word is just helping you proofread your document. Spelling and grammar checking are covered in Lesson 7, "Using Editing and Proofing Tools."

Impact Public Relations provides a forum for professional public relations consultants throughout the state to meet, to exchange views about general business issues, and to further individual skills development.

The text is displayed in the document window as you type, wrapping to the next line when the insertion point reaches the right margin.

Keep this file open for the next exercise.

W2000.3.17

Click And Type

Click And Type is available only in Print Layout view or Web Layout view. Your document must be displayed in Print Layout view for the next exercise. To verify that your document is in Print Layout view, or to change the view to Print Layout, on the View menu, click Print Layout.

Using Click And Type

Click And Type is a feature that you can use to quickly position the insertion point in any blank area of a document. You move the mouse pointer to the desired location in the blank document, click, and then begin typing. As you move the mouse pointer to different areas of the page, the mouse pointer shape indicates whether the text you type will be left-aligned, centered, or right-aligned. Click And Type is an especially useful feature if you want to start text centered on a line or on a page; you don't have to use the Center button to center text on a line, nor do you have to create blank lines to center a line on a page. You simply position the pointer where you want to begin typing text, and Word creates formatting and alignment attributes based on the location where you click.

Mouse Pointer	Aligns Text
I≡	Left.
I≝	Left with the first line indented.
I	Center.
≡I	Right.

For example, suppose you are in the middle of a multi-page document. You need to insert a list of names and add more text. Double-click the center of the blank area where you want to insert the text and type your list. Word applys center alignment to the text.

After you are finished entering the list, double-click in the left area of the document and type your additional text. Word applies left-alignment to the text.

In this exercise, you use Click And Type to insert a centered subtitle, which will identify the next section of the brochure that you are creating.

1 To verify that you are in Print Layout view, on the View menu, click Print Layout.

2 Move the pointer back and forth across the page to observe how it changes to indicate how the item will be formatted.

If you don't want to type text where you double-clicked, just double-click another area. If you've already typed text, on the Standard toolbar, click the Undo button to remove the text that you inserted, and then click the Undo button again to remove the Click And Type formatting.

The Undo button reverses the last action, so in the example above, the Undo button removes the inserted text. But if you had removed text, the Undo command would have replaced it. You can also find the Undo command on the Edit menu. You'll learn more about the Undo button in Lesson 2, "Editing a Document."

3 Position the pointer at the center of the page slightly below the introductory paragraph that you typed in the previous exercise.

The pointer shape indicates that the item will be centered.

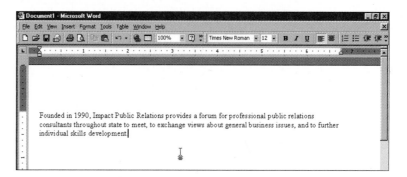

4 Double-click, and type **Membership Information**.

Saving a Document

W2000.4.1

Save

The text that you enter is stored in the computer's memory, which is temporary. To keep the **file** for future use, you must store the document on your hard disk. A file is a collection of related data or information that is assigned a specific name and stored on a disk. To permanently store a document, you must save it to your hard disk. Otherwise, when you quit Word, your document is deleted. You save a document by clicking the Save button on the Standard toolbar. When you save the document, you give the document a unique file name so that you can retrieve the document for future use.

The first time you save a document, the Save As dialog box appears so that you can name the document and put it in a **folder**. A folder is a container in which to store and organize documents, programs, graphics, and files, and is represented by the icon of a file folder. If you make any changes to a document and need to save it, click the Save button and the newest version of the document is saved, but the Save As dialog box does not appear.

A file name can contain as many as 255 characters. Word uses the first words of the document, up to the first punctuation mark or line break, as the file name when you save the file for the first time. You can also delete Word's default file name to assign a file name yourself. Because you have up to 255 characters to work with, you should strive to make your file names as descriptive as possible. An example of a vague and cryptic file name would be *Questions*. You might not remember what the questions are, or what they are for. A better file name would be *Questions for Lesson 3 Test Bank*. When you save a file, you cannot include any of the following characters in the file name.

* \ / < > ? : ; "

In this exercise, you save your new document to your hard disk and save the document again after you make changes.

Save

The Places Bar in the Save As dialog box provides convenient access to commonly used locations for saving and storing files.

The Places Bar also provides access to your list of Internet favorites and a list of recently opened documents (in the History folder).

Notice that the text *Founded in 1990.doc* is selected in the File Name box. The selected text is deleted as you begin typing new text.

You can also click the Save In box to display a list of resources (such as your hard disk, a floppy disk, or a network drive) and available folders.

You can save a copy of the active document with a different name or in a different location. You might want to do this if you are using one document as a starting point to create another document or if you want to have a copy of the original document before you make changes to it. You will learn how to do this in Lesson 2, "Editing a Document."

Save

1   On the Standard toolbar, click the Save button to display the Save As dialog box.

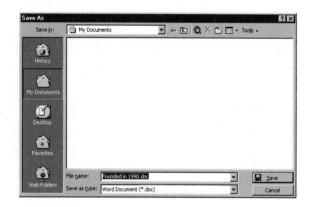

2   In the File Name box, type **Brochure 01**.

3   Click the Save In down arrow, and click the icon for your hard disk.

4   Click the Word Core Practice folder.

     The Save In box displays the text *Word Core Practice*, and the dialog box displays the contents of the Word Core Practice folder.

5   Double-click the Lesson01 folder.

     The Lesson01 folder opens.

6   Click the Save button.

     The file is saved to your hard disk with the new name, which is now displayed in the Microsoft Word title bar.

7   Click at the end of the first paragraph to position the insertion point there.

8   Press the Spacebar, and type the following sentence:

     Meetings are held monthly where an expert guest speaker presents timely and pertinent information.

9   On the Standard toolbar, click the Save button.

     Word saves the document.

     Keep this file open for the next exercise.

Closing a Document and Quitting Word

After a file is stored on your hard disk, you can clear it from the screen by closing the document window or quitting Word. If the document has not been saved, Word prompts you to save the file before closing the window.

To clear a document from the document window, on the File menu, click Close, or in the top-right corner of the screen, click the Close button. Closing the current document window leaves Word still running. When you click Exit on the File menu, the Word program quits.

When you have one document open in Word, two Close buttons are displayed in the top-right corner of the Word window. These buttons each have an X on them, and one is just above the other one. The lower Close button is used to close the current document, and the top Close button is used close the document and exit Word.

New Blank Document

When you start Word, a blank document is displayed in the Word window. After you save and close this new document, Word remains open, but does not automatically display a new blank document in the window like it did when you started Word. You must click the New Blank Document button on the Standard toolbar to create a new document.

In this exercise, you close the current document, exit Word, and then start Word.

1   On the File menu, click Close.

The document closes, leaving Word open but no documents open.

2   On the File menu, click Exit.

Word closes.

3   To restart Word, Click the Start button at the left end of the Windows taskbar, point to Programs, and click Microsoft Word.

Word 2000 starts.

W2000.4.9

To change the character of Office Assistant, right-click the Office Assistant and click Options. Click the Gallery tab, click the Next or Back buttons until you see the Office Assistant that you want, and then click OK.

If you select an assistant and receive an alert box saying that the selected assistant is not available, insert the requested Office 2000 or Word 2000 CD-ROM to install the assistant on your hard disk.

Using the Office Assistant

The first time that you start Word, the Office Assistant appears. The Office Assistant helps you find answers and instructions for your Word questions. The default Office Assistant character is an animated paper clip, but it can take other forms, such as an animated cat or dog. You can save time by using the Office Assistant, rather than searching a table of contents or an index.

To use the Office Assistant to get help, click the Office Assistant, and then type a question in the What Would You Like To Do? box. The Office Assistant provides information whether you type complete sentences or just key words. After you enter a question or keyword, click the Search button or press Enter. The Office Assistant displays a variety of Help topics that are related to the question that you asked. Click the topic that most closely relates to your question to read more about it.

Sometimes the Office Assistant appears on its own if you're doing something that it might be able to help you with, such as writing a letter or using an advanced feature. If you already have the Office Assistant displayed, a light bulb might appear next to it to signal that the Office Assistant has a tip for you that might help you with what you're doing.

In this exercise, you display the Office Assistant, use it to get help, and then close the Office Assistant.

1   If necessary, on the Standard toolbar, click the New Blank Document button to create a new document.

2   If the Office Assistant is not displayed, on the Help menu, click Show The Office Assistant.

3 Click the Office Assistant.

The Office Assistant appears with a yellow help box.

4 Type **How do I use the Office Assistant?** in the box.

5 Click the Search button.

The Office Assistant displays a list of Help topics that are related to the question that you asked.

You can permanently turn off the Office Assistant by right-clicking the Office Assistant, clicking Options, clicking the Options tab, clearing the Use The Office Assistant check box, and then clicking OK. You can turn on the Office Assistant again by clicking Show The Office Assistant on the Help menu.

6 Click Display Tips And Messages Through The Office Assistant.

The Word Help window displays the related help information.

Underlined text indicates a link to another topic.

7 Click the underlined text Hide, Show, Or Turn Off The Office Assistant.

A new Help topic is displayed.

8 When you're finished using Help, in the top-right corner of the Help dialog box, click the Close button.

9 To close the Office Assistant, right-click the Office Assistant, and then click Hide.

Lesson Wrap-Up

In this lesson, you learned how to start and quit Word, how to use menus and toolbars, how to enter text and save a document, how to close and open a document, and how to use the Office Assistant to get help in Word 2000.

If you are continuing to the next lesson:

● On the File menu, click Close to close the file. If you are prompted to save changes, click No.

Word closes the file without saving the changes.

If you are not continuing to other lessons:

Close

1 On the File menu, click Close to close the file. If you are prompted to save changes, click No.

Word closes the file without saving the changes.

2 In the top-right corner of the Word window, click the Close button.

The Word program closes.

Lesson Glossary

button A square or rectangular element with a picture or abbreviated label on it. A button instructs a program to perform a particular action when the button is clicked.

cascading menu A list of commands that appears when the mouse pointer is positioned over a menu command that has a right pointing arrow. Cascading menus are also called submenus.

character Any single letter, number, or symbol that is entered in a document. Tabs, page breaks, spaces, paragraph marks, and other formatting symbols are also considered characters.

Close button A button that ends or shuts down the current window or application. The Close button is located in the top-right corner of the window.

dialog box A screen element that appears when you need to communicate with a program. A dialog box displays current information and options that can be selected before completing a command.

document A self-contained piece of work created by using a program.

file A collection of related data or information that is assigned a specific file name and stored on disk.

folder A storage area for files and other folders.

Formatting toolbar A toolbar that contains buttons for quick access to formatting functions.

icon A small picture that represents a program or document.

insertion point A blinking vertical bar resembling a capital I that indicates the location at which the next character typed or item inserted will appear. The insertion point can be moved anywhere within the document window by clicking any visible location or by pressing various keys.

Maximize/Restore button A button that toggles between displaying a window in its maximum size and restoring a window to its previous size. The button is located in the top-right corner of the window.

menu The area that, when clicked, displays available commands. Menus allow access to commands specific to the active window or object.

menu bar The area at the top of a window that lists the names of the menus available in a program.

minimize To reduce a document window to an button on the Windows taskbar. The document is still open; you just can't see the document when it's minimized.

Minimize button A button that, when clicked, reduces a window to a button on the Windows taskbar. The Minimize button appears as a button with a horizontal line and is located in the top-right corner of the window.

mouse pointer An icon that moves to reflect the position of the mouse.

navigation buttons Buttons that are used to move around in a document. These buttons are located on the vertical scroll bar.

Office Assistant An animated, interactive Help feature. The first time that Word is started, the Office Assistant appears. The Office Assistant prompts you to type a question or topic, and then the Office Assistant displays several responses. You can select the option that best meets the current need or type another query.

ruler An on-screen scale marked with inches or other units of measurement. The ruler changes the indentation of paragraphs, resets page margins, and adjusts the width of columns. The ruler is located below the toolbars.

ScreenTip A help item that briefly explains what an element is. ScreenTips appear when the mouse pointer is positioned over a button or screen element for a few seconds.

scroll bars Navigational tools that are used to move through a document. The vertical scroll bar is located along the right side of the window, and the horizontal scroll bar is located along the lower portion of the window just above the status bar.

selection area The area between the left edge of the window and the left edge of a line of text. You position the mouse pointer in the selection area to select an entire line of text. The pointer changes to a right-pointing arrow when it is positioned in the selection area.

Standard toolbar A toolbar that contains buttons for editing functions. The Standard toolbar is located below the menu bar.

status bar An area that contains brief information about programs that are currently in use. Some programs might display explanations of currently selected menu commands at the lower edge of the program window.

taskbar The strip along the bottom of the screen that typically shows, from left to right, the Start button, the Quick Launch bar, icons for certain utilities, such as the Volume Control for the computer's sound system, and the time. Programs that are running also appear as buttons on the taskbar.

title bar The area at the top of a window or dialog box that displays the name of the current dialog box or application and the name of the current document.

toggle To alternately turn an option on or off each time that the option is selected.

toolbar A group of buttons used to carry out commands. For instance, the Formatting toolbar contains buttons such as Bold, Underline, Italic, and alignment buttons—all of which you use to format text.

window An area in which information is displayed on the screen. Windows can be maximized (sized to fit the full screen), minimized (compressed into buttons on the taskbar), or restored to their original sizes.

word wrap A feature that flows text continuously from one line to the next each time the insertion point reaches the right margin. With word wrap, it is not necessary to press Enter at the end of each line unless you want to insert a blank line or a new paragraph.

Quick Quiz

1   How do you save a copy of the current document without changing the original version?

2   What are two ways that you can close a document?

3   What happens when you click the button labeled with an *X* in the top-right corner of the Word window?

4   What is the difference between an expanded menu and a personalized menu?

5   How do you use Click And Type?

6   What is the Office Assistant?

7   How do you separate the Standard and Formatting toolbars?

8   What is the Start menu used for?

Putting It All Together

Exercise 1: If necessary, start Word. Open Word by using the Start menu. In a blank document, use the Click And Type feature to insert the following heading, centered about one-quarter of the way down the page:

Expense Report Reminders

Use Click And Type again to position a left-aligned paragraph below the title. Type the following information:

When filing your expense reports, make sure to attach your original receipts, record beginning and ending mileage figures, and record the itemized expenses on your hotel bill separately. These are the most common reasons for expense reimbursement delays.

Save the document in the Lesson01 folder located in the Word Core Practice folder on your hard disk with the name **Expense Reminders 01**, and then close the document.

Exercise 2: Use the Office Assistant to find information on how to type over existing text.

LESSON 2

Editing a Document

After completing this lesson, you will be able to:

✔ *Open a file.*

✔ *Navigate through a document.*

✔ *Scroll through text.*

✔ *Insert text in a document.*

✔ *Select text.*

✔ *Edit a document by deleting and restoring text.*

✔ *Create a folder.*

✔ *Save a file with a different name.*

Before the days of computer and word processing programs, any correspondence done by hand or on a typewriter could include crossed-out words, correction fluid, or spelling and punctuation errors. People simply couldn't edit without starting over or having flaws in their document. Now that most personal and business correspondence is typed on a computer using a word processing program, there are no more excuses for crossed-out words or correction fluid.

With Microsoft Word you can quickly and efficiently edit letters, documents, reports, newsletters, memos, and faxes. Word displays a red wavy line if a word is misspelled or unknown and displays a green wavy line to indicate incorrect or questionable grammar usage.

In this lesson, you will learn how to open a file that you already created. Then, because the Word window often displays only a portion of a document at a time, you'll learn how to scroll to view different parts of a document. You'll move the insertion point around the document by using the mouse pointer and by pressing keys on the keyboard.

After learning how to navigate through a document, you'll begin to edit. To edit, you first need to identify the text that you want to change. Word provides shortcuts so that you can select text by the word, line, sentence, paragraph, or the entire document. After you select the desired text, you'll learn how to delete the selection. When you're finished editing the document, you'll save the file.

In this lesson, you will learn how to create a folder in which to save the file and how to save the file with a different name. You'll also save the file in a different format so that it can be used by other word processing programs.

To complete the procedures in this lesson, you will need to use the practice file Brochure 02 in the Lesson02 folder in the Word Core Practice folder that is located on your hard disk. You'll use this file to navigate through the document, edit text, and save the file with a new name.

For additional information on how to find and open files used in this book, see the "Using the CD-ROM" section at the beginning of this book.

Sample files for the lesson

W2000.4.2

Opening an Existing File

After you save a Word document, you can reopen it later to review its contents or make changes. You'll need to navigate to the folder containing the document and then open the document itself.

Word keeps track of the last four documents that you opened. Word displays the names of these files at the bottom of the File menu so that you can open them with only a couple of mouse clicks. To open a file that is not listed at the bottom of the File menu, you use the Open dialog box.

In this exercise, you open an existing file.

1   If necessary, start Word.

2   On the Standard toolbar, click the Open button.

The Open dialog box appears.

Open

3   Click the Look In down arrow, click the icon for your drive, double-click the Word Core Practice folder, and double-click the Lesson02 folder.

The contents of the Lesson02 folder appear in the Open dialog box.

> Word remembers the folder in which you last saved a document. When you display the Open dialog box or the Save As dialog box, the contents of that folder are displayed so that you can easily find what you are looking for.

> To open a recently used document from the Open dialog box, on the Places Bar, click the History icon, and double-click the file that you want to open. The Places Bar is located along the left side of the Open dialog box.

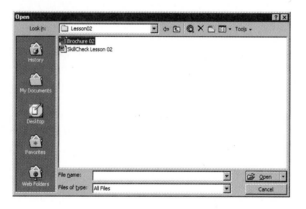

You can also open a file by double-clicking the file name in the Open dialog box.

In the following exercises, the Standard and Formatting toolbars are separated. For information on how to separate the toolbars, see the "Using the CD-ROM" section at the beginning of this book.

4   Click the file Brochure 02, and click the Open button.

The file Brochure 02 appears in Word, and the Open dialog box closes.

Keep this file open for the next exercise.

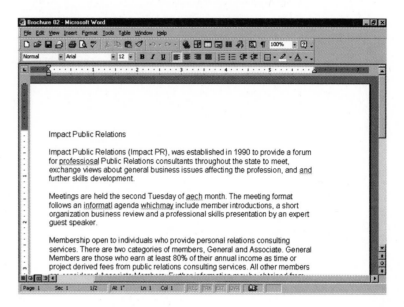

W2000.3.4

When the mouse pointer looks like the I-beam, you can move around and make edits to the text. You can tell when the mouse pointer is in the selection area because the I-beam changes to a right-pointing arrow. The selection area is any location to the left of the left margin of your document.

Navigating Through a Document

To change existing text in a document, or to edit, you first move the insertion point to the location where you want to make a change. The mouse pointer, the **arrow keys** on the keyboard (used to move the mouse pointer or insertion point up, down, left, or right), and the scroll bars are all navigation tools that help you to move through a document.

To move the insertion point by using the mouse, simply move the I-beam pointer (the pointer that looks like a capital I) to the location where you want the insertion point to appear, and click.

important

In a new, blank document, you cannot move the insertion point with the arrow keys or the mouse. You can move the insertion point only to places in the document that include text, tables, or graphics.

For more information about key combinations, see lesson 4, "Formatting Text."

The following table lists each keyboard key or **key combination** that can be used to quickly move the insertion point. A key combination is a combination of keyboard keys used to perform a function, instead of using the mouse pointer to perform the same task. For example, if the key combination is Ctrl+Home, you press and hold the Ctrl button while pressing the Home button. Word moves the insertion point to the beginning of the document.

Press	To move the insertion point
Left arrow key	Left one character (one unit of space, such as a letter, number, punctuation mark, or other symbol).
Right arrow key	Right one character.
Down arrow key	Down one line.
Up arrow key	Up one line.
Ctrl+Left Arrow	Left one word.
Ctrl+Right Arrow	Right one word.
Home	To the beginning of the current line.
End	To the end of the current line.
Ctrl+Home	To the beginning of the document.
Ctrl+End	To the end of the document.
Page Up	Up one full screen.
Page Down	Down one full screen.
Ctrl+Page Up	To the beginning of the previous page.
Ctrl+Page Down	To the beginning of the next page.

In this exercise, you move the insertion point using the keyboard and the mouse.

1   Click after the letter *M* in the word *Meetings*, which is the first word in the second paragraph, and press the Left arrow key to move the insertion point one character to the left.

The insertion point moves one character to the left. It is positioned in front of the letter *M* in *Meetings*.

2   Press the Down arrow key.

The insertion point moves one line down. It is positioned at the beginning of the second line in the paragraph.

3   Press the Up arrow key.

The insertion point moves up in front of the *M* once again.

4   Press the Right arrow key.

The insertion point returns to where you started, directly after the *M*.

5   Press Ctrl+Right Arrow.

The insertion point moves to the beginning of the word *are*.

Word keeps track of the last three locations where you typed or edited text. To return to a previous editing location, press Shift+F5 until you reach the location that you want.

6   Press Ctrl+Left Arrow.

The insertion point moves to the beginning of the word *Meetings*.

7   Press the End key.

The insertion point moves to the end of the line.

8 Press the Home key.

The insertion point moves to the beginning of the line.

9 Press Ctrl+Home.

The insertion point moves to the beginning of the document.

10 Press Ctrl+End.

The insertion point moves to the end of the document.

Keep this file open for the next exercise.

Scrolling Through Text

Because the document window normally displays only a portion of a page at one time, you might need to move (or **scroll**) the view of the document to view another section of it. If your document has more than one page, you'll need to scroll to see the other pages of the document. The vertical scroll bar, scroll arrows, and scroll box move the document up and down. The horizontal scroll bar, scroll arrows, and scroll box move the document window left and right.

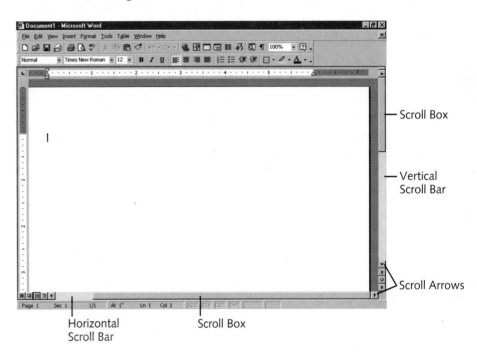

The following table lists available scrolling tools and their functions.

Do this	Button	To move the document view
Click the Up scroll arrow	▲	Up one line at a time.
Click the Down scroll arrow	▼	Down one line at a time.
Click the Left scroll arrow	◄	Left a few characters at a time.
Click the Right scroll arrow	►	Right a few characters at a time.

Do this	Button	To move the document view
Click above the scroll box on the vertical scroll bar		Up one screen at a time.
Click below the scroll box on the vertical scroll bar		Down one screen at a time.
Click left of the scroll box on the horizontal scroll bar		Left one screen at a time.
Click right of the scroll box on the horizontal scroll bar		Right one screen at a time.
Drag the vertical scroll box		Continually forward or backward through the document.
Drag the horizontal scroll box		Continually left or right through the document.
Click the Previous Page button	⬆	To the beginning of the previous page.
Click the Next Page button	⬇	To the beginning of the next page.

"One screen" is the amount of a document that can be displayed in the document window at one time. This amount will vary depending on your screen area settings and whether the document window is maximized.

The Previous Page and Next Page buttons, located below the vertical scroll bar, are not always set to move forward or backward by a page. You can use the Select Browse Object button, located between the Previous and Next buttons, to select the type of item by which you want to browse, such as page, bookmark, footnote, table, graphic, or other item. To browse by page, click the Select Browse Object button, and click the Browse By Page button.

In this exercise, you use the scroll bars and scroll arrows to move through a document.

Up Scroll Arrow

1   Click the Up scroll arrow once.

The document moves up one line.

The insertion point stays in the same place while the view of the document itself moves up, sliding the text down the screen.

Down Scroll Arrow

2   Click the Down scroll arrow.

The insertion point stays in the same place while the document itself moves down, sliding the text up the screen.

The horizontal scroll bar works the same way as the vertical scroll bar.

3   Click the scroll bar above the scroll box.

The document moves down one screen. The first line of text on the previous screen is now the last line of text on the current screen.

Scrolling does not move the insertion point. If you scroll to a new location and you want to edit at that spot, you must click that location to place the insertion point there. If you simply start typing without clicking the location, the view jumps back to where you left the insertion point, and the text will be inserted there.

4   Click the scroll bar below the scroll box.

The content moves down one screen.

5   Drag the scroll box up to the top of the scroll bar.

The text that you see in the window moves along with the scroll box, and a yellow ScreenTip tells you which page you are currently scrolling.

6   Press Ctrl+End.

The insertion point moves to the end of the document.

Select Browse Object

7   On the vertical scroll bar, click the Select Browse Object button.

The Select Browse Object menu appears.

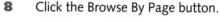

Browse By Page

8   Click the Browse By Page button.

The view and the insertion point move to the beginning of the next page.

9   Click the Previous Page button.

Previous Page

The view and the insertion point move directly to the beginning of the previous page. If the insertion point is already on the first page of the document, the Previous Page button moves the insertion point to the beginning of that page.

10   Click the Next Page button.

Next Page

Both the view and the insertion point move directly to the beginning of the next page. If the insertion point is already on the last page of the document, the Next Page button moves the insertion point to the beginning of that page.

11   Press Ctrl+Home.

The insertion point moves back to the beginning of the document.

Keep this file open for the next exercise.

W2000.1.8

> When Overtype mode is activated and you insert new text in the middle of a sentence or paragraph, it's easy to lose existing text by mistake because the new words that you type replace existing text.

Overtype

Inserting Text in a Document

One of the first steps to being able to edit a document is learning to insert text. Word provides two modes to insert more text. For example, if the annual report for your company was typed without a current list of all the board members, the names of the board members can be inserted later. Word uses **Insert mode** when you start the program. In Insert mode, when you type new text, the existing text moves to the right. The other choice is **Overtype mode**. In Overtype mode, existing text is deleted and replaced by the next text you type, including spaces.

Research shows that a majority of users prefer Insert mode, so Insert mode is Word's default mode. Double-clicking the Overtype button toggles between Insert and Overtype modes. A toggle is a button that alternately turns an option on or off each time that the option is selected.

In this exercise, you insert text into a document.

1   In the last line of the first paragraph, click just before the first *s* in the word *skills* to position the insertion point.

2   Type **individual**, and press the Spacebar.

The new text is added at the insertion point, moving the existing text to the right.

Keep this file open for the next exercise.

Selecting Text

To edit text in a document, you must first select the desired text. One way to select text is to hold down the mouse button and then drag the insertion point over the text that you want to select. You deselect text by clicking anywhere within the document window. You can tell when text is selected because it appears highlighted (selected text usually appears white with a black background). Any changes will affect the selected text.

To select blocks of text quickly, Word uses a selection area. The selection area is any location to the left of the left margin of the document. You can tell when the pointer is in the selection area because the I-beam changes to a right-pointing arrow.

The following table summarizes the methods for selecting blocks of text.

To select	Do this
One word	Double-click the word.
A line	Click the selection area to the left of the line. (The mouse pointer changes to a right-pointing arrow when it is in the selection area.)
A sentence	Hold down the Ctrl key and click anywhere in the sentence.
A paragraph	Double-click the selection area to the left of any line in the paragraph, or triple-click anywhere in the paragraph.
An entire document	Hold down the Ctrl key and click anywhere in the selection area, or triple-click anywhere in the selection area.

You can also select text by using the keyboard. Click in front of the text that you want to select and press Shift+Right Arrow to select text to the right of and before the mouse pointer, or Shift+Down Arrow to select text to the right of the mouse pointer. Notice that if you press Shift+Down Arrow in the middle of a line, the selected text includes part of the next line. Likewise, if you press Shift+Down Arrow at the beginning of a line, the entire line is selected. You can also click at the beginning of the text that you want to select, hold down Shift, and then click at the end of the text to select a block of text.

When you drag the mouse pointer past the first word, Word automatically selects entire words instead of one letter at a time.

In this exercise, you select and deselect text.

1   Double-click the word *Tuesday* in the second paragraph.

  The entire word is selected.

2   Click within the word *Tuesday* to deselect it.

3   Move the mouse pointer to the selection area of the first line in the second paragraph.

4   Click once in the selection area.

  The entire line of text is now selected.

5   Hold down the Ctrl key.

6   Click within the sentence containing the word *Tuesday*, and release the Ctrl key.

  The entire sentence is now selected.

7   Move the mouse to the selection area, keeping the mouse pointer level with the paragraph containing the word *Tuesday*.

8   Double-click the selection area.

  The entire paragraph is now selected.

9   Click within the document outside the selection area.

  The paragraph is no longer selected.

10 Triple-click within the paragraph.

The entire paragraph is now selected.

11 Hold down the Ctrl key.

12 Click the selection area.

The entire document is selected.

13 Click within the document.

The document is no longer selected.

14 Triple-click the selection area.

The entire document is selected.

15 Click within the document to deselect it.

Keep this file open for the next exercise.

> If you drag the mouse pointer to select an entire sentence, don't forget to select the ending punctuation.

> You can also select an entire document. On the Edit menu, click **Select All**, or press the key combination Ctrl+A. You'll learn more about key combinations in Lesson 4, "Formatting Text."

W2000.1.1

Deleting and Restoring Text in a Document

Now that you know how to select text, you can easily delete a selected block of text. To delete a large section of text, select the text, and press Delete or Backspace. You can save time by selecting large areas of text to be deleted, rather than deleting the text character by character.

For example, in the annual report that you prepared for your company, you typed the introduction message from your company's president; however, the president has now decided to write it himself. You don't have to delete the letter one character at a time, instead select the entire letter, and press Delete. Now the page is blank and ready for the President to add his own letter.

To delete a single character, position the insertion point to the left of the character and press Delete, or to the right of the character and press Backspace. To delete text using the keyboard, you use the key combinations listed in the following table.

Press	To delete a word
Ctrl+Backspace	To the left of the insertion point.
Ctrl+Delete	To the right of the insertion point.

tip

If you use either of these key combinations while the insertion point is positioned within a word, you delete the part of the word before or after the insertion point, respectively.

Overtype

Another way to delete text is to use Overtype mode. Double-click Overtype on the status bar to turn on Overtype mode. When Overtype mode is turned on, you type over the existing text.

Word keeps track of the editing changes that you make in a document so that you can easily remove a change and restore the text to the way it was prior to making the edits. If you make a mistake while editing, on the Standard toolbar, you can click the Undo and Redo buttons to change and restore text.

Undo   Redo

You can also click Undo and Redo on the Edit menu. If your toolbar does not show the Undo and Redo buttons, on the Standard toolbar, click the More Buttons button, click the Add Or Remove button, and click the Undo and Redo buttons.

To **undo** an action, click the Undo button. If you undo an action by mistake and need to restore or **redo** the action, you can do so by clicking the Redo button. To undo or redo multiple actions, click the down arrow to the right of the Undo or Redo button and select the action that you want to undo or redo. All actions completed after the one that you select in the list are also undone. Although most actions can be undone, actions such as saving and printing cannot.

In this exercise, you delete and restore text to fix some of the errors in the document.

Word marks any word not found in its standard dictionary with a red wavy line. After you correct the word, the wavy line is removed. You'll learn more about the dictionary and spelling check in Lesson 7, "Using Editing and Proofing Tools."

1   Click the insertion point to the right of the last *s* in the misspelled word *professiosal* in the first paragraph.

2   Press the Delete key.

The letter *s* is deleted, and the remaining text is shifted to the left.

3   Type **n**.

The red wavy line is removed.

4   In the second paragraph, position the insertion point to the right of the letter *t* in the word *Informatl*.

5   Press Backspace.

The *t* is deleted, and the red wavy line is removed.

6   In the second paragraph, position the insertion point in front of the *a* in the misspelled word *aech*.

Overtype

7   On the status bar, double-click Overtype.

The Overtype mode is turned on.

8   Type **ea**.

The word is changed, and the red wavy line is removed.

9   On the status bar, double-click Overtype.

The Overtype mode is turned off.

10   Double-click the word *personal* in the third paragraph.

The word *personal* is selected.

11   Type **public**.

The word *personal* is replaced with the word *public,* and the rest of the text moves to the right as you type.

12   Double-click the selection area to the left of the first paragraph.

The paragraph is selected.

13   Press Delete.

The paragraph is deleted.

Undo

Redo

14 On the Standard toolbar, click the Undo button.

The deleted paragraph is restored and is also selected.

15 On the Standard toolbar, click the Redo button.

The paragraph is deleted again.

16 Click the Undo button again.

The deleted paragraph is restored and is also selected.

17 Press the Down arrow key.

The paragraph is deselected.

18 Click after the second occurrence of the word *and* in the last sentence of the first paragraph.

19 Press Ctrl+Backspace.

The word *and* is deleted.

20 Press Ctrl+Right Arrow twice to move the insertion point to the word *individual*.

21 Press Ctrl+Delete.

The word *individual* is deleted.

Keep this file open for the next exercise.

W2000.4.4

You can now delete files and folders from within the Open and Save As dialog boxes. Select the file or folder that you want to delete, and click the Delete button.

Delete

You can also create folders in any other Microsoft Office 2000 application, in Windows Explorer, or in My Computer.

Creating a Folder

After you create a document, you might want to save the document in a folder. A folder is a storage area on your computer's hard disk or a network drive. A **network** is a system of computers connected by communications links. When a computer is connected via a network, you can use one computer to access the hard disk of another computer on the network. You can create folders to store files by project, author, file type, or just about any organization scheme you can imagine.

For example, you might have a folder named Memos. In this folder, you store all the memos that you send to your boss. You might choose to have a *subfolder* (a folder within a folder) in your Memo folder named Sent Marketing. This is where you store memos that you send to the marketing department. You could even have another subfolder in your Memo folder called Sent Finance. This folder contains the memos that you send to the finance department. Now when you open the Memo folder, you won't have to wade through all the memos you have sent; instead, you have sorted and saved them in subfolders, so they are quick and easy to find and retrieve.

Word makes creating folders easy directly from the Save As dialog box. With Word's file management features, you can easily organize, locate, and create folders to store documents and save files with different names.

In this exercise, you create a folder.

1   On the File menu, click Save As.

The Save As dialog box appears and displays the content of the Lesson02 folder, which is the last folder that you used.

Create New Folder

2   Click the Create New Folder button.

The New Folder dialog box appears.

You can also create new folders in Windows Explorer. You don't have to create them from within Word. To create a new folder in Windows Explorer, click the Start button, point to Programs, and then click Windows Explorer. In the Folders pane on the left side of Windows Explorer, navigate to and double-click the folder in which you want to create a new folder. On the File menu, point to New, and click Folder. A new folder appears with the name *New Folder* selected. Type the name of the new folder, and press Enter to rename it.

3   Type **My Exercises** in the Name box, and click OK.

The New Folder dialog box closes, and the Save As dialog box appears and displays the My Exercises folder. The file Brochure 02.doc is listed in the File Name box because it is the file that is currently open.

4   Click the Cancel button.

The Save As dialog box closes and the file is not saved.

W2000.4.3

Saving a File with a Different Name

You might find it necessary to make a copy of a file. You can keep the original on hand for safekeeping or for comparison and then make changes to a new version. For example, the marketing manager at Lakewood Mountains Resort creates a revised brochure each year. When it's time to create a new brochure, she opens the previous version and saves it with a new name. Using the previous brochure helps create the new brochure quickly and efficiently with just a few updates. Saving the new brochure with a new name preserves previous versions to maintain a historical archive.

In this exercise, you save the current file with a different name in the My Exercises folder.

The My Exercises folder doesn't appear in the Save In box because it isn't the last folder in which you saved a document.

1   On the File menu, click Save As.

The Save As dialog box appears. The content of the Lesson02 folder appears.

2   Double-click the My Exercises folder.

The My Exercises folder opens.

3   Click after *Brochure 02* in the File Name box.

4   Press the Spacebar, and type **Edited**.

5   Click the Save button.

The Save As dialog box closes, and the file is saved with the name Brochure 02 Edited.doc. The file's new name appears in the title bar of your document.

tip
You should make a **backup** copy of important files to protect against losses from computer crashes, viruses, accidental changes, or deletions. You can save copies of files to floppy disks or to a network disk (a disk that is physically located on another computer, but is available to users on the same network), if one is available. The best way to safeguard files is to use a *tape backup system*.

W2000.4.3

Saving a File in a Different Format

Your computer at work has Office 2000 installed, but you have a different word processing program installed on your computer at home. You need to take work home with you to meet deadlines, but if you don't have the same computer software as your company, how will you be able to work at home on your computer? Luckily, Word allows you to save a document in another format. Saving a file in a different format is useful when the document needs to be used in another word processing program, in an earlier version of Word, or if you want to use the document as a Web page. You can save your document at work in Rich Text Format (.rtf) so you'll be able to read the document at home using other Microsoft programs such as Windows Notepad or WordPad.

A **file format** is the way in which information is stored in a file so that a program can open and save the file. A file's format is indicated by the three-letter extension after the file name. For example, when you save a new document in Microsoft Word 2000, by default, Word stores it in Word 2000 format with a .doc file extension. Files saved in Rich Text Format have the .rtf extension, and files saved in text-only format have the .txt extension.

To save a file in Rich Text Format:

1   On the File menu, click Save As.
2   In the File Name box, type a new name for the document.
3   Click the Save As Type down arrow.
4   Click Rich Text Format.
5   Click Save.
    The file is saved in the selected format.

Lesson Wrap-Up

In this lesson, you learned how to open an existing file and navigate through a document using the scroll bars, arrow keys, and insertion point. You also learned how to edit a document by inserting, selecting, and deleting text, and how to manage files by creating a folder and saving a file with a different name and in a different format.

If you are continuing to the next lesson:

Save

1 On the Standard toolbar, click the Save button to save changes made to the Brochure 02 Edited file.

The changes are saved to the file.

2 On the File menu, click Close to close the file.

The file closes.

If you are not continuing to other lessons:

Save

1 On the Standard toolbar, click the Save button to save changes made to the Brochure 02 Edited file.

The changes are saved to the file.

Close

2 In the top-right corner of the Word window, click the Close button.

The file closes, and the Word program closes.

Lesson Glossary

arrow keys Keys on the keyboard that are used to move the mouse pointer or insertion point up, down, left, or right to various locations in a document.

backup A copy of a file or an entire disk for use in the event that the working copy becomes damaged or lost.

file format The way in which information is stored in a file so that a program can open and save the file. A file's format is indicated by a three-letter extension after the file name.

Insert mode A mode of operation used to place text or a graphic at the location of the insertion point. When you type new text, existing text is moved over, not deleted. Text or graphics before and after the insertion point adjust to accommodate the inserted item.

key combination A combination of keyboard keys used to perform a function, instead of using the mouse pointer to perform the same task.

network A system of computers connected by communications links. When a computer is connected via a network, you can use one computer to access the hard disk of another computer on the network.

Overtype mode A mode of typing, in which existing text is replaced by new text.

redo An operation that allows the last action undone to be reversed or redone.

scroll To move the on-screen view to reveal other portions of a document.

undo An operation that allows the last action performed to be reversed, or undone.

Quick Quiz

1   How do you delete a document in Word?

2   What are three ways that you can scroll forward through a document?

3   If you make a mistake when editing a document, what can you do to fix the problem?

4   What keys do you press to select text to the right of the insertion point?

5   What is the Select Browse Object button used for?

6   What are two ways to open a recently opened document?

7   What menu command do you use to open an existing file? What tool-bar button?

8   What is the difference between scrolling and moving the insertion point?

9   How can you select a sentence within a paragraph?

important

In the Putting It All Together section below, you must complete Exercise 1 to continue to Exercise 2.

Putting It All Together

Exercise 1: If necessary, start Word. Open the file SkillCheck Lesson 02, in the Lesson02 folder in the Word Core Practice folder that is located on your hard disk, and make the following edits.

- Type the word **provides** before the misspelled word *comprejensive* in the first sentence.

- Replace the first occurrence of the word *for* with the word *to* in the first sentence of the first paragraph.

- Delete the second occurrence of the word *has* in the sentence beginning *A full service agency.*

- Replace the Senior Vice President's name at the end of the letter with your own.

■ Select the last sentence in the third paragraph, which begins with *We believe,* and delete it.

■ At the end of the document, add three blank lines after *Sincerely* to allow room for the signature.

■ Change the date to January 1, 2000.

■ Make spelling corrections as needed.

The finished document should look similar to the following illustration.

January 1, 2000

Mr. and Mrs. George Billingsley
Billingsley Inc.
5678 Elm Street
Hinesburg, VT 50265

Dear Mr. and Mrs. Billingsley,

This letter is in response to your request for information about the services provided by Impact Pubic Relations (Impact PR). Impact PR provides comprehensive public relations services including advertising and marketing communications services for a variety of diverse corporations, businesses and non-profit organizations. A full service agency, Impact PR has handled public relations and advertising for everything from sewing machines and frozen foods to computer software applications and book promotions.

Impact PR works with a variety of clients in the Northern New England area, Boston, New York, and New Jersey in the fields of manufacturing, healthcare, financial services, education, and computer software. Impact PR also offers in-house graphic design capabilities to produce distinctive, results-oriented advertising and collateral including annual reports, brochures, corporate identity, logos and more.

With a philosophy of providing hands-on attention and personalized service for our clients, Impact PR is committed to creative, high-quality work, innovative solutions and responsive service.

Please feel free to contact me for more information. I can be reached by phone at 303-555-0120, or by e-mail at someone@microsoft.com.

Sincerely,

[your name]
Senior Vice President

Exercise 2: Create a subfolder named **Putting It All Together** in the Lesson02 folder, and then save the edited file from Exercise 1 in the new folder as **SkillCheck Lesson 02 Edited**.

LESSON 3

Using Templates and Wizards

After completing this lesson, you will be able to:

✔ *Use a Word template.*

✔ *Create a template.*

✔ *Use a wizard to create a document.*

When you use Microsoft Word templates and wizards, you save yourself a lot of time. For example, suppose that your boss has decided that you will be in charge of all the internal company correspondence. Your new job duties include sending out a weekly memo to all employees, faxing updates to various departments, and creating a monthly newsletter. Rather than having to recreate the layout and design each memo or newsletter that you create or even having to retype standard information each time that you create a letter or fax, you can use a **template**. A template is a document that contains built-in text, styles, and other formatting that can be used to create other documents that will share the same basic formatting.

You can use an existing document to create a customized template. Creating a customized template is ideal when you've already spent significant time adding text, character and paragraph formatting, graphics, or styles to a document and want to use the same or similar formatting for other documents that you create. By creating a template from an existing document, you can avoid having to apply similar formatting to the other documents. You save the document as a custom template and modify it for further use.

You also use a **wizard** to create a document. A wizard prompts you for information one step at a time and then generates a formatted document based on your answers.

In this lesson, you will learn how to create a document using a template, create a template, and use a Word wizard to create a document.

Sample files for the lesson

To complete the procedures in this lesson, you will need to use a file named IPR January 00 Flyer 03 in the Lesson03 folder in the Word Core Practice folder that is located on your hard disk. You'll use this file to create and save a custom template.

For additional information on how to find and open files used in this book, see the "Using the CD-ROM" section at the beginning of this book.

W2000.4.7

Using a Word Template

Every Word document is based on a template. The template determines the basic properties of the document, such as the margins and the layout (how text is displayed on paper). The template also defines the characteristics of the text, such as its font, font size, and font style. Most documents are generated from a generic template called the **Normal template**. The Normal template is the **default** template in Word. When you click the New Blank Document button on the Standard toolbar, a new blank document is created based on the Normal template.

Word has many built-in templates, each categorized by type. These templates allow you to create documents for specific uses such as fax sheets, memos, resumes, and letters. Templates contain both **preformatted text** and **placeholder text**. Preformatted text includes headings and other entries that you don't need to change. For instance, a memo template might contain the title *Memorandum*, displayed in a particular font, font size, and font style. Other preformatted memo text includes *To:*, *From:*, and *Re:*. Placeholder text is temporary because you will either delete it or replace it with your own text. Placeholder text usually provides a brief explanation of what you can type to replace the placeholder text. For example, a memo template might contain the placeholder text *[Your name here]*, which indicates that you should replace the placeholder text with your name.

In this exercise, you use a ready-made Word template to create a fax sheet, enter text, and then save the new document.

1   On the File menu, click New.

The New dialog box appears.

2   Click the Letters & Faxes tab.

> A default is a setting that an application establishes when it is installed but can be changed by a user at any time.

> You can save a new Word file as either a document or as a template.

> In the following exercises, the Standard and Formatting toolbars have been separated. For additional information on how to separate the toolbars, see the "Using the CD-ROM" section at the begining of this book.

> There are two basic types of templates: global and document. A global template, such as the Normal template, contains formatting that is available to all documents. Document templates, such as memo or fax templates, contain formatting available only to documents that are created using that template. For example, if you create a memo using a memo template, formatting is applied using both the Normal template (a global template) and the Memo template (a document template).

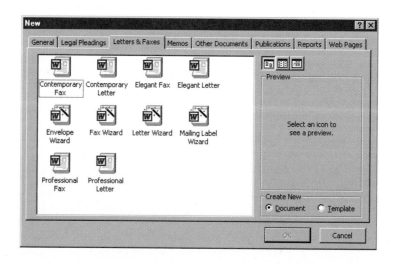

3   Double-click the Contemporary Fax icon.

The Contemporary Fax template appears.

> [Click here and type address]
>
> ## facsimile transmittal
>
> | To: | [Click here and type name] | Fax: | [Click here and type fax number] |
> | From: | [Click here and type name] | Date: | 10/1/99 |
> | Re: | [Click here and type subject of fax] | Pages: | [Click here and type number of pages] |
> | CC: | [Click here and type name] | | |
>
> ☐ Urgent   ☐ For Review   ☐ Please Comment   ☐ Please Reply   ☐ Please Recycle
>
> Notes: Select this text and delete it or replace it with your own. To save changes to this template for future use, choose Save As from the File menu. In the Save As Type box, choose Document Template. Next time you want to use it, choose New from the File menu, and then double-click

> **Use the Tab key instead of the mouse pointer to select all the placeholder text throughout the Contemporary Fax template.**

4   In the top-right corner of the document, click the placeholder text for the address.

The placeholder text is selected and you can begin typing.

5   Type **Impact Public Relations**, and press Enter.

6   Type **4567 Main Street**, and press Enter.

7   Type **Charlotte, VT 80227**, and press Enter.

8   Click the placeholder text to the right of the word *To:*.

The placeholder text is selected and ready for your entry.

9   Type **Mr. and Mrs. Bergman**.

> **Notice that the correct date is filled in by Word and will remain unless you select the date and type a new one.**
>
> **You can select the text *facsimile transmittal* and replace it with different text. For example, you could put your name or your company's name here to personalize the fax sheet. You could also insert clip art or a company logo on the fax sheet.**

10   Replace the rest of the placeholder text as follows:

Fax: **303-555-0100**

From: **Lisa Jacobson**

Re: **Services provided by Impact Public Relations**

Pages: **2**

CC: **Jeff Adell**

11   Double-click the box to the left of the words *For Review*.

A check mark is inserted in the box.

12   Scroll down, if necessary, and select the paragraph to the right of the word *Notes:*.

13   Type the following:

Please see the attached letter for a summary of our services. Please feel free to contact me for more information.

Save

14   On the Standard toolbar, click the Save button.

The Save As dialog box appears.

15   In the File Name box, type **ImpactPR Fax 03**.

16 If necessary, click the Save In down arrow, and navigate to the Lesson03 folder in the Word Core Practice folder on your hard disk.

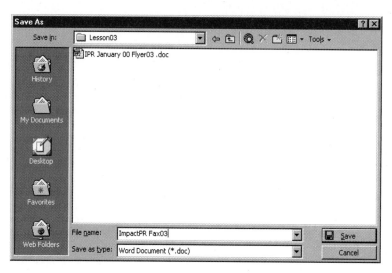

17 Click the Save button.

Word saves the document.

18 On the File menu, click Close to close the template. If you are prompted to save changes, click No.

Creating Your Own Template

After the meeting coordinator at Impact Public Relations finished creating the monthly meeting announcement flyer, she realized she would save time with future flyers by creating a template from the existing flyer. Now, when she creates a new flyer, she can save herself time by basing the new flyer on this template.

A template created from a document has the same characteristics, format, and text as the original document. You create a template by saving a document as a template, modifying the template so that it is more generic in nature, and saving any modifications that you make. The next time that you open the template, it is ready for you to update.

> **If your hard disk uses a letter other than C, substitute the appropriate drive letter in place of C.**

tip

If you save a template in the Templates folder, the template appears on the General tab when you click New on the File menu. To create custom tabs for templates in the New dialog box, create a new folder in the Templates folder and save your templates in that folder. The name that you give the folder will appear on a new tab. In Microsoft Windows 95 or 98, the Templates folder is located by default in the C:\Windows\Application Data\Microsoft folder or the:\Windows\Profiles\[User_name]\Application Data\Microsoft folder. In Microsoft Office 2000, the Templates folder is located in the C:\Windows\Profiles\[User_name] folder. The user name refers to your own name or the name of the person logged on the computer when this folder is opened.

In this exercise, you create a template from a file. You then create a file from the template.

1   On the Standard toolbar, click the Open button.

     The Open dialog box appears.

2   Click the Look In down arrow, click the icon for your drive, double-click the Word Core Practice folder, and then double-click the Lesson03 folder.

     The contents of the Lesson03 folder appear in the Open dialog box.

3   Click the file IPR January 00 Flyer 03 and click the Open button.

     The file IPR January 00 Flyer 03 appears in Word and the Open dialog box closes.

4   On the File menu, click Save As.

     The Save As dialog box appears.

> The file extension for document templates in Word is *.dot.

5   In the File Name box, type **IPR Flyer Template 03**, click the Save As Type down arrow, and click Document Template (*.dot).

     Notice that the template will be saved in the Templates folder.

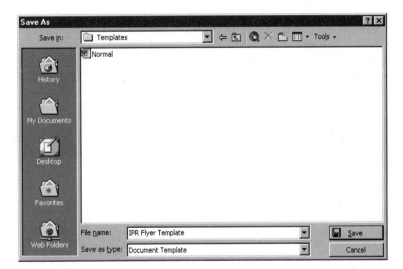

6   Click the Save button.

     The template is created.

7   Select the word *January* in the third line of the main title, and type **Month**. Then select *January 20th*, and type **Date**.

     The month and the date are replaced with generic text.

8   Select the title *Business Plans that Work!*, and type **Title**.

¶

Show/Hide ¶

9   On the Standard toolbar, click the Show/Hide ¶ button so that you can see the formatting marks in the document.

10   Select the following text, but leave the paragraph symbol at the end of the sentence unselected, and then press Delete:

     Carolyn Seeley will demonstrate how to create, review, and adjust a business plan for a startup company.

> As you enter and edit text, Word inserts special formatting marks—such as spaces, tabs, and paragraph marks—into the document. These formatting marks do not appear on the screen and are not printed, unless you use the Options dialog box or click the Show/Hide ¶ button to display them.

11 Select the bulleted list, but leave the paragraph symbol at the end of the sentence of the last bullet unselected, and then press Delete.

Show/Hide ¶

12 Click the Show/Hide ¶ button to hide the formatting marks.

The flyer should look like the one shown below.

Showing the formatting marks is useful when you cut and copy text and want to be sure that you have selected all the appropriate tabs, spaces, and hard returns. You will learn more about showing formatting marks in Lesson 5, "Changing the Layout of a Document."

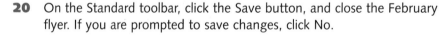

Save

13 On the Standard toolbar, click the Save button and close the template.

14 On the File menu, click New to create a document based on the template.

The New dialog box appears.

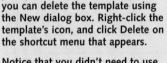

When you no longer need one of your previously created templates, you can delete the template using the New dialog box. Right-click the template's icon, and click Delete on the shortcut menu that appears.

Notice that you didn't need to use the Save As command to avoid altering the template. Word automatically created a new document and left the template unchanged.

15 If necessary, click the General tab, and double-click the IPR Flyer Template 03 icon.

A new document is created based on the template.

16 Double-click the word *Month,* and type **February**.

17 Double-click the word *Date,* and type **February 17th**.

18 On the Standard toolbar, click the Save button.

19 In the File Name box, type **IPR February 00 Flyer**. Click the Save In down arrow, and navigate to the Lesson03 folder in the Word Core Practice folder on your hard disk.

Save

20 On the Standard toolbar, click the Save button, and close the February flyer. If you are prompted to save changes, click No.

Word saves and closes the document.

Creating a Template from a Template

The letterhead for Impact Public Relations doesn't show the new company logo. You could create a letterhead template from a template so that you don't have to insert the logo every time that you need to use the letterhead. To create a template from an existing template, on the File menu, click Save As, type the name of the template in the Save As dialog box, click the Save As Type down arrow, click Document Template, and then click the Save button. Your newly saved template will appear on the General tab in the New dialog box.

W2000.4.5

Using a Wizard

You can also automate the creation of a document by using one of Word's many wizards. You can use wizards to create memos, letters, faxes, and many other business documents. The major difference between a wizard and a template is that a wizard walks you through text entry for many parts of a document. By contrast, a template simply displays placeholder text that you replace on your own. After you create a document by using a wizard, you will still need to replace some placeholder text. However, you'll notice much less placeholder text than if you had created the same document by using a template.

In this exercise, you create a document using the Memo Wizard, and you modify and save the memo.

1 On the File menu, click New.

The New dialog box appears.

2 Click the Memos tab.

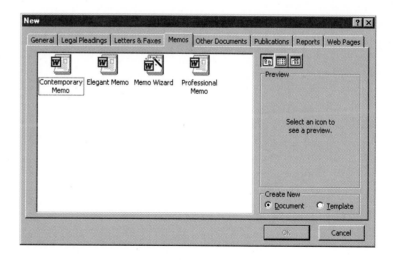

3   Double-click the Memo Wizard icon.

The first Memo Wizard dialog box appears.

Notice the flowchart on the left side of the Wizard dialog box. The green square indicates the stage that you're at in the wizard's process. You can move to a specific step in the process by clicking a box on the flowchart. If you make a mistake, click the Back button as many times as necessary to return to previous steps.

4   Click the Next button.

The next wizard dialog box appears, asking which style of memo that you want to use.

5   Click the Elegant option, and click Next.

The next wizard dialog box appears. The *Yes. Use This Text* option is already selected.

6   Type **IPR Memo 03** it the Title box, and click Next.

The next wizard dialog box appears.

7   In the From box, select the default text, and type **Lisa Jacobson**.

8   In the Subject box, type **Expense Report Reminders**.

Because Word automatically enters today's date in the Date section of the memo, your Memo Wizard dialog box will differ slightly from the one shown here.

If you are using a wizard to create a document for future use, you can select the date and type the new date that you want.

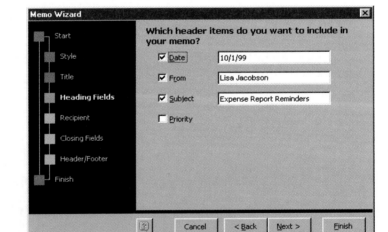

9   Click Next.

The next wizard dialog box appears.

10   In the To box, type **All employees**, and click Next.

The next wizard dialog box appears.

11   Select the Writer's Initials check box, and type **LJ** in the Writer's Initials box.

12   Click Next.

The next wizard dialog box appears.

13   Clear the Confidential check box, and click Next.

The last wizard dialog box appears.

14   Click Finish

The Memo Wizard closes. Your customized memo appears in a new document window.

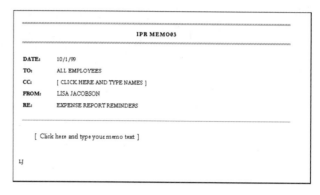

15   Click the placeholder text next to the CC: line.

16   Press Delete.

The unwanted line is deleted.

17   Click the placeholder text in the body of the memo and type: **When filing your expense reports, be sure to attach your original receipts.**

Lesson Wrap-Up

In this lesson, you learned how to create a document by using a template, how to create a template from a document, and how to use a wizard to create a document.

If you are continuing to other lessons:

Save

1   On the Standard toolbar, click the Save button.

The Save As dialog box appears.

2   Navigate to the Lesson03 folder, and then save the memo as **IPR Memo 03**.

3   Click the Save button.

Word saves the document.

4   On the File menu, click Close. If you are prompted to save changes, click No.

Word closes the file.

If you are not continuing to other lessons:

Save

1   On the Standard toolbar, click the Save button.

2   Navigate to the Lesson03 folder, and then save the memo as **IPR Memo 03**.

Word saves the document.

Close

3 In the top-right corner of the Word window, click the Close button. If you are prompted to save the changes, click No.

Word closes the file and the Word program closes.

Lesson Glossary

default A setting that an application establishes when it is installed. It can be changed at any time.

Normal template A general-purpose collection of page, paragraph, and character formats that you can use for any type of document. When you start Word or click the New Blank Document button, Word creates a new blank document based on the Normal template.

placeholder text Temporary text that is in the position of the text that you'll replace. Placeholder text is already formatted in the document so that you don't have to worry about the layout or formatting when you replace the text. Placeholder text includes formatted characters, words, and paragraphs, including headings and other entries.

preformatted text Text that includes headings and other entries displayed in a particular font, font size, and font style that you don't need to change.

template A document that contains built-in text, styles, and other formatting that can be used to create other documents that will share the same basic formatting.

wizard A feature that asks questions and then uses the answers that you enter to automatically layout and format a document.

Quick Quiz

1 From what dialog box do you open a Word template?

2 What is the difference between a template and a wizard?

3 What are two built-in wizards that Word provides?

4 Under what circumstances would you want to create a template?

5 Name three of the built-in templates that Word provides.

6 When you create a document from a template, how can you be sure that you're not saving the document as the template that you used to create the document?

important

In the Putting It All Together section below, you must complete Exercise 1 to continue to Exercise2.

Putting It All Together

Exercise 1: If necessary, start Word. Use the Fax Wizard and the following information to create a fax that contains just a cover sheet with a note and is set up to print so that it can be sent from a separate fax machine. Address the fax to Mr. and Mrs. Ken Bergman, using the fax number 303-555-0188. Select the
Professional cover sheet and include your name and the following address in the proper places:

IPR

4567 Main Street

Charlotte, VT 80227

303-555-0100

Save the fax sheet as **Bergman Fax 03** in the Lesson03 folder in the Word Core Practice folder.

Exercise 2: Create a template from the fax that you created in the previous exercise. Open the Bergman Fax 03 document, and delete the information in the To: line and the Fax: line. Save the document as a template, name it **Fax Template 03,** and then close it.

LESSON 4

Formatting Text

After completing this lesson, you will be able to:

✔ *Use the Formatting toolbar to format text.*

✔ *Align text.*

✔ *Cut and paste text.*

✔ *Use drag and drop to edit text.*

✔ *Use collect and paste.*

✔ *Apply styles.*

✔ *Create a paragraph border.*

✔ *Add shading to a paragraph.*

✔ *Preview a document.*

✔ *Print a document.*

Have you ever wished that you could change the format and layout of a document to place emphasis on key words and phrases? Or have you ever read a document that you created and printed, only to find that the information on page 3 should be where the information on page 2 is? Microsoft Word has numerous features to help you create and format the documents in just the way you want. Word also lets you move and copy information throughout the document or even to another document.

In this lesson, you will learn how to apply formatting to make text bold, underlined, and italic, and you'll learn how to change the size and font **style** of text. When you edit a document, you often need to move or copy text or other objects from one place to another. In this lesson, you will learn different methods for cutting and copying text and objects. You'll practice copying and pasting text between different documents. You'll learn how to modify the appearance of a paragraph by aligning text, creating a border, and adding shading.

Sample files for the lesson ➡️

For additional information on how to find and open files used in this book, see the "Using the CD-ROM" section at the beginning of this book.

To complete the procedures in this lesson, you will need to use a file named Brochure 04 in the Lesson04 folder in the Word Core Practice folder that is located on your hard disk. This document has been created to publicize the services of Impact Public Relations. You'll change the text, formatting, borders, and shading. For the section in this lesson on moving and copying text, you'll use the files Memorandum 04 and Logo 04. These files contain text that you will paste in the brochure.

Using the Formatting Toolbar to Format Text

W2000.1.2
W2000.1.11

Although in Word you can change the appearance of text in several different ways, using the Formatting toolbar is the quickest and easiest way to make most text changes. The Formatting toolbar has several buttons and lists that you can use to change text attributes. An **attribute** is a characteristic such as bold formatting, italics, lowercasing, underlining, font (the style of the characters), font size, and even text color.

The boxes at the left end of the Formatting toolbar are, from left to right, the Style box, the Font box, and the Font Size box, as shown in the following illustration. These boxes tell you the name of the style, the name of the font, and the size of the font currently in use. (Styles are covered later in this lesson.) You click the down arrows on the right sides of the boxes to open the boxes to display a content list.

In the following exercises, the Standard and Formatting toolbars have been separated. For addi-tional information on how to separate the toolbars, see the "Using the CD-ROM" section at the beginning of this book.

The buttons on the toolbars toggle on and off. That is, when you click a button, you turn on the attribute. When you click the button again, you turn off the attribute.

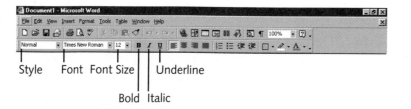

When you select formatted text, the font and font size of the selected text appear on the Formatting toolbar, in the Font and Font Size boxes, only if the font and font size of the selected text is the same. If the font, font style, or font size varies throughout the selected text, the Font, Font Size, and Font Style boxes appear blank on the Formatting toolbar. If the selected text is bold, italic, or underlined, the relevant button on the Formatting toolbar appears recessed and in a lighter shade.

You can also use the Formatting toolbar to remove formatting. For example, if you want to remove the bold formatting from a title, you simply select the title text and click the Bold button.

In this exercise, you use the Formatting toolbar buttons to make text bold, italic, and underlined, and you use the Formatting down arrows to open lists on the Formatting toolbar to change the font and size of a heading.

1   On the Standard toolbar, click the Open button.

The Open dialog box appears.

Open

2   Click the Look In down arrow, click the icon for your hard disk, double-click the Word Core Practice folder, and then double-click the Lesson04 folder.

The contents of the Lesson04 folder appear in the Open dialog box.

> When you create a new document, Word uses New Times Roman as the font in 12-point type as the default setting. A point is the equivalent of 1/72 of an inch in height. So 12-point text is one-sixth inch in height.

3   Verify that the file Brochure 04 is selected and click the Open button.

The file Brochure 04 appears in Word, and the Open dialog box closes.

4   Select the heading line, *Impact PR Network*.

5   On the Formatting toolbar, click the Bold button, and click the Italic button.

Bold

The title appears bold and italic.

I

Italic

6   Double-click the last word of the heading, *Network*, to select it.

7   On the Formatting toolbar, click the Underline button.

8   Click anywhere outside the selected text.

> You can also apply the Bold attribute to selected text by pressing the key combination Ctrl+B. Similarly, you can italicize selected text by pressing Ctrl+I.

The text is no longer selected, and the word *Network* is underlined.

9   Triple-click the selection area (the area of the document to the left of the text).

All text in the document appears selected.

10   On the Formatting toolbar, click the Font down arrow.

<u>U</u>

Underline

A list of available fonts appears.

> You can also apply the Underline attribute to selected text by pressing Ctrl+U.

> Note that the styles listed in the Font list on your computer screen might be different from the styles shown in this figure.

11   Scroll down, if necessary, and click Century Schoolbook.

The text changes to the Century Schoolbook font.

> The most recently used fonts are listed first in the Font list, followed by an alphabetical listing of all available fonts.

12   On the Formatting toolbar, click the Font Size down arrow (to the right of the number *12*).

A list of font sizes appears.

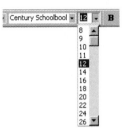

> The Font Size list displays whole numbers, but you can specify font sizes in half-point increments by typing the font size (for example, *10.5*) in the Font Size box.

13   Click 10.

The selected text is displayed in a smaller, 10-point font size.

14   Click anywhere outside the selected text

The text is no longer selected.

15   On the File menu, click Save As.

The Save As dialog box appears.

16   Save the document as **Brochure 04 Edited**, and click Save.

Word saves the document.

Keep this file open for the next exercise.

W2000.1.13
W2000.3.16

Applying Character Effects to Text

You can apply formatting attributes and effects that are not available on the Formatting toolbar, such as superscript, subscript, strikethrough, and small caps character effects from the Font dialog box. When you use the Font dialog box, you can also change multiple attributes at once and display a sample of the selected attributes before you apply them to the text. Other attributes that are available only from the Font dialog box include special effects such as shadowed or embossed text and color for underlined text.

(continued)

continued

To use the Font dialog box, you select the text that you want to format, and on the Format menu, click Font. Or before you begin typing text, on the Format menu, click Font. Then all text that you type will appear in the format that you selected in the Font dialog box until you change the formatting again.

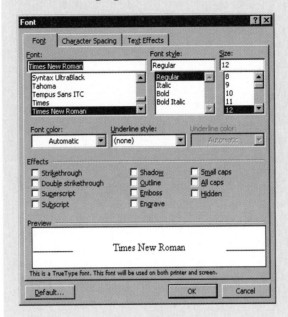

Since all the font attributes are visible in the Font dialog box, modifications can be made quite easily. You can use the Preview box to see how the modifications will look in the document.

W2000.2.1

Aligning Text in a Document

By default, text that you type has the **Align Left** alignment attribute applied. That is, text is aligned with the left margin. However, you can use the **Center, Align Right,** or the **Justify** attributes to align text. Centered text is placed equally between the left and right margins, right-aligned text is placed at the right margin, and justified text fills out all the space between the right and left margins. To align an existing paragraph, click anywhere in the paragraph and click one of the following buttons on the Formatting toolbar.

As is true with text attributes, when an alignment attribute is turned on, all text typed from that point on is affected until you turn the attribute off.

Center   Justify

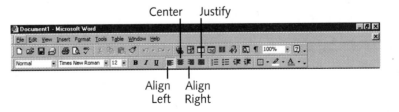

Align   Align
Left   Right

Use the alignment buttons on complete paragraphs rather than on characters or phrases. You do not need to select all the text in a paragraph before you apply an alignment. You only need to click to place the insertion point somewhere in the paragraph.

The following illustration shows the four different types of alignment attributes.

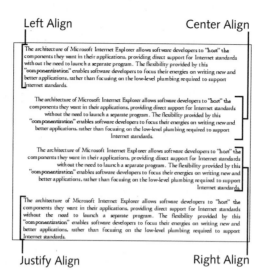

In this exercise, you center, right-align, left-align, and justify text.

1   Select the first heading line, *Impact PR Network*.

Center

2   On the Formatting toolbar, click the Center button.

The heading line moves to the center of the document.

3   Click anywhere in the first paragraph.

Align Right

4   On the Formatting toolbar, click the Align Right button.

The paragraph moves to the right margin.

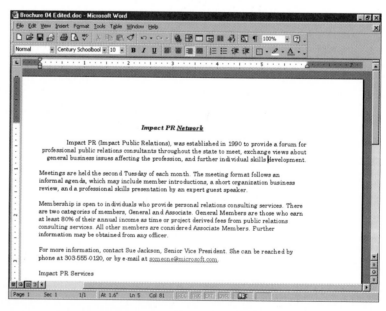

Align Left

5   On the Formatting toolbar, click the Align Left button.

The paragraph moves back to the left margin.

Justify

6 On the Formatting toolbar, click the Justify button.

The lines in the paragraph now extend to both the left and right margins, except for the last line of the paragraph, which doesn't extend all the way to the right margin because it is shorter than the other lines.

7 On the Formatting toolbar, click the Align Left button to return the text to its original alignment.

Keep this file open for the next exercise.

W2000.1.9

> You can also access the Cut, Paste, and Copy commands on the Edit menu.

Cutting and Pasting Text

When you cut and paste text, you are removing text from one location in a document and placing it in another location in the same document or in a different document. Copying and pasting duplicates the original information in another location or document. There are various methods for cutting and pasting text: you can click Cut and Paste on the Edit menu, use the mouse pointer to drag and drop text, or click the Cut and Paste buttons on the Standard toolbar. For example, the marketing manager at Impact Public Relations is updating the company brochure. The new brochure will contain information from an internal memorandum that was distributed to company employees. To save time, she will copy the information in the memo, rather than retyping it, and will paste the information into the brochure that she is updating.

Copy

Cut

When you use the Copy command, text that you select is duplicated in a new location while remaining in the original spot. When you use the Cut command, the text that you select is taken from its original position and moved to another location.

In this exercise, you copy selected text from one document to another, and cut and paste selected text within the same document.

1 On the Standard toolbar, click the Open button.

Open

The Open dialog box appears with the contents of the Lesson04 folder displayed.

2 Select the file named Memorandum 04 and click Open.

Word opens the file.

3 Triple-click the main paragraph of the memo to select it.

Copy

4 On the Standard toolbar, click the Copy button.

Nothing changes on the screen, but the text is copied. The main paragraph remains selected.

> To use a shortcut menu to copy or cut and paste, right-click the selected text, and on the shortcut menu, click Cut or Copy. To paste text, right-click the location where you want to paste the text, and on the shortcut menu, click Paste.

5   On the File menu, click Close to close the memorandum document.

The brochure document is now visible.

6   Scroll down and click at the end of the document after the word *Photography*.

7   Press Enter twice.

The insertion point moves two lines below the word *Photography*.

Paste

8   On the Standard toolbar, click the Paste button.

The paragraph remains in the original document, and a copy of the paragraph is inserted at the new location in the brochure.

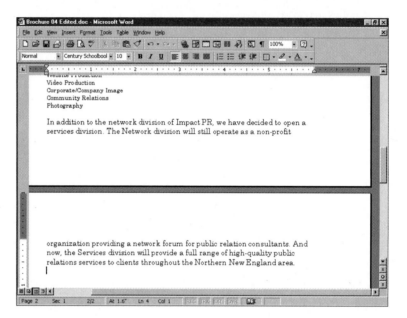

9   Select the paragraph that you just inserted, and on the Formatting toolbar, click the Font Size down arrow, and then change the font size to 10.

10   Select the fourth paragraph which begins *For more information*.

Cut

11   On the Standard toolbar, click the Cut button, and press Delete to remove the extra blank line.

The paragraph is removed from its location in the document and is placed on the Clipboard.

12   Click the blank line below the word *Photography* (the last item in the list of services).

Paste

13 Press Enter to separate the paragraph with a blank line, and on the Standard toolbar, click the Paste button.

The paragraph appears at the new location after the list of services.

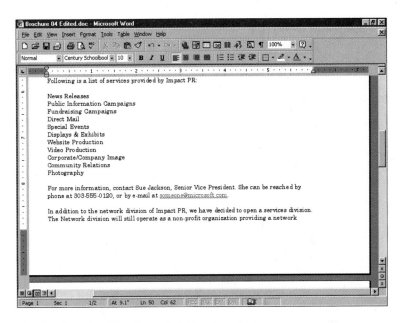

Save

14 On the Standard toolbar, click the Save button.

Keep this file open for the next exercise.

W2000.1.9

The Clipboard is a temporary storage area designed to hold text and/or pictures that have been cut or copied.

Using Paste Special

The Paste Special command extends the capabilities of the Paste command. In Microsoft Word, the Paste Special command uses Microsoft's **object linking and embedding (OLE)** technology to integrate data created by other Microsoft Office programs. To understand the difference between Paste and Paste Special, consider what happens you paste part of an Excel worksheet into a Word document by using the Paste command on the Edit menu or the Paste button on the Standard toolbar. You begin by copying a range of cells from the worksheet to the Windows **Clipboard**. You then switch to your Word document, position the insertion point where you want to paste the data, and the use the Paste command or Paste button to insert the data into the Word document. The data from the worksheet appears in the Word document as a Word table, and you can format and edit the table text just as you would edit any table.

When you paste data that originated from a different program into a Word document, as in the above example, the pasted data is no longer associated with the original program. If you want to maintain an association between the pasted content and the original application, you use the Paste Special command. You can use two basic approaches: you can either **embed** or **link** the Clipboard contents.

(continued)

continued

An object is a collection of data that is treated as a single element within a document.

If you use Paste Special to embed the pasted contents, Word converts the pasted contents to an **object** and retains its association with the program in which the contents originated. In the Excel example, if you paste and embed the contents of an Excel worksheet into a Word document, the contents are converted to an Excel object that can be edited in Excel but not in Word. If you double-click the object, Word launches Excel, which you can then use to make changes to the data. The pasted contents are no longer associated with the original workbook file, but they are associated with the Excel program.

Why is this useful? Suppose the cells that you copied from the Excel worksheet contained several formulas that make calculations on other cells. If you simply paste the data into Word, you lose all of these formulas. If you paste and embed the worksheet data as an Excel object, you can double-click the object, change formulas, or change other values and then have Excel recalculate the formulas. When you exit Excel and return to your Word document, the changes you made in Excel appear in the Excel object.

A source file is the file that contains the information that was used to create a linked object or an embedded object.

If you use Paste Special to link your pasted contents, Word creates a connection, or link, between the pasted data and the file (called the **source file**) in the originating application. For example, in the Excel example, if you copy a range of cells from an Excel workbook, and then paste and link the data in a Word document, Word converts the data to an Excel object and links it to the original workbook. If you double-click the Excel object, Excel launches Excel and opens the workbook that contains the pasted data. You can make changes to the workbook, and save your changes. Then in the Word document, you can update the Excel object to reflect the changes that have been made in the Excel workbook.

So how is linking different than embedding? When you embed an object in Word, the object becomes part of the Word document. A connection is made to the program in which the object originated, but not to the source file where the data originated. In other words, there is no longer any relationship between the Excel object in Word and the contents of the original workbook (source file). However, if you link pasted contents, the data are not truly part of the Word document—they remain part of the source file. Suppose you save and close your Word document after pasting and linking an Excel object. Now suppose you or anybody else opens the Excel workbook and makes changes to values or formulas in the workbook, and then saves the workbook. When you reopen the Word document, you can click the Excel object, and then use the Link dialog box in Word to update the Excel object to reflect the changes you have made in the Excel workbook.

W2000.1.9

To copy text using drag and drop, position the mouse pointer over the selected text, hold down the mouse button, hold down Ctrl, and then drag to the new location.

Using Drag and Drop to Edit Text

To cut and paste without using the buttons, you can use the drag-and-drop technique. As is true with other editing techniques, you begin by selecting the desired text. To drag and drop, select the text, position the mouse pointer over the selected text, hold down the left mouse button, and then drag the selection to a new location.

In this exercise, you use drag and drop to move text within a document.

1   Click the selection area to the left of the word *Photography* to select the entire line.

2   Position the mouse pointer over the selected text, and press and hold down the left mouse button.

A dotted rectangle appears near the mouse pointer.

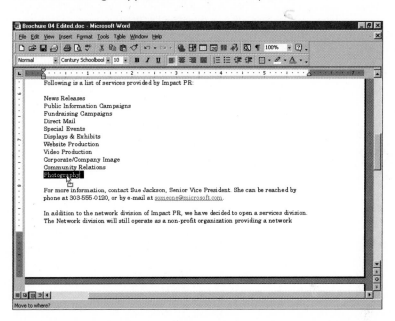

3   Drag the text, with the dotted rectangle, until the dotted line mouse pointer is directly in front of the *N* in *News Releases* (the top line in the list of services).

4   Release the mouse button.

The text moves to the new location.

5   On the Standard toolbar, click the Save button.

Save

Word saves the document.

Keep this file open for the next exercise.

W2000.1.9

Although the Windows Clipboard has been available in every version of Windows and Microsoft Office, the ability to cut or copy multiple items at a time to the Office Clipboard and then paste one or more items (called collect and paste) is new in Office 2000.

The Office Clipboard is available in Word, Excel, PowerPoint, and Outlook 2000. However, it is not available in FrontPage 2000 or any non-Office 2000 programs.

Using Collect and Paste

Office 2000 actually uses two clipboards—the Windows Clipboard (which you have already used in this lesson) and the **Office Clipboard**. The Windows Clipboard can store only one selection at a time. However, the Office Clipboard can hold up to 12 items at a time, and you can paste any of these items into documents—not just the item that you most recently copied or cut to the Clipboard. You need to view the Office Clipboard's toolbar so that you can see its contents.

When you position the mouse pointer over a Clipboard item that contains text, Word displays the first 50 characters of text. When you position the pointer over a Clipboard item that contains a picture, Word displays a ScreenTip labeled *Picture 1*, *Picture 2* (or *Item 1*, *Item 2*), and so forth in the order in which the pictures were added to the Office Clipboard.

The Clipboard toolbar appears automatically when you copy or cut two items consecutively. If you close the Clipboard toolbar three times in a row without using Paste All or any of the item buttons, the Clipboard toolbar will no longer appear automatically. You'll have to manually open the Clipboard toolbar. To manually open the Clipboard toolbar, on the View menu, point to Toolbars, and click Clipboard. You can also show the Clipboard toolbar again by copying an item two times consecutively.

The Office Clipboard can hold up to 12 items. If you try to copy a thirteenth item, a message asks if you want to discard the first item on the Office Clipboard and add the new item to the end of the Clipboard. If you click OK, the next time you copy an item from any program, the Office Clipboard automatically discards the first item and adds the new item. If you click Cancel, any new items that you copy won't be added to the Office Clipboard until you make space on the Office Clipboard by pasting or cutting items already stored there. You won't see the message again until the Office Clipboard is full. Note that the collected items remain on the Office Clipboard until you quit all open Office programs on your computer.

In this exercise, you open the Clipboard toolbar, see how the Office Clipboard handles multiple items, and then paste from it and clear it.

1   On the View menu, point to Toolbars, and click Clipboard.

The Clipboard toolbar opens.

Clear Clipboard

2 Click the Clear Clipboard button.

If there were any cut or copied items in the Clipboard, they are cleared.

Open

3 On the Standard toolbar, click the Open button. In the Open dialog box, select the file named Logo 04, and click Open.

Word opens the file.

4 Click the text *Impact PR*.

Little boxes appear around the logo, indicating that the logo is selected.

Copy

5 On the Standard toolbar, click the Copy button, and close the logo document.

The logo is copied from the document and placed in the Clipboard. There is one item available in the Clipboard. The logo document closes, and the brochure document appears.

6 Double-click the last paragraph of the brochure document that begins *In addition to the network*.

Cut

7 On the Standard toolbar, click the Cut button.

The paragraph is removed from the document and placed on the Office Clipboard. The Clipboard toolbar now contains two items.

8 Move the mouse pointer over the first item in the Clipboard toolbar.

A ScreenTip appears, displaying the words *Picture 1*.

9 Move the mouse pointer over the second item in the Clipboard toolbar.

The ScreenTip displays the beginning contents of the paragraph that you cut.

10 Scroll up to the top of the document, and click in front of the letter *I* in the heading *Impact PR Network*.

11 Press Enter eight times to move the title down.

12 On the Clipboard toolbar, click the first item.

The text *Impact PR* now appears at the top of the brochure.

13 Scroll down and click the blank line above the second heading, *Impact PR Services*, and then press Enter to insert another blank line.

14   On the Clipboard toolbar, click the second item.

The paragraph is inserted at the bottom of the first section in the document.

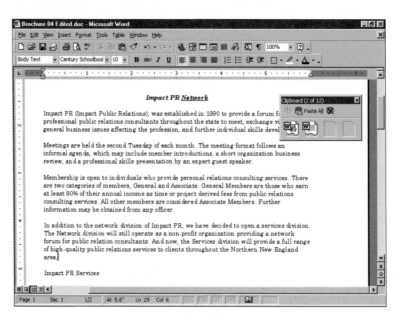

 15   On the Clipboard toolbar, click the Clear Clipboard button.

Clear Clipboard

16   In the top-right corner of the Clipboard, click the Close button.

The Clipboard toolbar closes.

 17   On the Standard toolbar, click the Save button to save the document.

Save

Word saves the document.

Keep this file open for the next exercise.

W2000.3.15
W2000.3.16

Applying Styles to Text

Styles save you time when formatting a document and help you maintain a consistent format within the same document and from document to document. For example, suppose you are creating a document that contains several subheadings. You want these subheadings to be in a different font than your text and green. Instead of using the formatting options on the Formatting toolbar every time you type a subheading in the document, you can create a style.

> A style is a named set of formatting instructions, used to apply multiple formatting characteristics to text in a single step.

After you create the style, you simply insert the insertion point anywhere in the exhisting text or anywhere in the document you want the style to start and click the Style down arrow. Select the style you want and the text is modified with the chosen style.

Whenever you open a new, blank document, Word automatically attaches a standard template to the document. A template is a preformatted document that has its own set of styles. When you type in a new, blank document, the characters are set in a default style that is called Normal. The words that you type are automatically formatted in the font Times New Roman, at 12 points in size, and aligned against the left margin. The Normal template has five styles, three of which are designed to be used as headings. The names of styles are located on the Formatting toolbar, in the Style list, as shown below.

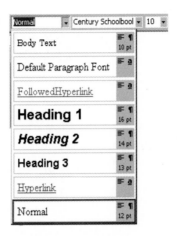

You can use styles to quickly apply multiple formatting attributes to text. For example, you could specify attributes such as bold, left align, italicize, and even font color, and then apply all those attributes at the same time by applying a style. Simply select or click the text, and on the Formatting toolbar, click the Style down arrow, and click the style that you want to apply. If you want to apply a style to an entire paragraph, you need only click anywhere in that paragraph and click the style name in the Style list. You can also apply a style by clicking a blank line, selecting a style from the Style list, and typing. The text that you type from then on appears in the style that you selected.

In this exercise, you apply styles to paragraphs.

1   Scroll down in the document, and click anywhere in the word *Photography*, which is the first item in the list of services near the end of the document.

2   On the Formatting toolbar, click the Style down arrow, and click Heading 3.

   The style is applied to the current paragraph—in this case, the single line *Photography*.

3   Select the remaining list items, click the Style down arrow, and click Heading 3.

   The Heading 3 style is applied to all the paragraphs in the list.

On the Edit menu, click the Repeat command to apply styles to multiple paragraphs that are scattered throughout the document. Apply the style that you want to the first paragraph, click or select the next paragraph, and press Ctrl+Y or F4. Use this method until you are finished applying the style.

4   Click outside of the list to deselect the paragraphs.

The list should look like the one in the following illustration.

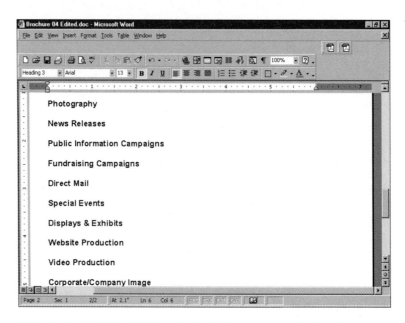

5   Click in front of the first line in the last paragraph in the document.

6   On the Formatting toolbar, click the Style down arrow, and click Heading 1.

The style is applied to the entire paragraph.

Undo

7   On the Standard toolbar, click the Undo button to remove the formatting that you just applied.

8   In the last paragraph in the document, select the words *For more information,*.

9   On the Formatting toolbar, click the Style down arrow, and click Heading 3.

The style is applied only to the selected text and not to the entire paragraph.

10   Select the *P* in the word *Photography*, which is the first item in the list of services.

11   Click the Style down arrow, and click Heading 1.

The character becomes larger.

Undo

12   On the Standard toolbar, click the Undo button to remove the formatting you just applied.

13   On the Standard toolbar, click the Save button.

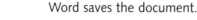

Word saves the document.

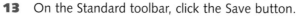
Save

Keep this file open for the next exercise.

Creating a Paragraph Border

W2000.2.4

You can use borders to enhance the appearance of the documents that you create and to help distinguish blocks of text. Borders are a great way to catch a person's eye. Suppose you are creating a corporate memo reminding your co-workers about the upcoming company picnic. The information in the memo includes the date, time, location, menu and activities planned. You need to remind your co-workers to bring $5 with them to the picnic. Important information like this can get lost in a document, so you add a border around this sentence so they'll be sure not to miss the message.

You can create a border around entire pages in a document or around only selected paragraphs. Word provides a variety of preset borders to choose from, and all borders are customizable.

A border is based on a rectangular design, used to frame text in a document. Borders do not have to surround the text on all four sides of a document; you can display or hide any combination of the four borders that form the rectangle. For example, you could display only a bottom border for a paragraph. The marketing manager at Impact Public Relations likes to create a two-line border (one line along the bottom and the other to the right) for the introductory paragraphs in her brochures. You can apply a border to a single paragraph or to multiple paragraphs.

One way to customize a border is to alter its *line weight*, which is the width of the lines that make up the border. To change the line weight, on the Tables And Borders toolbar, click the Line Weight down arrow, and click a point size for the border width. You can then click the Border Color button to choose a color for the lines.

Border Color

You can also create and format paragraph borders by clicking Borders And Shading on the Format menu, clicking the Borders tab, and then setting border characteristics.

Another option is to apply the border to a particular side of the paragraph. For example, if you want the border to appear below the paragraph, rather than surrounding it on all four sides, click the Border down arrow to specify the side of the paragraph that you want the border to appear on.

In this exercise, you use the Tables And Borders toolbar to create and apply a border to an introductory paragraph.

1 Click anywhere in the paragraph that begins with the words *With a philosophy* (the eighth paragraph, located above the list of services).

Tables And Borders

2 On the Standard toolbar, click the Tables And Borders button.

The Tables And Borders toolbar appears on your screen, and the mouse pointer looks like a pencil.

3   On the Tables And Borders toolbar, click the Line Style down arrow.

A list of line styles appears.

4   Scroll down until you see a double squiggly line, and click it.

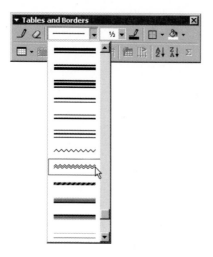

Border Color

5   On the Tables And Borders toolbar, click the Border Color button.

A color palette appears.

6   Click the Gold square (fourth row, second square).

Border Down Arrow

7   Click the Border down arrow.

A list of border buttons appears, each button displaying a type of border.

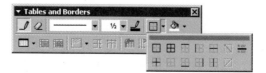

tip

You can remove a border by clicking the affected text, and clicking the Border down arrow. When the border choices are displayed, click the No Border button. You can also display the Borders And Shading dialog box, and in the Setting section, click None to remove a border.

Outside Border

8 On the Tables And Borders toolbar, click the Outside Border button.

The line style, color, and border type that you specified are applied to the paragraph. The paragraph should look similar to the one on the following page.

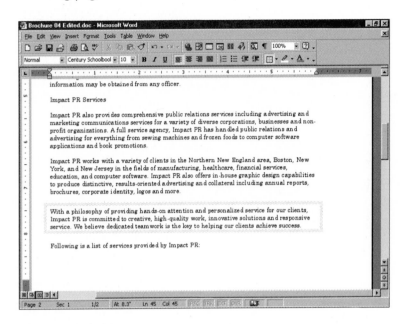

Save

9 Click the Save button.

Word saves the document.

Keep this file open for the next exercise.

W2000.2.4

If the Tables And Borders toolbar is not displayed, on the Standard toolbar, click the Tables And Borders button.

Adding Shading to a Paragraph

You can call attention to selected paragraphs by adding **shading**—either as a shade of gray or in color. If you apply color shading to a paragraph but print the document on a black-and-white printer, the color shading will be printed as a shade of gray.

To expand the shading color list, on the Tables And Borders toolbar, click the Shading Color down arrow, and click the desired color square to add shading to selected text.

In this exercise, you add a shading color to the last paragraph in your document.

1 Click anywhere in the last paragraph (the one beginning with the words *For more information*).

Shading Color

2 On the Tables And Borders toolbar, click the Shading Color down arrow.

A color palette is displayed.

3 Click the Light Yellow square (eighth row, third square).

The paragraph is now shaded in light yellow. Notice that the color on the Shading Color button is also light yellow.

4 Scroll up to the paragraph that has a border surrounding it, and click the paragraph.

5 Click the Shading Color button.

The bordered paragraph is now shaded in light yellow, too.

The light yellow color on the Shading Color button indicates that this is the color that you most currently used. If you select another paragagraph and click the Shading Color button, the paragraph changes to light yellow. If you change the color to sea green, the Shading Color button turns sea green, and any text or paragraph that you select before clicking the button again will turn sea green too.

If the shade that you pick is dark, Word automatically converts the text to white for readability. To remove shading, first select the shaded text. On the Tables And Borders toolbar, click the Shading Color down arrow, and click No Fill.

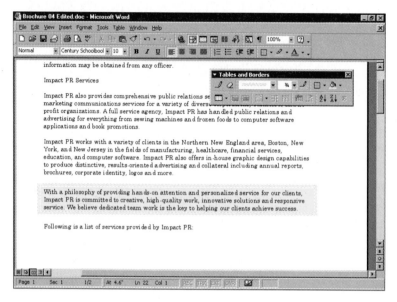

6 On the Standard toolbar, click the Undo button.

Word removes the shading from the paragraph.

Close

7 In the top-right corner of the Tables And Borders toolbar, click the Close button.

Save

8 On the Standard toolbar, click the Save button.

Word saves the document.

Keep this file open for the next exercise.

W2000.3.2

Previewing a Document

To see exactly how your document will look after it is printed, you can use Print Preview. The Print Preview window shows you exactly how the lines on the page will appear when they're printed and where page breaks will occur. If you don't like the layout, you can make adjustments before you print. Using Print Preview can help you identify desired formatting changes without wasting paper.

In this exercise, you preview a document before printing it.

important

You must have a printer to complete the following exercise.

Print Preview

1   On the Standard toolbar, click the Print Preview button.

The screen should look similar to the one shown here.

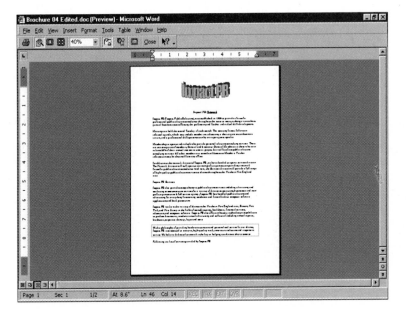

If the ruler isn't visible, click the View Ruler button.

View Ruler

Multiple Pages

2   On the Print Preview toolbar, click the Multiple Pages button, and click the second button in the top row to view two pages at a time.

3   Click the One Page button to return to the single-page view.

One Page

4   On the Print Preview toolbar, click Close.

The Print Preview closes, and Word returns to the previous view of the document.

Keep this file open for the next exercise.

tip

To print a document in Print Preview, on the Print Preview toolbar, click the Print button.

W2000.3.1

The default printer is the specific printer that is selected automatically as the location where documents will be printed on your computer.

Printing a Document

You can use two methods to print a document in Word. One way is to use the Print button to print one copy of all pages in the current document using the default printer. This method is convenient when you want to print the entire document. The other method is to use the menu to display the Print dialog box. If you want to print multiple copies of the document, print from a different printer, print a selected page or pages range, you use the Print dialog box to specify. Instead of printing out the entire document to review and edit page 6, you can use the Print dialog box to print page 6 only.

In this exercise, you practice printing a document by using both the Print button and the Print dialog box, and then you print only a selected block of text.

Print

1 On the Standard toolbar, click the Print button.

One copy of the current document is printed on the default printer.

2 Click anywhere on the first page of the document.

3 On the File menu, click Print.

The Print dialog box appears.

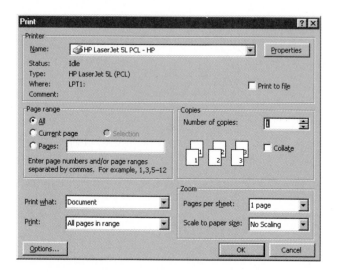

You can also print a specific page other than the current page by typing the number of the page that you want to print in the Pages box in the Print dialog box. To print multiple pages but not the entire document, you can type the page numbers, inserting a comma between page numbers for non-sequential pages or using a dash to indicate a continuous range of sequential pages. For example: 1,3,5 or 4-6.

4 In the Page Range section, click the Current Page option, and click OK.

The first page of the document is printed.

5 Select the first paragraph which begins *Impact PR*.

6 On the File menu, click Print.

The Print dialog box appears.

7 In the Page Range section, click the Selection option, and click OK.

The selected text is printed.

Lesson Wrap-Up

In this lesson, you learned how to format text. You also learned how to use various text attributes, how to cut or copy and paste text, and how to use the Clipboard to paste multiple selections. In addition, you applied styles, paragraph borders, and shading and then previewed and printed the document.

If you are continuing to the next lesson:

Save

1 On the Standard toolbar, click the Save button.
   Word saves the changes to the file.

2 On the File menu, click Close to close the file.
   Word closes the file.

If you are not continuing to other lessons:

1 On the Standard toolbar, click the Save button.
   Word saves the changes to the file.

✕ **2** In the top-right corner of the Word window, click the Close button.
Close   Word closes the file and the Word program closes.

Lesson Glossary

Align Left A formatting attribute in which each line of a block of text is positioned with the left margin. By default, each paragraph that you type is left-aligned unless you change the alignment setting.

Align Right A formatting attribute in which each line of a block of text is positioned with the right margin.

attribute A characteristic that is applied to text in a Word document, such as the font, font size, bold, underline, or italics.

Center An attribute that aligns each line of a block of text an equal distance from the left and right margins.

Clipboard A temporary storage area designed to hold text and/or pictures that have been cut or copied.

embed The act of placing an object in a document.

Justify An attribute that aligns a block of text flush with both the left and right margins. Spaces between words are enlarged proportionally so that each line fills the space between the margins.

link Connects an embedded object with the original program.

object A collection of data that is treated as a single element within a document.

object linking and embedding (OLE) A technology for transferring and sharing information among programs.

Office Clipboard An extension of the Windows Clipboard and is available in Word, Excel, Outlook, and PowerPoint 2000 for collecting multiple selections in memory. You can use the Office Clipboard to choose which selection among multiple paste objects to paste into a different location.

shading A rectangle of color surrounding a block of text used to emphasize specific information in a document.

source file A file that contains the information that was used to create a linked object or an embedded object.

style A named set of formatting instructions. You use a style to apply multiple formatting characteristics to text in a single step.

Quick Quiz

1   What key combination and shortcut key allow you to apply styles to multiple nonconsecutive paragraphs?

2   What are four methods to cut and paste a selection of text?

3   Before you print a document, how can you be sure that the margins will look right?

4   What is a style?

5   What are two ways that can you apply bold formatting to a selection of text?

6   How can you view multiple selections of text in the Office Clipboard?

7   What is the difference between cutting and copying text?

8   How do you change the line style of an existing border?

9   How can you edit a linked object in a Word document?

important

In the Putting It All Together section below, you must complete Exercise 1 to continue to Exercise 2.

Putting It All Together

Exercise 1: If necessary, start Word. Open the document named Invitation 04 from the Lesson04 folder. Center all the text in the document. Change the second paragraph from the bottom to a 20-point font size, in small caps, blue, and bold. Select the lines of text *You're invited to...*, *When*, and *Where*, and change them to 16 points and bold. Change all text to the font Garamond. Finally, move the last three paragraphs to the top of the document. Print two copies of the document. Save the document as **Invitation 04 Edited** in the Lesson04 folder.

Exercise 2: Select all the text in the invitation and create a blue border. Add light turquoise shading inside the border. Save the document and close it.

LESSON 5

Changing the Layout of a Document

After completing this lesson, you will be able to:

✔ *Adjust page margin settings.*

✔ *Insert a forced page break.*

✔ *Set paragraph alignment, indentation, and spacing.*

✔ *Change indents and tab settings.*

✔ *Insert and clear tabs.*

✔ *Add page numbers to a document.*

✔ *Create and customize headers and footers.*

✔ *Change page orientation.*

Rather than using the default settings that Microsoft Word provides, you can use other settings and tools to change how your letters, lists, proposals, and general correspondence look. One way to quickly customize a document is by changing the way the text appears on the page by altering page margins, resetting paragraph alignments, changing tab settings, and customizing headers and footers. When you create a document, you are doing more than just formatting text; you have the capability to change the page layout of the document by altering how text appears on the page.

You start this lesson by changing a **page margin**. A page margin is the amount of space at the top, bottom, or sides surrounding the text on a page. Another setting that you can manipulate is where a page breaks. A **page break** occurs when text or objects on a page run out of space. Word "breaks" up the overflow text or objects by creating a new page. Word automatically inserts page breaks, but you can also insert a **hard page break**, which manually forces a page to break at a specific place in the document.

You can also use a **header** or a **footer** on a document with multiple pages. A header is the text that appears at the top of a page that usually includes the title of the work, the date, and page numbers. A footer is text printed at the bottom of the page, which might include the date, author's name, and the title of the document.

You'll also set tab stops for a particular paragraph within the document. A **tab stop** or **tab** is used to indent the first line of a paragraph or to align text or numbers in columns. You can also use Tabs to align columns of text within a parpgraph. Other settings, include **indents** and **spacing**. Indents determine the alignment of the paragraph in relation to the page margin setting, and spacing indicates the area above and below the paragraph as well as the space between the lines.

In this lesson, you will learn how to adjust page margin settings, insert page breaks, and set paragraph alignment, indentation, and spacing. You'll also learn how to change indents, insert and clear tabs, and add page numbers to a document. In this lesson, you will also create headers and footers, and change the page orientation of a document.

To complete the procedures in this lesson, you will need to use the practice file named Salary Survey 05 in the Lesson05 folder in the Word Core Practice folder that is located on your hard disk. This document was created to publicize the results of a salary and benefits survey administered to a random sampling of Impact Public Relations membership.

Changing Page Margins Using the Page Setup Dialog Box

When you use the Page Setup dialog box, you determine how the document appears on the printed page. The Page Setup dialog box is most commonly used for setting page margins. Page margins affect the entire document because after the page margins are changed, the number of pages in the document might increase or decrease depending on how much text the page margin allows per page. To change the page margins in a document, you can use the ruler at the top of the document or the Page Setup dialog box, which is accessed by clicking Page Setup on the File menu.

By default, Word includes left and right page margins of 1.25 inches and top and bottom page margins of 1 inch. You use the Page Setup dialog box to adjust top, bottom, left, and right page margin settings, determine the placement of headers and footers, and select the amount of text that you want the settings to affect.

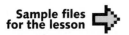

Sample files for the lesson

For additional information on how to find and open files used in this book, see the "Using the CD-ROM" section at the beginning of this book.

W2000.3.7

In the following exercises, the Standard and Formatting toolbars have been separated. For additional information on how to separate the toolbars, see the "Using the CD-ROM" section at the begining of this book.

You can click the Apply To down arrow to define whether you want the setup changes to apply to the whole document, the selected text only, or from the position of the insertion point forward.

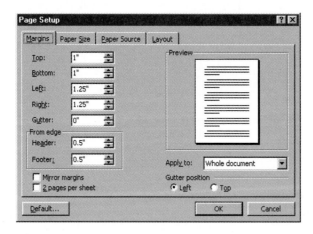

In this exercise, you change the page margin settings using the Page Setup dialog box.

Open

1   On the Standard toolbar, click the Open button.

The Open dialog box appears.

2   Click the Look In down arrow, click the icon for your hard disk, double-click the Word Core Practice folder, and then double-click the Lesson05 folder.

The contents of the Lesson05 folder appear in the Open dialog box.

3   Double-click the file Salary Survey 05.

The file Salary Survey 05 appears in Word, and the Open dialog box closes.

4   On the File menu, click Page Setup.

The Page Setup dialog box appears. The current top margin setting (1″) is selected.

> You can also use the up and down arrows to the right of the settings to select preset sizes. The up arrow increases the page margin size, and the down arrow decreases the page margin size.

5   In the Top box, type **1.5**, and press Tab.

In the Preview section to the right of the page margin settings, the top page margin shifts down to show what the text will look like.

6   In the Bottom box, type **1.5**, and press Tab.

In the Preview section, the bottom page margin shifts up.

7   Click OK.

The top and bottom page margins are now 1.5 inches instead of 1 inch.

> There is no visible change to the text in Normal view, which is the currently selected view for the document.

8   On the File menu, click Save As.

The Save As dialog box is displayed.

9   In the File Name box, type **Salary Survey 05 Edited**.

10   Click Save to save the file in the Lesson05 folder.

Word saves the document.

Keep this file open for the next exercise.

W2000.3.7

Changing Page Margins Using the Ruler

You can also change page margins using the **ruler**. The ruler is a scale shown in the document window that is marked in inches or other units of measurement. A horizontal ruler in Normal view and both horizontal and vertical rulers in **Print Layout view** are provided in Word.

> To turn the rulers on or off in Normal view and Print Layout view, on the View menu, click Ruler.

To use the ruler, you should use Print Layout view, not the default setting of **Normal view**, so that you can see the page margin settings relative to the page borders. You use Normal View to edit and format the document, but Normal View doesn't show the page margins relative to the page borders. You can also use **Print Preview** to view your document as it will be printed, but you will not be able to make changes in this view.

The **horizontal ruler** along the top of the document window shows the left and right page margins as well as the left and right paragraph indents, such as first line and hanging indents (you'll learn more about these indents later in this lesson). Often, the paragraph indents and page margins are the same; however, it's important to recognize that you can adjust the page margins or indents of paragraphs independent of the page margins. The **vertical ruler** along the left edge of the document shows the top and bottom page page margin boundaries.

To change page margins using the ruler, you use Print Layout view, which is shown below. This view allows you to see the page margins on the vertical and horizontal rulers. When you position the mouse pointer over the page margin, the mouse pointer appears as a horizontal double-arrow. You can then drag the **first line indent**, hanging indent, left indent, or right indent marker to a new location to reset the page margin. You'll learn more about these indents in this lesson.

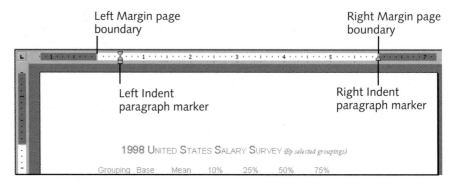

In this exercise, you change the page margins of the document using the ruler.

> To display the page margin measurements as you adjust them, hold down the Alt key as you drag a marker. This technique also allows you to adjust the page margin in smaller increments.

1   On the View menu, click Print Layout.

The document is displayed in Print Layout view. The 1.5-inch top page margin setting is reflected on the vertical ruler.

2   Position the mouse pointer above the Left Margin marker on the horizontal ruler until the pointer is displayed as a double-arrow.

> You can also change the document view with the layout buttons along the bottom-left edge of the document window.

3   Hold down the Alt key.

The double-arrow disappears.

4   Drag the marker to the left until the measurement of 6.5″ is displayed in the white portion of the ruler.

The left page margin shifts to the left, and all the text in the document is adjusted. Notice that the tabs and columns in the document are disrupted.

5   Release the Alt key.

6   Position the mouse pointer over the Right Margin marker until the pointer is displayed as a double arrow.

7 Hold down the Alt key, and drag the marker to the right until the measurement of 7" is displayed in the white portion of the ruler.

The right page margin shifts to the right, and the text is adjusted. Both the left and right page margins are now set at .75 inches.

8 Release the Alt key when the page margin is set.

Save

9 On the Standard toolbar, click the Save button.

Word saves the document.

Keep this file open for the next exercise.

W2000.3.11

Aligning Text Vertically on a Page

You can change the **vertical alignment** of text using the Layout tab of the Page Setup dialog box. Vertical alignment is the way the lines of text line up between the top and bottom page margins. (Horizontal alignment can be adjusted by using the Left, Center, Right, or Justify buttons on the Formatting toolbar; vertical alignment of text, on the other hand, can be set only from the Page Layout dialog box.) Normally you want text to align with the top margin. That is, when you begin typing text on a new page, the text appears at the top of the page and new lines of text are added below. However, you can change the text alignment on a page so that it aligns with the bottom of the page (the first line starts at the bottom, and each new line appears at the bottom of the page, causing previously typed lines to be "pushed" upward) or is centered vertically on the page (the first line of text appears at the midpoint on the page, and new lines are positioned so that an even amount of space is maintained between the top and bottom page margins).

To change vertical text alignment, on the File menu, click Page Setup, and click the Layout tab. In the Vertical Alignment box, click the down arrow, and click Top, Center, Justified, or Bottom to define how the text is aligned vertically on the page. The default vertical alignment is the Top setting. The Justified setting fills in paragraphs (rather than individual lines, which is the case with the Center alignment setting) evenly between the top and bottom margins. For example, when you type the first paragraph on a page, the text appears at the top of the page. When you press Enter to begin a new paragraph, the next paragraph begins at the bottom of the page. When you press Enter and begin a third paragraph, the second paragraph moves to the top of the page, and the new paragraph is entered near the bottom of the page.

W2000.1.6

Inserting Page Breaks

At times, you might want to begin a new page before you have typed a full page of text. Perhaps you are creating your resume and want to make sure that each section stays on the same page; you don't want to have the section on education split between two pages. Instead you can insert a hard page break to put all the education information on the second page. To insert a hard page break, you position the insertion point at the location where you want to add the break, and press Ctrl+Enter. You can delete a hard page break by positioning the insertion point on the page break and pressing Delete.

An automatic page break, called a **soft page break**, is inserted when text wraps to a line below the bottom page margin. Soft page breaks, which appear as dotted horizontal lines in Normal view, are adjusted by Word as you modify text within a document. For example, when your text runs out of room on the first page, a soft page break is displayed on the screen and subsequent text is displayed on the second page. If you only have a line or two on the second page and you delete a paragraph from the first page, the soft page break disappears because now all the text has room to fit the first page. The soft page break does not reappear on the screen until you continue to type more text that fills up the first page and carries over to the next page.

In this exercise, you view soft page breaks and insert hard page breaks.

1 On the View menu, click Normal.

The document is displayed in Normal view.

2 Scroll down the document to view the soft page breaks.

3 Scroll to the heading *Median U.S. Salary,* and click to the left of the letter M.

4 Press Ctrl+Enter.

A hard page break is inserted. Notice that the soft page break on this page has now moved further down the page.

5 Scroll to the heading *Salary Percentiles,* click to the left of the first S and press Ctrl+Enter.

A hard page break is inserted.

6 Press Ctrl+End to move to the end of the document, and press Ctrl+Enter.

A hard page break is inserted at the end of the document. (You will add text to this page later).

7 Save the document using the current name.

Word saves the document.

Keep this file open for the next exercise.

> Soft page breaks are displayed as dotted horizontal lines in Normal view, but appear as separate pages in Print Layout view.

Save

W2000.2.3

> As you enter and edit text, Word inserts special characters or formatting characters—such as spaces, tabs, and paragraph marks—into your document. These characters are not printed and do not appear on the screen unless you click the Tools menu, click Options, and select the Formatting Marks check boxes on the View tab or the Show/Hide ¶ button on the Standard toolbar. For more information on using the Show/Hide ¶ button, see Lesson 3, "Using Templates and Wizards."

Formatting a Paragraph

Word defines a **paragraph** as any amount of text that ends with a hard return. Each time you press Enter, a **paragraph mark** (a hidden formatting character that designates the end of a paragraph) is inserted into the document. Although you see the actual paragraph mark only if the display of nonprinting characters (or formatting marks) is turned on, the paragraph mark is still present. Even a blank line is considered to be a paragraph because it ends with a hard return.

The formatting that you select for a paragraph is applied to the next paragraph that you type. This process occurs because all formatting associated with a paragraph is stored in the paragraph mark. When you begin a new paragraph, the paragraph takes on the formatting characteristics of the previous paragraph. Alternatively, when you delete a paragraph mark, the preceding paragraph takes on the formatting characteristics of the next paragraph.

Paragraphs are set by default to be single-spaced and left-aligned with no indentation. You change the default paragraph settings for single paragraphs or groups of paragraphs by using the Paragraph dialog box. To access the Paragraph dialog box, on the Format menu, click Paragraph.

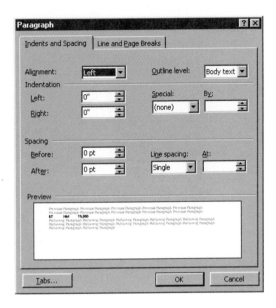

As with most Word formatting commands, you either select the paragraphs that you want changed and then apply formatting, or apply the formatting first and then type the desired text.

> To format only one paragraph, click anywhere in that paragraph. To format multiple paragraphs, first select the paragraphs that will be affected.

You can use the Indents And Spacing tab of the Paragraph dialog box to use and modify **alignment** and indention:

Alignment   The arrangement of text in fixed or predetermined positions. If the paragraph is left-aligned, all the text in the paragraph will begin on the left side of the document.

Indentation   Determines the position text is moved in from the page margin. You can also specify positions for hanging indents (indenting all but the first line of a paragraph to the same point) and first line indents (only indenting the first line of a paragraph) by clicking the Special down arrow, and then selecting the desired indent type.

In this exercise, you change paragraph spacing and create hanging indents using the Paragraph dialog box.

1   Scroll to the heading *Salary Percentiles*, if necessary, and select the heading and all the text under the heading.

2   On the Format menu, click Paragraph.

    The Paragraph dialog box appears.

3   Click the Indents And Spacing tab, if necessary.

4   In the Spacing section, in the After box, click the up arrow twice.

The paragraph spacing is changed to 12 points, and a preview of the change is shown in the Preview section.

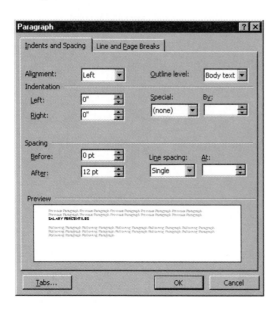

5   Click OK, and click outside the paragraph to deselect the text.

The Paragraph dialog box closes, and 12 points of space are added after each paragraph in the document.

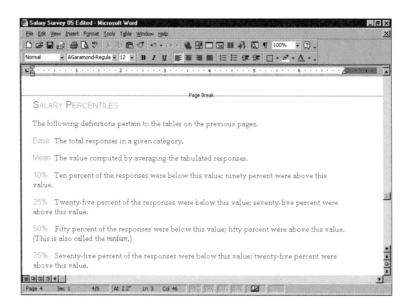

You don't have to select all text in every paragraph before you apply a paragraph format. You need to include only part of the first and last paragraphs in the selection. The formatting that you apply still affects all the partially selected paragraphs.

6   In the same section of the Word document, select the definitions under the text *The following definitions pertain to*….

7   On the Format menu, click Paragraph.

The Paragraph dialog box appears.

8   Click the Special down arrow, click Hanging, and then click OK.

Word creates a hanging indent for the definition paragraphs, where the first line *hangs* farther out from the following lines. The default value for a hanging indent is 0.5 inch, which is what you use for this exercise.

9   Click anywhere in the document to deselect the text.

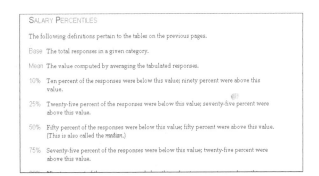

Save

10   On the Standard toolbar, click the Save button.

Word saves the document.

Keep this file open for the next exercise.

W2000.2.5

Indenting Text Using the Ruler

To quickly create a hanging or first line indent, you can use the ruler. The ruler contains markers for both of these indents, as well as a right indent, as displayed below.

First line Indent   Right Indent

Left Indent   Hanging Indent

You begin indenting paragraphs by selecting the text and dragging the appropriate marker to the desired position on the ruler.

To	Do this
Fully indent a section	Drag the Left Indent marker. All three formatting markers move.
Indent only the first line	Drag the First Line Indent marker only.
Create a hanging indent	Drag the Hanging Indent marker only.

In this exercise, you change indent settings using the ruler.

1   Under the sentence *The following definitions pertain to...*, select the seven definition paragraphs.

Be precise with the mouse while working with the ruler because it is easy to click and drag the wrong marker. Take your time and make sure that you grab the right marker by checking the ScreenTip. If you find that you dragged the wrong marker and your text is indented incorrectly, press Ctrl+Z to undo the change before you try again.

Although you don't need to hold down the Alt key when you drag one of the paragraph markers, doing so allows you to see the measurement that you want to set.

2   Position the mouse pointer over the Hanging Indent marker on the ruler (the bottom triangle).

The ScreenTip Hanging Indent appears.

3   Hold down the Alt key, and drag the Hanging Indent marker to the right until a measurement of .75" appears to the left of the marker. Release the mouse button, but do not deselect the text.

The paragraphs are indented 0.75 inch from the first line of each paragraph.

4   Release the Alt key.

5   With the definition paragraphs still selected, drag the Left Indent marker (the square) to the 2-inch mark on the ruler.

Notice that all three formatting markers move and the paragraphs are fully indented.

6   With the definition paragraphs still selected, drag the right Indent marker (the triangle on the lower-right side of the ruler) to the 5.5-inch mark on the ruler.

The right margin of the selected text moves to the left.

7   Click anywhere outside the paragraphs to deselect the text.

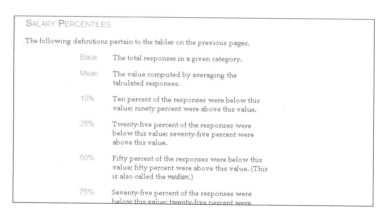

8   Scroll through the document to view the various paragraph formats.

9   On the Standard toolbar, click the Save button.

Word saves the document.

Keep this file open for the next exercise.

Save

W2000.2.6

Changing Tab Settings

Word automatically left-aligns tab stops and spaces them at every half inch. Each time that you press the Tab key, the insertion point moves to the next tab stop on the current line. Unless you specify otherwise, Word inserts a left tab stop each time that you press Tab. A left tab aligns text at a specific distance from the left page margin. The following table explains the types of tabs that are available. You can change the tab alignment by clicking the Tab button to the left of the horizontal ruler or by clicking Tabs on the Format menu and clicking the desired alignment option in the Tabs dialog box.

Tab Type	Button	Effect
Left	L	Aligns text to the right of the tab.
Right	⌐	Aligns text to the left of the tab.
Center	⊥	Centers text on either side of the tab.
Decimal	⊥	Aligns numbers along a common decimal position.
Bar	I	Inserts a vertical bar at the tab stop.

While automatic spacing between tab stops might be acceptable for most documents that you create, you have the option of changing the spacing. For example, if you are working on a document that had several columns of data, you can change the tab settings so that the data is spaced evenly and is legible on the page. When you use tabs, you might find that the columns created are not always wide enough to accommodate your text.

In this exercise, you widen columns using the Tabs dialog box to change tab settings.

1   Scroll to the heading *Median U.S. Salary by Two-Digit Zip Codes*, and select all the zip code lines below the heading (from *01* through *98*).

2   On the Format menu, click Tabs.

    The Tabs dialog box appears.

3   In the Tab Stop Position box, type **1**.

4   Click the Set button.

    The tab is set, and the tab position number appears in the Tab Stop Position list.

> If you have problems selecting the text, click to the left of the first line *01 MA $51,920*, hold down the Shift key, and then select this line. Release both the Shift key and the mouse button. Scroll down to line number 98. Notice that as you scroll, line 01 remains selected. When you reach line number 98, press Shift and select this line. Word automatically selects lines 02 through 97 for you.

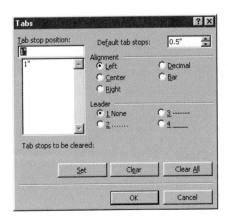

5   Type **2.5**, and click the Set button.

    The second tab is set, and the tab position number appears in the Tab Stop Position list.

6   Click OK to close the Tabs dialog box.

The columns of information are neatly spaced and aligned according to the tab stops that you just inserted.

7   Click anywhere on the page to deselect the text.

Keep this file open for the next exercise.

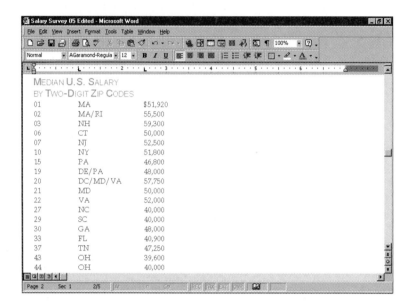

W2000.2.6
W2000.2.8

> You can also select the type of tab and insert tab stops using the horizontal ruler which is explained later in this lesson.

Setting and Clearing Specific Tab Stops

When making lists, charts, or other highly formatted sections of text, it can be helpful to create tabs at special intervals to break up information in a visually appealing way. The type of tab alignment that you select in the Alignment section of the Tabs dialog box determines how the text is aligned at that tab stop. There are five types of tab stops available in Word.

You can also create a **leader tab,** which is displayed as a row of dots from the insertion point to the next tab stop. Leader tabs can be left-aligned, right-aligned, centered, or decimal-aligned as well. You might have seen a leader tab before in a ledger or on a bill, where the *total* line has a row of dots leading to the total of the bill to distinguish it from other entries that are above the leader tab.

You set and clear tabs using the Tabs dialog box. Here you can set one or multiple tabs, determine the alignment of the text to the tab stop, or clear all existing tabs.

In this exercise, you set tabs using the Tabs dialog box. You then enter text to see the results of the tabs that you add, and you clear a tab setting.

1   Press Ctrl+End to move the insertion point to the end of the document.

2   On the Format menu, click Tabs.

The Tabs dialog box appears.

If you intend to set a lot of custom tabs, it is best to clear the defaults first. To clear the defaults, in the Tabs dialog box, click the Clear All button before setting the custom tabs. If you leave the default tabs you have to press the Tab key more often.

3 In the Tab Stop Position box, type **1**, and click the Set button.

4 In the Tab Stop Position box, type **3**, and click the Set button.

5 In the Tab Stop Position box, type **4**.

6 In the Alignment section click the Decimal option, click the Set button, and then click OK.

Two left-aligned tabs and a decimal tab are displayed on the ruler, and the Tabs dialog box closes.

7 Press Tab, type **Employment Level**, and press Tab again.

8 Type **Base**, and press Tab.

9 Type **Mean**, and press Enter.

The headings appear as you type.

10 To enter the first line of information, press Tab, and type the following, pressing Tab between each entry and Enter after the last entry.

Entry

52

$36,100.00

The information for the first line in the table is entered.

11 Press Tab, and type the following, pressing Tab between each entry and Enter after the last entry.

Mid Level

207

$42,410.00

The information for the second line in the table is entered. Notice that the number is aligned at the decimal point rather than at the default left.

12   Press Tab, and type the following, pressing Tab between each entry.

Senior Level

186

$55,500

Press Enter. Notice that even though you didn't type a decimal point in the number, it is still aligned properly with the other numbers.

---Page Break---
Employment Lever	Base	Mean
Entry	52	$36,100.00
Mid Level	207	$42,410.00
Senior Level	186	$55,500

13   On the Format menu, click Tabs.

14   Click the 3" setting in the Tab Stop Position list, and click the Clear button.

The 3" tab setting is cleared.

15   Notice that Word automatically selected the 4" setting in the Tap Stop Position list. Now that the 4" setting is selected, click the 2 option in the Leader section.

16   Click the Set button, and click OK.

17   Press Tab, and type **Average**.

18   Press Tab, and type **$44,670**.

The space before the second tab is filled with leader dots.

---Page Break---
Employment Lever	Base	Mean
Entry	52	$36,100.00
Mid Level	207	$42,410.00
Senior Level	186	$55,500
Average		.........$44,670

Save

19   On the Standard toolbar, click the Save button.

Word saves the document.

Keep this file open for the next exercise.

Using the Ruler to Set and Clear Tab Stops

You can also quickly set and clear tab stops using the ruler. This tactic works well when you want to set tab stops visually by lining them up with the text below, rather than specifying a set number to place the stops at.

To set a tab stop using the ruler, you select the paragraph(s) to be affected. Then you click the Tab Align button at the far left side of the ruler to specify the tab alignment type. Click the ruler at the desired position to place the tab stop marker. A tab stop marker appears at that position.

In this exercise, you enter more text and set tabs using the ruler.

1   Click to position the insertion point after the last *0* in the number *$55,500* and press Enter two times.

2   Type the following four lines of information, using the Tab key to move to each tab setting and pressing Enter after each line. Press Tab and type:

Age	Base	Mean
20-29	82	$37,800
30-44	178	$47,290
45 and over	200	$50,440

Now that there is more text on your screen, the results of the alignment settings are apparent.

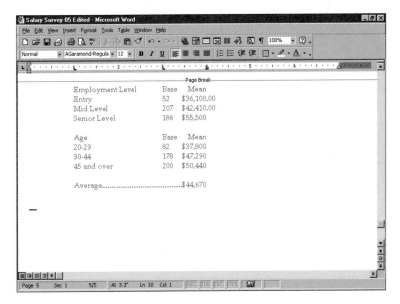

3   Select all the rows of text on this page, except for the row labeled *Average,* which is the last row.

4   Drag the second tab marker (located on the 3-inch mark) off the ruler.

The tab is cleared and the text shifts.

Left Tab

You can also use the Tab Align button to set the first line indent and the hanging indent. Click the Tab Align button until the First Line Indent or Hanging Indent symbol appears. Then on the ruler, click the position where you want to set the indent.

First Line Indent

Hanging Indent

Save

5 On the left side of the ruler, click the Tab Align button, which now appears as the Left Tab button on the ruler.

The Tab Align button changes to a Center Align button.

6 Click the ruler at the 3-inch mark.

A centered tab is set, and the text is realigned.

7 Click anywhere outside the selected text to deselect it.

Employment Level	Base	Mean
Entry	52	$36,100.00
Mid Level	207	$42,410.00
Senior Level	186	$55,500
Age	Base	Mean
20-29	82	$37,800
30-44	178	$47,290
45 and over	200	$50,440
Average...$44,670		

8 On the Standard toolbar, click the Save button.

Word saves the document.

Keep this file open for the next exercise.

Inserting a Page Number

W2000.3.5
W2000.3.9

When you create a document that has more than one page, you might consider using page numbers to mark each page. Using page numbers comes in handy when you are presenting the document to other people. The people reading your document do not know the information inside-out, like you do. So instead of telling them to find the paragraph "under the picture towards the middle of the document," simply tell them to turn to page six and follow along under the picture. Page numbers also come in handy when you are creating a lengthy document. Page numbers allow you to keep the document in order, especially if you print random pages from the document or are making edits. Page numbers remind you where you are in the document.

You can add page numbers to a document using the Page Numbers command on the Insert menu. By default, page numbers are displayed at the bottom-right corner of each page. You can change the page number position to either the top or bottom of the page, and then you can specify the left, right, or middle of the page. You also have the option to show a page number only on the first page.

If you are using Normal view, you won't be able to view any page numbers that you inserted. You can, however, view the page numbers in Print Preview or Print Layout view.

In this exercise, you add page numbers to the document.

1 Press Ctrl+Home to move the insertion point to the top of the document.

2   On the Insert menu, click Page Numbers.

The Page Numbers dialog box appears, and the page number's current position is displayed in the Preview section.

If you want to change the position of the page number, click the Position down arrow and select either the top or the bottom of the page.

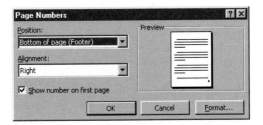

3   Click the Alignment down arrow, and click Center.

The page number is centered in the sample in the Preview section.

4   Click OK, and scroll down to the bottom of the page to view the page number.

Keep this file open for the next exercise.

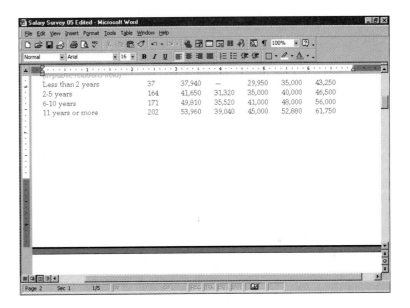

Less than 2 years	37	37,940	—	29,950	35,000	43,250
2-5 years	164	41,650	31,320	35,000	40,000	46,500
6-10 years	171	49,810	35,520	41,000	48,000	56,000
11 years or more	202	53,960	39,040	45,000	52,880	61,750

W2000.3.10

Creating Headers and Footers

Along with page numbers, headers and footers are great for documents that contain more than one page. Headers and footers work great in documents containing chapters or sections, because you can let the reader know where they are in the document by using the header or footer to show them what section they are reading.

In Normal view you cannot see the header and footer, but in Print Layout view you can.

You can add header or footer text to a document in the upper or lower page margins. This text can be a document identifier such as a file name, or perhaps a page number or information about the author.

In this exercise, you open the header, and then add text to the header.

1   On the View menu, click Header And Footer.

The Header And Footer toolbar and the Header and Footer boxes appear, and you now have access to the header. Notice that the Header box is at the top of the page and the Footer box is at the bottom of the page.

2   On the Header And Footer toolbar, click the Switch Between Header And Footer button.

The insertion point moves from the header to the footer.

3   Click the Switch Between Header And Footer button again.

The insertion point is back in the header.

4   Type your name.

Your name appears in the top-left corner of the header.

5   Scroll to the second page and look at the header.

Your name also appears there.

6   On the Header And Footer toolbar, click the Close button.

The Header And Footer toolbar closes.

Keep this file open for the next exercise.

> If the Header And Footer toolbar is in your way, drag the toolbar to move it.

Switch Between Header And Footer

Switch Between Header And Footer

Customizing Headers and Footers

W2000.3.10

> You can use the Formatting toolbar while editing headers and footers to make the text as plain or as ornate as you want.

While creating the header or footer, you have access to both the Formatting toolbar and the Header And Footer toolbar. The Header And Footer toolbar offers a variety of tools specifically used for customizing headers or footers. You might customize a header or a footer for the company's annual report. The report is divided into several sections (or chapters), and you can use a footer to insert the page number and the title of the section on each page. You can create a header to go on each page with the title of the annual report, and you can include your company name on the header, too.

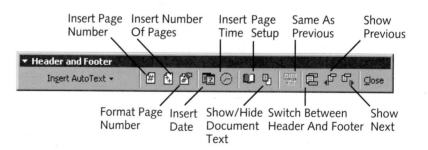

In this exercise, you use the Header And Footer toolbar to edit the header and footer.

1   On the View menu, click Header And Footer.

The Header And Footer toolbar appears, and the headers and footers are available for editing.

2   Scroll to any footer within the document.

> You can also open an existing header or footer by double-clicking the header or footer in Print Layout view.

3   Click the page number.

A box made up of short diagonal lines now surrounds the page number.

4   Move the mouse pointer over the box until it changes from the I-beam to a four-headed arrow, and click the box surrounding the page number.

A group of smaller black boxes forms within the dashed box.

5   Press Delete.

The page number disappears, and the insertion point moves to the left side of the footer.

6   Type **Page**, and press the Spacebar.

The text appears on the left of the footer box. As you type the *e*, a ScreenTip appears with the text *Page X of Y*.

Insert Page Number

7   On the Header And Footer toolbar, click the Insert Page Number button.

The current page number appears.

Insert Number Of Pages

8   Press the Spacebar, type **of**, and press the Spacebar again.

9   On the Header And Footer toolbar, click the Insert Number Of Pages button.

The total number of pages in the document appears.

Center

10   On the Formatting toolbar, click the Center button.

The custom page number is centered in the Footer box.

Switch Between Header And Footer

11   On the Header And Footer toolbar, click the Switch Between Header And Footer button.

The view of the document moves up to the header on the same page.

Align Right

12   On the Formatting toolbar, click the Align Right button.

Your name moves to the right of the header box.

13   Close the Header And Footer toolbar.

> You can create a different header and footer for the first page of the document than for the other pages. To vary the header and footer on the first page, on the Header And Footer toolbar, click the Page Setup button. In the Headers And Footers section of the Page Setup dialog box, select the Different First Page check box.

14   On the Standard toolbar, click the Save button.

Word saves the document.

Keep this file open for the next exercise.

W2000.3.6

Switching Page Orientation

You can lay out the text on a page in two ways: **portrait** orientation and **landscape** orientation. Text placed in portrait orientation appears horizontally on a vertical page. This is the default page orientation in Word. Text placed in landscape orientation appears horizontally on a page that is turned on its side. Diplomas and awards are usually oriented in this manner.

The figures below illustrate portrait and landscape orientation.

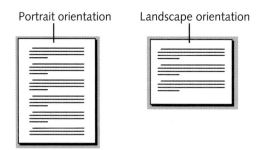

You can change orientation even after you've started creating a document.

In this exercise, you change the page orientation from portrait to landscape.

1   On the File menu, click Page Setup.

The Page Setup dialog box appears.

2   Click the Paper Size tab.

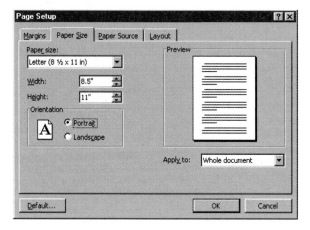

3   Click the Landscape option, view the Preview box, and click OK.

The text appears in landscape orientation.

Notice in the Preview box that the page orientation changed from portrait (8.5" x 11") to landscape (11" x 8.5").

4   On the Standard toolbar, click the Zoom down arrow, and click Whole Page.

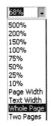

The first page of the document should now look similar to the following.

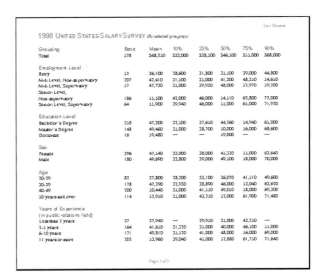

Lesson Wrap-Up

In this lesson, you learned how to change the page margins of the document, format paragraphs, and set and change tab stops. You also learned how to create headers and footers, insert page numbers and page breaks, and change the orientation of a document.

If you are continuing to other lessons:

Save

1   On the Standard toolbar, click the Save button to save changes made to the file that you edited.

Word saves the changes.

2   On the File menu, click Close to close the file.

Word closes the file.

If you are not continuing to other lessons:

1   On the Standard toolbar, click the Save button to save changes made to the file that you edited.

Word saves the changes.

Close

2   In the top-right corner of the Word window, click the Close button.

The Word program closes.

Lesson Glossary

alignment The arrangement of text in fixed or predetermined positions. If the paragraph is left aligned, all the text in the paragraph will begin on the left side of the document.

first line indent A paragraph setting that specifies the indent for the first line of a paragraph.

footer Text that appears at the bottom of all pages or selected pages of a printed document.

hanging indent A formatting attribute that aligns the first line of a paragraph flush with the left page margin and indents all subsequent lines a specified distance to the right.

hard page break A forced page break inserted manually in a specific place in the document.

header Text that appears at the top of all pages or selected pages in a printed document.

horizontal ruler The bar along the top of the document window that shows the left and right page margins, the left and right paragraph indents, and any customized tab stops. You can use the horizontal ruler to adjust the page margins, indents, and tab stops.

indents Indents are the specified spacing between the block of text and the left or right page margin.

landscape A page layout in which text appears horizontally on a page that is turned on its side.

leader tab A tab stop that displays a row of dots from the insertion point to the next tab stop. Leader tabs can be left-, right-, center-, or decimal-aligned.

Normal view The editing view that is used for most word processing tasks, such as typing, editing, and formatting. This is the default page layout view in Word. In Normal view, you cannot see the headers and footers and the page margins relative to the page borders, but you can see them in Print Layout view.

page break The point at which one page ends and another begins. Word allows page breaks to be manually inserted and also uses an automatic pagination feature to determine the locations of page breaks.

page margin An area of blank space between the edge of the paper and the text.

paragraph Any amount of text that ends with a hard return. A blank line is also considered to be a paragraph because it ends with a hard return.

paragraph mark A hidden formatting character that designates the end of a paragraph. Paragraph marks can be displayed by pressing the Show/Hide ¶ button.

portrait A page layout in which text appears horizontally on a vertical page. This is the default page orientation in Word.

Print Layout view An editing view in Word that displays the document as it will be printed but still allows use of Word's editing and formatting commands. In this view, you can see the headers and footers and the page margin setting relative to the page borders, whereas you cannot see these in Normal view.

Print Preview A document view that displays the file as it will be printed. Unlike Print Layout view, Print Preview does not allow access to all Word's editing and formatting functions.

ruler A graphic scale, showing measurements that can be used to apply paragraph formatting and customize tab stops to a document.

soft page break The point in a document where text wraps to a line below the bottom page margin and begins a new page. Soft page breaks, which appear as dotted horizontal lines in Normal view, are adjusted automatically by Word as you modify text within a document.

spacing The vertical distance that appears between paragraphs, as well as the distance between the lines within a paragraph.

tab (tab stop) A measured space that places and aligns text at a specific horizontal page location. Also a hidden formatting character that is inserted into text whenever the Tab key is pressed.

vertical alignment The way the lines of text on a page are aligned vertically between the top and bottom page margins.

vertical ruler The bar along the left edge of the document that shows the top and bottom page margins. You can also use the ruler to adjust the top and bottom page margins.

Quick Quiz

1   Name three ways in which you can change the page margins in Word.

2   How is vertical alignment similar and different from horizontal alignment?

3   How do you display the measurements of the page margins?

4   How do you display the Headers And Footers toolbar?

5   What's the difference between the Left Indent marker and the Left Page Margin marker on the ruler?

6   How do you clear a tab stop?

7   How do you specify that you want to insert a page number in the top-right corner of the document?

8   When the headers and footers boxes are displayed, what two ways can you switch between the header and the footer?

9   When you delete a paragraph mark, what formatting characteristics does that paragraph take on?

important

In the Putting It All Together section below, you must complete Exercise 1 to continue to Exercise 2.

Putting It All Together

Exercise 1: If necessary, start Word. Open a new, blank Word document. Adjust the left and right page margins to 2 inches and change the orientation to landscape. Insert tab stops at 2 inches, 4 inches, 6 inches, and 8 inches. The 6-inch tab stop should be a decimal tab and the 8-inch tab stop should be a right tab. Type the following headings in the first line:

Years Experience, Base, Mean, and **90%.**

Insert a new line, make heading text bold, and then save the document as Practice 05.

You will use Exercise 1 to complete the following exercise.

Exercise 2: Type the following information on the following two lines, pressing Tab between the entries.

| Less than 2 years | 37 | $37,940 | $43,250 |
| 2-5 years | 164 | $41,650 | $55,000 |

Create a centered heading with the title **Survey Results** and a footer with the current date on the left and **Page** *X* **of** *Y* on the right (where *X* is the current page and *Y* is the number of pages). Save the file in the Lesson05 folder, and close the document.

LESSON 6

Using Automated Formatting

After completing this lesson, you will be able to:

✔ *Set AutoFormat options.*

✔ *Add automatic borders.*

✔ *Create automatic bulleted lists.*

✔ *Create automatic numbered lists.*

✔ *Modify an automatic list.*

✔ *Use the Format Painter.*

✔ *Create an AutoText entry.*

✔ *Insert an AutoText entry.*

✔ *Create and print envelopes.*

✔ *Create and print mailing labels.*

Microsoft Word 2000 helps you save time by automating the process of entering and formatting text as you type. For example, when the marketing manager at Impact Public Relations needs to create a numbered list, she types the number 1 at the start of the line. The number indicates that the list will be numeric. Since Word automatically numbers the list for her, she doesn't have to type other numbers for the items in the list. If she wants to delete or insert a list item in the middle of the list, Word automatically renumbers the list.

The marketing manager also uses the **Format Painter** and **AutoText** features to save time when she formats a document. By clicking the Format Painter button on the Standard toolbar, she is able to copy the formatting of the currently selected paragraph or characters. After she has copied the formatting, she can apply it to other paragraphs within the same document.

AutoText contains stored text entries that have an abbreviated name associated with each entry. You use AutoText for frequently used words or phrases, such as your company's name or even your own name. You can use the AutoText abbreviation instead of typing each character of your name. For example, if your name is Catherine Turner, you might choose the abbreviation Cath. When you want to insert your name in a document, you type the abbreviation *Cath*, press F3, and the text *Catherine Turner* is inserted into the document.

You can also use AutoText for pictures.

Word can also save you time when you want to print an envelope. After you finish typing a letter, you can use the Envelopes And Labels dialog box to create an envelope for your letter. Word automatically inserts a pre-defined user address, return address, and any address listed in the current document is inserted as the recipient's address. You can also use Word to create labels in a similar manner.

In this lesson, you will learn how to create and modify bulleted and numbered lists, and you'll use Format Painter to copy formatting and the AutoText feature to automate text entry. You will also practice creating and printing envelopes and mailing labels.

Sample files for the lesson ⇨

For more information on how to find and open files used in this book, see the "Using the CD-ROM" section at the beginning of this book.

To complete the procedures in this lesson, you will create a new document called Expense 06. This document explains expense reporting procedures at Impact Public Relations. It will include borders, a numbered list, and a bulleted list. You'll also use the documents Letter 06 and Logo 06, located in the Lesson06 folder in the Word Core Practice folder on your hard disk.

Setting AutoFormat Options

You can easily create a **border, bulleted list,** and **numbered list** by using Word's automated formatting features. A border is a line placed around one or more sides of a paragraph, table, or picture. You can also add borders, including graphical borders, around entire pages. A bulleted list is a series of paragraphs with a symbol (or bullet—usually a dot, square, or other graphic) inserted at the start of each paragraph. A numbered list is a series of paragraphs with a number inserted at the start of each paragraph.

The marketing manager at Impact Public Relations has a busy day ahead of her. The company's shareholders are meeting tonight. She has several things to do today, and she must also gather various documents and materials to create an information packet for each shareholder.

In the following exercises, the Standard and Formatting toolbars have been separated. For additional information on how to separate the toolbars, see the "Using the CD-ROM" section at the beginning of this book.

She uses Word to create an automated bulleted list for all the things she needs to do today. She also uses Word's automated numbered list as a guide for all the materials she needs for the packets and in what order to place the information in the packets. Because her desk is a bit cluttered, she decided to put a border around her To Do List to distinguish the list from other papers on her desk and make it easier to find. The illustration on the next page shows the marketing manager's list.

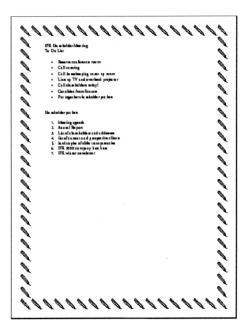

You can add borders and lists to a document manually, or you can let Word's AutoFormat feature format a document for you as you type. By setting AutoFormat options, you instruct Word to add borders or bulleted and numbered lists to your documents when you start typing the borders or the lists. Before Word can format the text in your document as you type, you must verify that AutoFormat is on.

In this exercise, you select AutoFormat options for your document.

1   If necessary, on the Standard toolbar, click the New Blank Document button to create a blank document.

New Blank Document

2   On the Tools menu, click AutoCorrect.

The AutoCorrect dialog box appears.

3   Click the AutoFormat As You Type tab.

New!

AutoCorrect now has a more powerful dictionary for detecting and correcting spelling errors. You'll learnmore about using the dictionary and checking spelling in Lesson 7, "Using Editing and Proofing Tools."

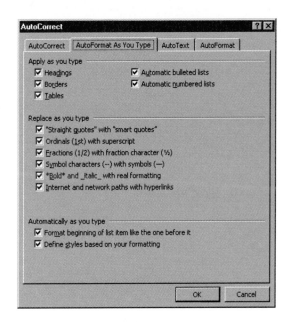

4   In the Apply As You Type section, select the Borders, Tables, Automatic Bulleted Lists, and Automatic Numbered Lists boxes, if necessary, and then click OK.

The AutoFormatting options are activated.

Adding Automatic Borders

Have you ever created a border in a document by holding down the Shift key and pressing and holding down the Hyphen key? That method isn't very accurate, and the border you created probably continued into the following line, so you had to use the Backspace key to even it out. You don't have to type hyphens across a page to create a horizontal border, instead, you can type just a few equal signs or dashes to create a border for a page.

The marketing manager at Impact Public Relations is creating a memo to her marketing staff reminding them of the appropriate steps to take when they report their company expenses. She wants to use different borders in the document to separate various topics.

In this exercise, you add double-line and single-line borders to a document.

1   In the blank document that you just created, type the heading **Reporting Expenses**.

2   On the Formatting toolbar, click the Style down arrow, click Heading 1, and then on the Formatting toolbar, click the Center button.

The Heading 1 style is applied to the heading, and the heading is centered.

3   Press Enter.

4   Type three equal signs (===), and press Enter.

A double-line border appears at the insertion point, extending from page margin to page margin.

5   Press Enter to move the insertion point to the next line, and type **The Reporting Process**.

6   On the Formatting toolbar, click the Style down arrow, click Heading 3, and then press Enter.

The Heading 3 style is applied to the new heading, and the insertion point is positioned on the next line.

7   Type three hyphens (---), and press Enter.

The paragraph is automatically underlined with a single-line border.

8   Press Enter twice, and type **Expense Report Reminders**.

9   On the Formatting toolbar, click the Style down arrow, click Heading 3, and then press Enter.

In step 4, select the indicated check boxes only if they are not already selected.

Center

When you center a paragraph that uses one of Word's default heading styles and then press Enter, Word applies the Normal style to the following paragraph. Because the Normal style is not centered, the centering attribute is not used.

10 Type three hyphens (---), and press Enter twice.

The Heading 3 format is applied to the new heading, and it is underlined with a single-line border.

Reporting Expenses
_____

The Reporting Process
_____

Expense Report Reminders
_____

Save

11 On the Standard toolbar, click the Save button.

The Save As dialog box appears.

12 Use the Save In down arrow to navigate to the Word Core Practice folder.

13 Double-click the Word Core Practice folder.

The folder contents are displayed.

14 Double-click the Lesson06 folder, and in the File Name box, type **Expense 06**.

15 On the Standard toolbar, click the Save button.

Word saves the document.

Keep this file open for the next exercise.

Creating an Automatic Bulleted List

W2000.2.2

You can convert an existing list to a bulleted list by using the Bullets button. Select the list items to which you want to add a bullet, and on the Formatting toolbar, click the Bullets button.

You can quickly create a bulleted list by simply typing an asterisk(*) before the first list item. Word formats the item as a bulleted list and continues to add a bullet each time you press Enter. A bulleted list comes in handy when you are working on a project as simple as a grocery list or as complex as listing all the supplies or vendors you need to reach for a company event.

To create an automatic bulleted list, you click to position the insertion point at the desired location, type an asterisk, and press Tab or the Spacebar. Type the desired list data, pressing Enter after each list item.

In this exercise, you create an automatic bulleted list.

1 Press Ctrl+End to move the insertion point to the end of the document.

2 Type **After you fill out your expense report, check the following before you submit the report to the Accounting Department:**, and press Enter twice.

3 Type *****, and press the Spacebar.

4 Type **Attach the original receipts.**, and press Enter.

The text is indented to the right, the asterisk turns into a bullet symbol, and another bullet symbol appears.

To stop Word from creating new automatic bulleted or numbered entries after you have completed the list, either press Enter twice to move the insertion point to the next line and remove the number or bullet, press Backspace, or on the Formatting toolbar, click the Bullets button.

5 Type **Verify that beginning and ending mileage figures are included.**, and press Enter.

6 Type **Verify that the expenses on your hotel bill are itemized separately.**, and press Enter.

7   Type **Verify that you signed the expense report.**, and press Enter twice.

The bulleted list is completed and no more bullets appear when you press Enter.

To remove bullets after they've been applied, select the paragraphs from which you want to remove the bullets, click the Bullets button on the Formatting toolbar, and then click the Decrease Indent button.

Reporting Expenses

The Reporting Process

Expense Report Reminders

After you fill out your expense report, check the following before you submit the report to the Accounting Department:

- Attach the original receipts.
- Verify that beginning and ending mileage figures are included.
- Verify that the expenses on your hotel bill are itemized separately.
- Verify that you signed the expense report.

Save

8   On the Standard toolbar, click the Save button.

Word saves the document.

Keep this file open for the next exercise.

W2000.2.2

Creating an Automatic Numbered List

Just as Word can generate bulleted lists as you type, it can also generate numbered lists. The paragraphs are formatted with a hanging indent so that the number of the entry appears to the left of the text.

You can learn more about hanging indents in Lesson 5, "Changing the Layout of a Document."

A hanging indent is a formatting attribute that aligns the first line of a paragraph flush with the left margin and indents all subsequent lines a specified distance to the right. In a numbered list, a hanging indent aligns each new line below the start of the first word in the first line, not below the number in the first line.

Numbered lists can save you time when you need to type a sequential list. Instead of having to type the number each time you make an entry, Word automatically inserts the numbers for you after you insert your first number and text and then press Enter. If you delete an item from an auto numbered list, Word will renumber the list. You can also insert additional items into your list and Word will number the new addition and renumber the rest of the list.

With Word's automatic numbering feature, the entries are numbered consecutively. The order of the numbers is updated as you insert or remove paragraphs. For example, if you forget to include a step in the series, you can insert the step, and the other steps are renumbered to account for the step that you just added.

In this exercise, you create an automatic numbered list.

1   Click to position the insertion point at the begining of the blank line under the heading *The Reporting Process*, and press Enter.

The insertion point is positioned under the heading, with a blank line between the heading and the current line.

2   Type **Follow these steps to fill out and submit your expense reports:**, and press Enter twice.

3   Type **1**, and press Tab.

4   Type **Open the Expense Report form from the network drive.**, and press Enter.

The text is indented to the right, Word recognizes you are starting a list, and the number 2 is inserted on the new line.

5   Type **Fill out the form online.**, and press Enter.

The insertion point moves to the next line, and the number 3 is inserted into the document.

6   Type **Save the form to your hard disk.**, and press Enter.

The insertion point moves to the next line, and the number 4 is inserted into the document.

7   Type **Print the form.**, and press Enter.

The insertion point moves to the next line, and the number 5 is inserted into the document.

> Pressing Enter twice terminates the numbered list, and pressing Backspace removes the extra line that was created when you pressed Enter the second time.

8   Type **Sign the form and attach the receipts.**, and press Enter.

The insertion point moves to the next line, and the number 6 is inserted into the document.

> To convert a numbered list to a plain list, select the paragraphs that contain the numbers that you want to remove. On the Formatting toolbar, click the Numbering button, and click the Decrease Indent button.

9   Type **Send the completed form and receipts to the Expense Report Manager in the Accounting Department.**, press Enter twice, and then press Backspace.

The automatic numbered list is completed.

Reporting Expenses

The Reporting Process

Follow these steps to fill out and submit your expense reports:

1   Open the Expense Report form from the network drive.
2   Fill out the form online.
3   Save the form to your hard disk.
4   Print the form.
5   Sign the form and attach the receipts.
6   Send the form and completed receipts to the Expense Report Manager in the Accounting Department.

Save

10   On the Standard toolbar, click the Save button.

Word saves the document.

Keep this file open for the next exercise.

W2000.2.7

Creating an Outline-Style Numbered List

You can also use Word's automatic formatting to create an outline-style numbered list (or simply an outline). Outlines are useful for planning the organization and content of documents and presentations—especially long documents. Items in an outline typically began with a Roman numeral, a number, or a letter, each denoting the item's level and sequence in relationship to other entries in the outline. The following illustration is a sample taken from an outline the marketing manager at Impact Public Relations has created for the speech she will give to shareholders later this month.

(continued)

continued

I.   Welcome to the 3rd Annual Shareholder Meeting

    a.   Brief History of Impact Public Relations

        1.   Company start date

        2.   Profits to date

        3.   List top clients

    b.   Introduce President

    c.   Introduce Board Members

II.   A plan for the future relies on strength from the past

    a.   Highlights throughout the year

    b.   New clients

        1.   Who are they

        2.   How do we cultivate relationships

            A.   Introduce marketing department

            B.   Introduce sales department

                a.   Mention growth in this department

                b.   Show sales brochure

To create an outline style numbered list, type I., and press Tab. Type the topic, sentence, or heading, and press Enter. Word recognizes you are creating an outline and inserts *II*. If you want to add more information under the *I*. heading, press Tab. Word inserts the letter *a*. and you are ready to enter the subtopic information. When you press Enter, Word inserts the letter *b*. When you are ready to begin the next topic or heading, press Backspace to move the insertion point back one tab space, so Word can automatically renumber the entry, based on the position of the insertion point.

Modifying an Automatic List

You can modify the numbers and bullets in your automatic lists. Word has many different number and bullet styles that you can use—such as letters, Roman numerals, boxes, or check marks. Depending on the list you are typing and the purposes of that list, you might want to change the number or bullet style to create a different look, add more professionalism to the document, or match the current design of a presentation that you show the list in.

Use the Bullets And Numbering dialog box to modify your lists. You can either use Word's preset bullets and numbers in the dialog box or modify the preset options to apply custom numbers or bullets. For example, in the Bullets And Numbering dialog box, you can choose either the Bulleted or Numbered tab to display different bullet or number styles. On one of these tabs, choose a bullet or number style and click the Customize button. You can customize the size, shape, font, and even color of the bullet or number style you choose.

In this exercise, you modify the bulleted and numbered lists that you created in the previous exercises.

1   Click to position the insertion point at the end of the line for the first numbered item (*Open the Expense Report form...*), and press Enter.

A new second step is inserted after the first step. The subsequent steps are renumbered to accommodate the new step.

2   Type **Note: The file is located in the Forms folder.**

3   Select the first item in the list.

4   On the Format menu, click Bullets And Numbering.

The Bullets And Numbering dialog box appears.

You can use the Outline Numbered tab to change the number format of an outline.

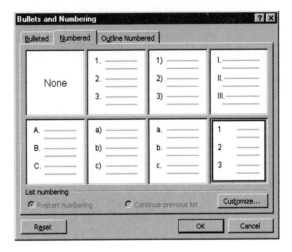

5   Click the second box in the first row, and click OK.

The numbered list is modified to include a period after each number.

6   Click the second item in the list, the one beginning with *Note:*.

7   On the Format menu, click Bullets And Numbering.

The Bullets And Numbering dialog box appears.

8   Click None, and click OK.

The numbering is removed from the second item in the list, and the remaining steps are renumbered to accommodate the change.

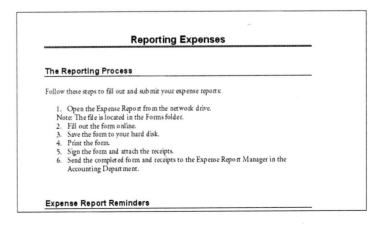

9   Right-click anywhere in the *Note:* line, and click Paragraph.

The Paragraph dialog box appears.

10   In the Indentation section, select the contents of the Left box, and type **.5**.

The paragraph will be indented one-half inch from the left margin.

> You can also click the Before and After up arrows twice to insert 12 points in the respective boxes.

11   In the Spacing section, select the contents of the Before box, and type **12**.

Word will insert 12 points of space before the paragraph.

12   In the Spacing section, select the contents of the After box, type **12**, and click OK.

The paragraph now is indented one-half inch from the left margin and has 12 points of space before and after the paragraph.

Reporting Expenses

The Reporting Process

Follow these steps to fill out and submit your expense reports:

1. Open the Expense Report form from the network drive.

    Note: The file is located in the Forms folder.

2. Fill out the form online.
3. Save the form to your hard disk.
4. Print the form.
5. Sign the form and attach the receipts.
6. Send the form and completed receipts to the Expense Report Manager in the Accounting Department.

> When you select a list, the number or bullet does not get highlighted along with the text entry.

13   Scroll down and select all the items in the bulleted list.

14   On the Format menu, click Bullets And Numbering.

The Bullets And Numbering dialog box appears. Notice that the Bulleted tab is displayed because Word recognizes that you are formatting a bulleted list.

> Bullets, like the letters and numbers on the keyboard, are also considered characters and can have different font settings. For example, a bullet in the Times New Roman font is different from a bullet in the Verdana font. To change the font for a bullet, on the Format menu, click Bullets And Numbering. In the Bullets And Numbering dialog box, click the Customize button, and click the Font button. Select the font you want, and click OK twice.

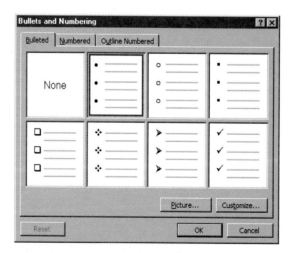

15   Click the first set of bullets in the second row (the check boxes), and click OK.

The bulleted list is modified.

You can also insert bullet characters from the Microsoft Office Clip Gallery. Select the items in the bulleted list, and in the Bullets And Numbering dialog box, display the Bulleted tab, and then click the Picture button. In the Picture Bullets dialog box, in the Picture table, click a bullet, and click Insert Clip.

16 Click anywhere outside the bulleted list.

The list is deselected.

Expense Report Reminders

After you fill out your expense report, check the following before you submit the report to the Accounting Department:

- ❑ Attach the original receipts.
- ❑ Verify that beginning and ending mileage figures are included.
- ❑ Verify that the expenses on your hotel bill are itemized separately.
- ❑ Verify that you signed the expense report.

Save

17 On the Standard toolbar, click the Save button, and on the File menu, click Close.

Word saves and closes the document.

W2000.1.10

Applying Multiple Attributes with Format Painter

Format Painter allows you to quickly copy the attributes of text that you have already formatted and apply these attributes to other text. The marketing manager at Lakewood Mountains Resort has created several custom styles for her newsletters. She is creating a brochure detailing information on the summer programs available at the resort and wants to reuse formatting that she has created for some paragraphs in the newsletters. Because she isn't using previous newsletters as a guide for the brochure, she'll have to duplicate all the custom formatting manually, unless she uses the Format Painter button.

To reapply formatting attributes to text, simply select the formatted text, and on the Standard toolbar, click the Format Painter button, and select the new text you want to be formatted. Format Painter *paints* (or copies) the selected formatting onto the selected text.

To copy a format multiple times, double-click the Format Painter button, and select each paragraph to which you want to copy the format. When you're finished, click the Format Painter button again to turn off Format Painter.

tip
Format Painter can be used to copy character formats, such as font, point size, and color. Format Painter can also copy paragraph formats, such as spacing, alignment, indentation, **kerning** (character spacing), and tabs. To copy character formatting, you select the text with the formatting that you want to copy. To copy paragraph formatting, you click anywhere in a paragraph with the formatting that you want to copy.

In this exercise, you format a paragraph and then use the Format Painter to copy character formatting and paragraph formatting characteristics.

1 On the Standard toolbar, click the Open button.

The Open dialog box appears.

Open

2 To display the Lesson06 folder, click the Look In down arrow, click the icon for your hard disk, double-click the Word Core Practice folder, and then double-click the Lesson06 folder.

The contents of the Lesson 06 appear in the open dialog box.

3 Double-click the file Letter 06.

The file is opened in Word, and the Open dialog box closes.

4 Select the date at the top of the letter.

5 On the Format menu, click Font.

The Font dialog box appears.

6 In the Font list, scroll up or down until you see Arial Narrow, and click Arial Narrow.

7 Click the Character Spacing tab.

The character spacing options appear in the dialog box.

8 Click the Spacing down arrow, and click Expanded.

The spacing between characters will be expanded by a number of points that you specify.

9 To the right of the Spacing box, select the contents of the By box, type **3**, and click OK.

The spacing between characters is expanded to 3 points, and the font is changed to Arial Narrow.

Format Painter

10 On the Standard toolbar, click the Format Painter button.

11 Select the four address lines (starting with *Ms. Amy Anderson*).

When you release the mouse button, the address lines are converted to the Arial Narrow font, and the character spacing is expanded to 3 points.

12 Click anywhere outside the address lines.

The address lines are deselected.

> December 15, 1999
>
> Ms. Amy Anderson
> Crescendo Music Society
> 1234 Johnson Road
> Charlotte, VT 98052
>
> Dear Ms. Anderson,
> This letter is in response for your request for information about the services provided by
> Impact Pubic Relations (Impact PR). Impact PR comprehensive public relations services
> including advertising and marketing communications services for a variety of diverse

13 Click anywhere in the next line beginning *Dear Ms....*

> Character spacing, or kerning, is the adjustment of text that involves increasing or decreasing the amount of space between letters. Kerning is used to enhance or improve how the text appears on the paper.

You can also display the Paragraph dialog box by right-clicking anywhere in the paragraph and clicking Paragraph on the shortcut menu.

14 On the Format menu, click Paragraph.

The Paragraph dialog box appears with the Indents And Spacing tab on top.

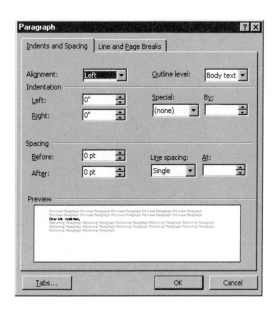

15 In the Spacing section, select the current contents in the After box, type **12**, and click OK.

Twelve points of space are inserted after the paragraph.

Format Painter

16 On the Standard toolbar, click the Format Painter button, and select the remaining paragraphs in the letter.

The paragraph spacing is applied to all remaining paragraphs in the letter.

17 Click anywhere outside the selected text.

The text is deselected.

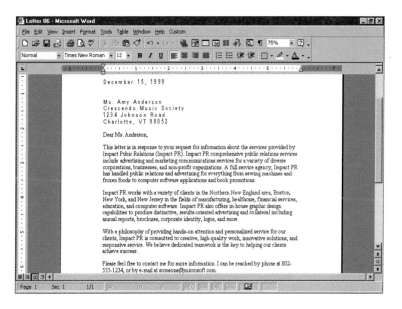

18 On the File menu, click Save As, and save the document with the name **Letter 06 Edited**.

Word saves the document.

Keep this file open for the next exercise.

Creating an AutoText Entry

An AutoText entry is a shorthand representation of a lengthy phrase, name, or other text that can be quickly inserted into a document. You might create an AutoText entry to store a frequently used address, a closing for a letter, or frequently typed names and terms. The marketing manager at Lakewood Mountains Resort created an AutoText entry for the company name. Whenever she types the letters *lmr* in a document, Word replaces them with the AutoText entry *Lakewood Mountains Resort*.

If you create an AutoText entry in a document that is based on the Normal template, the entry is stored globally, making it available in any document. If you create a document that is based on a template other than the Normal template, you can store the AutoText entry either globally or just in the template that you are using. If you choose the latter, the AutoText entry is available only in documents based on that particular template.

In this exercise, you create AutoText entries for a closing to a letter, the Impact Public Relations company name, and the company logo.

> You can find out more about using templates in Lesson 3, "Using Templates and Wizards."

1 On the Standard toolbar, click the New Blank Document button.

New Blank Document

2 Type **Sincerely,**.

3 Press Enter five times, and type **Lisa Jacobson**.

4 Press Enter, and type **Marketing Manager**.

5 Select the text, click the Font down arrow on the Formatting toolbar, and then click Arial Narrow.

> You can also display the Create AutoText dialog box by pointing to AutoText on the Insert menu and clicking New on the AutoText menu.

6 Press Alt+F3.

The Create AutoText dialog box appears. The first line of the selected text appears as the default name for the AutoText entry.

7 In the Please Name Your AutoText Entry box, type **lc** (shorthand for letter closing), and click OK.

The closing text for a letter is saved as an AutoText entry called *lc*, and it is added to the Normal template.

> When you make a change to the Normal template and then you quit Word, Word asks if you want to save the changes made to the Normal template. Click Yes to save the AutoText entries.

8 Press Ctrl+End to move to the end of the document, and press Enter twice.

9 Type **Impact Public Relations**.

10 Select the text that you just typed, and press Alt+F3.

The Create AutoText dialog box appears.

11 Type **ipr** in the Please Name Your AutoText Entry box, and click OK.

The company name is saved as an AutoText entry called *ipr*.

12 Close the document that you just created without saving the changes.

13 On the Standard toolbar, click the Open button in the Open dialog box, double-click the file Logo 06.

Open

14 Click the logo.

Resizing handles (small white boxes) appear around the border of the logo.

15 Press Alt+F3.

The Create AutoText dialog box appears.

16 In the Please Name Your AutoText Entry box, type **logo,** and click OK.

The company logo is saved as an AutoText entry called *logo*.

17 Close the document without saving the changes.

Inserting An AutoText Entry

At Impact Public Relations, Lisa Jacobson was recently promoted to marketing manager. One of her first duties in her new position is to continue with the correspondence handled by her predecessor. She has 12 different letters that require her name at the bottom of each. Instead of typing a closing for each letter, she created an AutoText entry and can insert the entry into each document.

After you create an AutoText entry, you can insert it anywhere in a document. If you know the name of the entry, you can simply type the name and press F3. If you are not sure of the name, you can select the entry from the AutoCorrect dialog box.

In this exercise, you insert the logo and closing AutoText entries into the file Letter 06 Edited.

1 Make sure the Letter 06 Edited document is displayed. If it is not displayed, click its button on the Windows taskbar.

2 Press Ctrl+End, and press Enter.

The insertion point moves to the end of the document, and a blank line is inserted after the last line.

3 Type **lc**, and press F3.

The letter closure lines are added to the end of the letter.

4 Press Enter, type **ipr**, and press F3.

The company name is added to the end of the letter.

> You can also display the AutoText toolbar to find AutoText commands. The toolbar includes buttons that allow you to create a new AutoText entry, select from a list of AutoText entries by category, or display the AutoText tab of the AutoCorrect dialog box. To display the AutoText toolbar, on the View menu, point to Toolbars, and select AutoText.

> The shorthand version of an AutoText entry is not case sensitive. In step 3, if you type LC and press Enter, Word will insert the same AutoText. However, because it's easier to type a shorthand entry in lowercase, this is the preferred approach.

With a philosophy of providing hands-on attention and personalized service for our clients, Impact PR is committed to creative, high-quality work, innovative solutions, and responsive service. We believe dedicated teamwork is the key to helping our clients achieve success.

Please feel free to contact me for more information. I can be reached by phone at 802-555-1234, or by e-mail at someone@microsoft.com.

Sincerely,

Lisa Jacobson
Marketing Manager

Impact Public Relations

You can print a complete list of the AutoText entries to help you keep track of them. On the File menu, click Print. In the Print dialog box, click the Print What down arrow, click AutoText Entries, and then click OK.

5   Press Ctrl+Home.

The insertion point moves to the top of the document.

6   Type **logo**, and press F3.

The logo is inserted at the top of the letter.

December 15, 1999

Ms. Amy Anderson
Crescendo Music Society
1234 Johnson Road
Charlotte, VT 98052

Dear Ms. Anderson,

This letter is in response to your request for information about the services provided by Impact Pubic Relations (Impact PR). Impact PR comprehensive public relations services include advertising and marketing communications services for a variety of diverse corporations, businesses, and non-profit organizations. A full service agency, Impact PR has handled public relations and advertising for everything from sewing machines and

Save

7   On the Standard toolbar, click the Save button.

Word saves the document.

Keep this file open for the next exercise.

W2000.3.14

Creating and Printing Envelopes

You can also use Word to format envelopes and mailing labels. Instead of using a typewriter to individually type each name and address on an envelope, Word can save you valuable time by printing the envelopes all at once. To create envelopes, you type the names and addresses using the Envelopes And Labels dialog box.

The marketing manager at Impact Public Relations is sending letters to all of last year's clients. Because her letter is a formal business letter, the addresses and names of all the clients have been entered into the letters. She can use Word to print envelopes for each letter without having to type each envelope individually.

The marketing manager also sends out the annual report to shareholders, but when she puts the report package together, she encloses a handwritten note, rather than a business letter. Because the addresses are not stored in Word, she must type the addresses in the Envelopes And Labels dialog box to print the envelopes one by one.

If a return address is not typed in the letter or Return Address text box, the return address (or user mailing address) is not defined and is left blank.

To create an envelope, on the Tools menu, click Envelopes And Labels. On the Envelopes tab of the Envelopes And Labels dialog box, you can type the recipient's address under Delivery Address, or if you're using an existing letter, this information will be captured from the letter. If the return address doesn't appear, or if you want to change it, you can type a return address. When you add the return address, the address information is added to the top of the letter.

In this exercise, you create and print an envelope using an existing letter.

1   On the Tools menu, click Envelopes And Labels, and click the Envelopes tab, if necessary.

The Envelopes And Labels dialog box appears with the Envelopes tab on top.

> For a quick way to insert an address that you have entered recently, click the Insert Address button down arrow and click a name in the list.

Insert Address

> Make sure that you clear the Omit check box above the Return Address box in the Envelopes And Labels dialog box. Otherwise the return address will not be printed on the envelope.

2   In the Return Address box, enter the mailing address so that it contains the following lines of text:

Lisa Jacobson

Impact Public Relations

4567 Main Street

Charlotte, VT 80227

3   Click the Add To Document button. When Word asks if you want to save the new return address as the default, click No.

The envelope information is added to the top of the letter.

W2000.3.14

<table>
</table>

If you don't want to add the envelope to the document, but would rather just print it, you can skip steps 3 through 5 and proceed to printing the envelope in step 6.

4   Click the Save button to save the document using the current name.

5   On the Tools menu, click Envelopes And Labels.

The Envelopes And Labels dialog box appears with the Envelopes tab selected.

6   Insert an envelope in the printer as shown in the Feed box, and click the Print button.

The envelope is printed. Your printer might require you to press a form feed button on the printer to indicate that the envelope has been inserted.

Creating and Printing Mailing Labels

You can also use Word to print a single label or an entire sheet of labels containing the same information for each label. The marketing manager at Impact Public Relations is developing a brochure for one of her clients. She sends the updated proofs to the client at least twice a week. She prints sheets of labels with the same address on each sheet so that she doesn't have to type the mailing address for each envelope.

When you select text before you begin creating a label, Word inserts that text as the label address. Otherwise, if there is an address in the current document, Word assumes that is the address to be used, and Word inserts this address. You can edit the text that Word inserts.

Before you select the type of label, measure the labels carefully. The actual label size might be smaller than the size indicated by the label manufacturer. For example, a 1-by-2-inch label might actually be 15/16-inch high and 1 15/16-inches wide.

If you want to print a full page of labels, in the Envelopes And Labels dialog box click the Labels tab, click the Option button, and select the Full Page Of The Same Label option. If you want to print an individual label, On the Labels tab of the Envelopes And Labels dialog box, select the Single Label option. You can use the Row and Column up and down arrows to indicate the location on the sheet of labels where you want the label to print.

If you want to create a sheet of labels and edit the labels, or save the labels and print them at another time, you can create a document just for the labels by clicking the New Blank Document button. You can then save the document and access it at another time.

In this exercise, you create a label, change the label size, print a single label, print an entire sheet of labels, and create a labels document.

1 On the Tools menu, click Envelopes And Labels, and click the Labels tab.

The Envelopes And Labels dialog box appears with the Labels tab on top. The address information is retrieved from the letter.

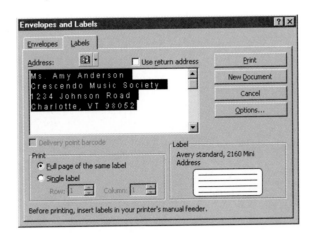

2 Click the Options button.

The Label Options dialog box appears.

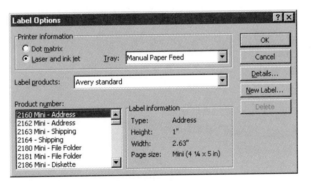

If you want to use a label size that is not listed in the Product Number box, in the Label Options dialog box, in the Product Number box, you can click a label type similar in size to the labels that you use. Click the Detail button to compare the label dimensions and the number of labels per sheet (for labels printed on laser and ink jet printers) or the number of columns on the label form (for labels printed on dot-matrix printers). You can also create your own custom labels. To create a custom label, click the New Label button in the Product Number box.

3 In the Product Number box, scroll down, and click the *8922 – Address* option, and then click OK.

The Envelopes And Labels dialog box appears. The Avery Standard, 8922 Address labels are selected.

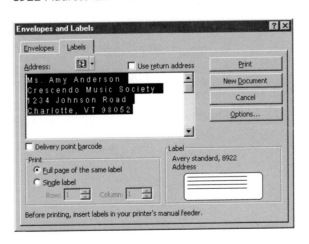

4 Click the Print button.

The label is printed. Your printer might require you to press a form feed

You would normally put a label manufacturer's label sheets in the printer (using the product number of the labels you specified in the Label Options dialog box). For classroom purposes, you print the labels on a blank sheet of paper.

button on the printer to indicate that the labels page has been inserted.

5   On the Tools menu, click Envelopes And Labels.

The Envelopes And Labels dialog box appears.

6   Verify the Full Page Of The Same Label option is selected, and click the Print button.

The same address is printed on the entire sheet of labels.

7   On the Tools menu, click Envelopes And Labels.

The Envelopes And Labels dialog box appears.

8   Click the New Document button.

A new document is created with a sheet of labels. You can use this document to edit the labels, or save it to print the labels at a later time.

New Blank Document

9   Save the labels document with the name **Labels 06**, and close the document.

Word saves and closes the document.

Lesson Wrap-Up

In this lesson, you learned how to set AutoFormatting options, add borders to documents, create bulleted and numbered lists, and use the Format Painter. You also learned how to create and insert an AutoText entry and how to create and print envelopes and mailing labels.

If you are continuing to the next lesson:

1   On the Standard toolbar, click the Save button to save any final changes made to the letter that you formatted.

2   On the Tools menu, click AutoCorrect, and click the AutoText tab.

Save

3   In the list of AutoText entries, scroll down until you see *ipr*, click this AutoText entry, and click the Delete button.

4   Repeat step 3 to delete the *lc* and *logo* AutoText entries.

5   Click OK.

6   On the File menu, click Close. If you are prompted to save the changes, click Yes.

Word saves and closes the document.

If you are not continuing to other lessons:

1   On the Standard toolbar, click the Save button to save any final changes made to the letter you formatted.

2   On the Tools menu, click AutoCorrect, and click the AutoText tab.

Save

3   In the list of AutoText entries, scroll down until you see *ipr*, click this AutoText entry, and click the Delete button.

4   Repeat step 3 to delete the *lc* and *logo* AutoText entries.

5   Click OK.

6   On the File menu, click Exit. If you are prompted to save the changes to the document, click Yes.

Word saves the changes to the file.

The file closes and the Word program closes.

Lesson Glossary

AutoText A feature in Word that allows you to store a phrase, name, title, text, or a picture and associate a shorthand abbreviation for the item. You can then quickly insert the item into a document by typing the shorthand abbreviation.

border A line placed around any side of a paragraph, table, or picture. You can also apply borders to cells within a table.

bulleted list A series of paragraphs with a bullet (a dot or other graphic) inserted at the start of each paragraph. The paragraphs are generally formatted with a hanging indent so that the bullet appears to the left of the paragraph text.

Format Painter A button on the Standard toolbar that allows you to copy all character or paragraph formatting and apply it to other selected text.

kerning The amount of space between letters. Kerning can enhance or improve how the text appears on the paper.

numbered list A series of paragraphs with a number inserted at the start of each paragraph. The paragraphs are generally formatted with a hanging indent so that the number appears to the left of the paragraph text.

Quick Quiz

1   How do you copy a format multiple times?

2   What settings need to be activated before you can create an automatic bulleted list and numbered list as you type?

3   If you know the name of an AutoText entry, what is the easiest way to insert the entry?

4   When you print an envelope, what option do you select so that the return address is not printed on the envelope?

5   How do you add an automatic single-line or double-line border to a document as you type?

6   What do you need to do if you want to print only a single label and not a full page?

7   What characters are used to automatically create a bulleted or numbered list as you type?

8   How do you create an AutoText entry?

9   How do you remove numbers from a numbered list?

Putting It All Together

Exercise 1: If necessary, start Word. Create a new document, and add the heading **Birthday Party** to the document using the Heading 1 style. Center the heading towards the top of the document, and create a double-line border below and above the heading. Using the information below, insert a numbered list and a bulleted list into the document, below the heading. (Don't worry about creating the accent character for piñata.) Save the document as **Border-Lists Practice 06,** and close the document.

Numbered list information:

    Book magician
    Order cake
    Pick-up balloons and streamers
    Buy party hats
    Get napkins, plates, spoons, and table cloth
    Clean living room
    Hang piñata in the backyard

Bulleted list information:

    Magic show
    Pin the tail on the donkey
    Musical chairs
    Open presents
    Birthday cake
    Piñata

important

You will need to have a printer to complete Exercise 2. You can print the envelope and labels on regular sheets of paper if you do not have these supplies with you.

Exercise 2: Using a new document, create an AutoText entry for the Madrona Community Orchestra. Name the AutoText entry **mco**. Insert the AutoText entry at the top of a new, blank document, and type the address:

    8765 Washington Road
    Sacramento, CA 80215

Create and print an envelope for this document using the above address for the recipient and return addresses, and print a full sheet of labels with the Orchestra address for the 5160 Address label type. Save the document as **Addresses 06.**

LESSON 7

Using Editing and Proofing Tools

After completing this lesson, you will be able to:

✔ *Check spelling in a document.*

✔ *Check for grammatical errors.*

✔ *Use the Thesaurus.*

✔ *Find specific text.*

✔ *Replace specific text.*

✔ *Create AutoCorrect entries and exceptions.*

✔ *Highlight text.*

✔ *Insert the date and time as text or as a field.*

✔ *Insert special characters.*

Before you deliver a Microsoft Word 2000 document to others, you should always proofread it carefully. Proofreading involves correcting all spelling and grammar errors and making any other final changes to the document. Fortunately Word's spelling and grammar capabilities can do some of this work for you.

The dictionary contains all words that Microsoft identifies as correct when you check the spelling of a document, including many proper nouns and acronyms. If you type *Our plans is to send the document after it has been proofread*, Microsoft will mark *plans is* as a grammatical error. On the other hand, if you type *Too whom it may concern*, Word will not mark the word *Too* as being a grammatical error. The bottom line: even after you use Word's spelling and grammar checking features to make corrections in a document, you still need to read through the document carefully to look for any additional errors.

You can also customize spelling and grammar checking feature by defining which grammar rules apply. For instance, you might want to use casual language (including contractions) when you compose a letter to a friend. When you compose letters to business associates, you might want to use more formal language. You can change the language style to suit your audience. Word will then mark grammatical errors based on the rules for the style of language that you want to use. If you specify that you want to use the Formal language style, and you type *I don't think this is an acceptable solution*, Word will mark *don't* as a grammatical error because contractions generally aren't permitted in formal English.

Word can also automatically correct common grammatical errors as you type them. For instance, if you type *Your my top candidate*, Word will change *Your* to *You're* as soon as it identifies the grammatical error.

You might also want to find a synonym for a particular word to give your document a more forceful or professional tone. Word has a thesaurus that you can use to improve the word choices in your document. In this exercise, you will use these and other proofing and editing tools to correct and improve documents.

In this lesson, you will check spelling and grammar in a document. Use the thesaurus, and find and replace specific text. You will also create AutoCorrect entries, highlight text, insert date and time fields, and special characters.

Sample files for the lesson

For additional information on how to find and open files used in this book, see the "Using the CD-ROM" section at the beginning of this book.

In the following exercises, the Standard and Formatting toolbars have been separated. For additional information on how to separate the toolbars, see the "Using the CD-ROM" section at the beginning of this book.

To complete the procedures in this lesson, you will use the file Brochure 07 in the Lesson07 folder in the Word Core Practice folder located on your hard disk. This document explains the services provided by Impact Public Relations.

Understanding Spelling and Grammar Checking Options

As you type the contents of a document, you might notice that some words or phrases are underlined with red or green wavy lines. These symbols are part of the **spelling checking** and **grammar checking** features in Word. A red wavy line identifies words that are not found in the dictionary, and a green wavy underline indicates phrases and grammatical constructions that Word detects as being potentially grammatically incorrect. To correct the error, you can manually edit the word or phrase, or you can use the Spelling And Grammar dialog box to view and select from suggested changes. After the word or phrase has been corrected, the red or green wavy line no longer appears.

Spelling And Grammar

You can check the spelling of a single word, or you can use the Spelling And Grammar dialog box to check the spelling and grammar in an entire document. This feature marks incorrectly spelled words, locates repeated words, and identifies capitalization and grammatical errors. To access the Spelling And Grammar dialog box, on the Standard toolbar, click the Spelling And Grammar button, or on the Tools menu, click Spelling And Grammar.

If you are correcting an individual spelling error, Word can display a list of possible corrections for a misspelled word. Simply right-click the text that is underlined in red to display a shortcut menu, and select the correct spelling from the list of possible corrections.

(continued)

continued

The spelling checking feature is now more powerful than earlier versions, with the capability to identify hundreds of additional names of people, organizations, companies, cities, countries, and even e-mail and Web addresses.

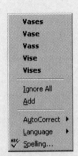

When you check the spelling for a complete document, Word compares each word in the document with words in its standard dictionary. If an error is found, the word is selected in the document window, and alternative selections are listed in the Suggestions list. After a possible misspelled word has been located, the following options are available, some of which appear as buttons in the Spelling And Grammar dialog box.

Button	Function
Ignore	Ignores only that occurrence of the selected word.
Ignore All	Ignores all occurrences of the word.
Add	Adds the word to the custom dictionary.
Change	Replaces the selected word with the selected word in the Suggestions list.
Change All	Replaces all occurrences of the word with the selected word in the Suggestions list.
Suggestions	Lists alternative suggestions for the misspelled word in the list.
AutoCorrect	Adds the word to a list that Word uses to automatically correct spellings of the word as you type it.
Undo	Returns a spelling correction to its previous state.
Delete	Appears if a double occurrence of a word is detected (such as *to to modify the document*), and can be used to delete the second occurrence of a word.
Options	Customizes spelling and grammar checking. For example, you can specify whether you want Word to ignore certain words with uppercase characters or words with numbers when Word checks spelling.

W2000.1.3

Spelling And Grammar

To complete the following exercise, you should verify that the Check Spelling As You Type option is in use. On the Tools menu, click Options. In the Options dialog box, click the Spelling And Grammar tab, and verify that the Check Spelling As You Type check box is selected.

Checking Spelling in a Document

There are three basic ways to check spelling in a document, depending on whether you want to correct errors as soon as Word identifies them or whether you want to wait and check spelling for the entire document after you have created it.

- Right-click a word that has a red wavy underline and then select a suggested correction from the list.
- On the Standard toolbar, click the Spelling And Grammar button to check spelling and grammar in the entire document.
- On the Tools menu, click Spelling And Grammar to check spelling and grammar in the entire document.

In this exercise, you correct a single spelling error, check a complete document for spelling errors, and then correct or ignore the potential errors that Word identifies.

1   On the Standard toolbar, click the Open button.

   The Open dialog box appears.

2   Click the Look In down arrow, double-click the icon for your hard drive, double-click the Word Core Practice folder, and then double-click the Lesson07 folder.

   The contents of the Lesson07 folder are displayed.

3   Double-click the file Brochure 07.

   The file Brochure 07 appears in Word and the Open dialog box closes.

4   In the first line of the second paragraph, right-click the misspelled word *aech*, and click *each* in the list of possible corrections that appears.

   The word is corrected in the document.

Spelling And Grammar

You can also start the spelling and grammar checker by pressing F7.

5   On the Standard toolbar, click the Spelling And Grammar button.

   The Spelling And Grammar dialog box appears with the word *IPRnetworks* selected in the document window.

   Word has no spelling suggestions for this term.

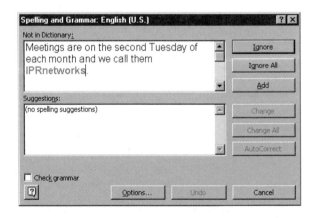

6   Clear the Check Grammar check box if it is currently selected.

7   Click the Ignore All button.

The word and all future instances of it in the document are ignored, and the word *an* is selected. Because this is an occurrence of a double word and not a misspelling, no alternative spellings are offered.

8   Click the Delete button.

The second occurrence of the word *an* is deleted, and the capitalization error *MEmbership* is selected. The correct usage of the capitalized word is displayed and selected in the Suggestions list.

9   Click the Change button to change the capitalization to Membership.

10   Word continues to check the document for spelling errors. When an error occurs, choose the best choice in the Suggestions list and click the Change button. Continue making the necessary corrections in the document.

When Word has finished locating all potential spelling errors, the following message box appears.

You can undo spelling corrections one-by-one immediately after closing the Spelling And Grammar dialog box. On the Standard toolbar, click the Undo button to undo the most recently corrected word. Click the Undo button again to undo the next corrected word. Repeat this procedure to undo any other spelling corrections.

Undo

11   Click OK.

The Spelling And Grammar dialog box closes.

12   On the File menu, click Save As, and Save the document as **Brochure 07 Edited**.

Word saves the document.

Keep this file open for the next exercise.

Using the Shortcut Menu for Words and Phrases

To identify the cause of a single grammatical error, you can right-click any word marked with a green wavy line to display a shortcut menu, and then make a selection from the shortcut menu as desired. The first item on the menu is a brief description of the error. If you click the About This Sentence item on the shortcut menu, Word displays a more thorough explanation of the grammatical problem and suggests ways to correct it.

If a red wavy line appears under a word that you know is spelled correctly (such as a proper name), you can add that word to the dictionary. To add a word to the dictionary and remove the red wavy line from all instances of that particular spelling, right-click the word to display a shortcut menu, and click Add.

W2000.1.5

Checking for Grammatical Errors

After you have typed your document, you can use Word to check the entire document for grammar and spelling errors. If an error is found, the word or phrase is selected in the Sentence box, and alternative words or phrases appear in the Suggestions list. You can ignore the error, check the grammar rule, or make changes to the existing document.

Normally Word checks for spelling and grammatical errors at the same time—with one exception. If you clear the Check Grammar With Spelling check box, Word checks only for spelling errors. You cleared this check box in the previous exercise to check for spelling errors only, so grammatical errors might still occur in your document. You can still check for grammatical errors at a later time.

To turn on grammar checking after you have checked spelling in a document, you must use the Options dialog box.

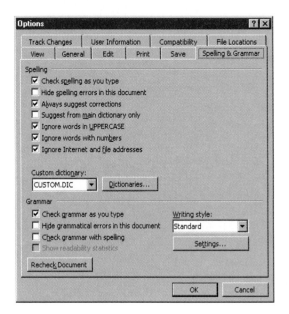

To check grammar in a document (after you've turned on grammar checking), on the Standard toolbar, click the Spelling And Grammar button to display the Spelling And Grammar dialog box. Click the Ignore button to ignore an error; click the Ignore All button to ignore the error wherever it occurs; or click the Change button to make the suggested replacement that appears in the Suggestions list.

If Word identifies a grammatical problem that can't be corrected with a simple replacement (such as a sentence fragment or words that appear to be out of order), the Change button will be grayed out (made unavailable). However, the dialog box will suggest that you consider revising the sentence.

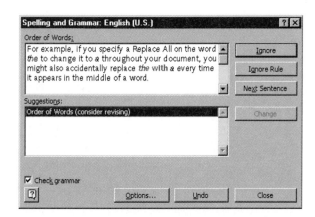

In this exercise, you check the grammar in a document.

1   Press Ctrl+Home to position the insertion point at the beginning of the document.

2   On the Tools menu, click Options.

The Options dialog box appears.

3   In the Options dialog box, click the Spelling And Grammar tab, if necessary.

4   In the Grammar section, verify that the Check Grammar With Spelling check box is selected, and click OK.

5   Scroll down until you see the sentence that is underlined with a green wavy line (the sentence begins *Membership open to individuals*).

6   Right-click anywhere in the sentence.

Word displays a shortcut menu that shows the grammar rule (fragment) that is being violated.

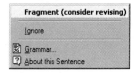

7   On the shortcut menu, click About This Sentence.

The Office Assistant appears and explains the meaning of a fragment and suggests ways to correct the grammatical error.

You can learn more about using the Office Assistant in Lesson 1, "Getting Started with Word."

> **Fragment**
> If the marked words are an incomplete thought, consider developing this thought into a complete sentence by adding a subject or a verb or combining this text with another sentence.
>
> • Instead of: Meteors the entire night.
> • Consider: We watched meteors the entire night.
>
> • Instead of: A rose by any other name.
> • Consider: A rose by any other name still smells sweet.

8   Click after the space following the word *Membership*, type **is**, and then press the Spacebar.

The error is corrected by adding a verb to the sentence, and the green wavy line no longer appears.

Keep this file open for the next exercise.

You can change other grammar checking options to reflect your own needs and preferences. You can use Casual, Standard, Formal, Technical, or Custom styles depending on the audience and the content of the document.

Specifying a Writing Style and Using Readability Statistics

Word checks the grammar of a document based on writing styles. A **writing style** is a set of grammatical rules and conventions that determine whether a particular phrase or sentence structure is appropriate for your intended audience.

For example, different departments at Impact Public Relations use different writing styles for their grammar checks. The marketing manager likes to set the grammar checker to use the Casual writing style because most of her documents are about upcoming events and are sent to previous and prospective hotel guests. The operations manager, on the other hand, prefers to set the grammar checker style to Formal, because he sends most of his documents to contractors and business partners.

By default, the grammar checker uses the Standard writing style. To change the writing style, on the Tools menu, click Options to display the Options dialog box, and then click the Spelling And Grammar tab, if necessary. In the Writing Style box, click the down arrow, and select the desired style.

You can also use the Spelling And Grammar dialog box to display your document's readability statistics. Readability statistics show useful information about the document, such as the average number of words per sentence and the average number of characters per word. For instance, if the readability statistics show that the average number of words per sentence is more than 20, you might want to consider breaking some sentences into two sentences to enhance readability. If you have selected the Show Readability Statistics check box prior to checking a document for grammatical errors, the Readability Statistics window appears after the spelling and grammar check is completed.

Using the Thesaurus

W2000.1.4

Word's thesaurus helps you look up alternatives or synonyms for a particular word. To use the thesaurus, click the word that you want to look up. On the Tools menu, point to Language, and click Thesaurus to display the Thesaurus dialog box.

You can also press Shift+F7 to display the Thesaurus dialog box.

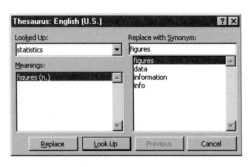

In the Thesaurus dialog box, if you see a word that you would rather use, click the word in the Replace With Synonym box, and click the Replace button. To look up additional synonyms, select a new word in the Meanings box, and click the Look Up button to view a new list of words in the Replace With Synonyms box.

You can also use the shortcut menu to look up synonyms. To do so, right-click a word, and point to Synonyms on the shortcut menu. Words with similar meanings are listed. The word that appears first in the list is the term that Word suggests as being the closest in meaning to the word. Click the desired word in the list.

In this exercise, you use the thesaurus to replace a word with a more appropriate synonym.

1   Scroll down until you see the paragraph that begins *Impact PR also provides.*

2   In the second line, right-click the word *variety*, and point to Synonyms on the shortcut menu that appears.

A list of synonyms for *variety* appears.

3   In the list of synonyms, click *range.*

Word replaces the word *variety* with *range.*

Keep this file open for the next exercise.

W2000.1.12

Finding Specific Text

When you edit long documents, you might want to move quickly to a particular location in the document so that you can review or edit text at this location. If you know the location of the document contains a unique word or phrase, you can use Word's Find and Replace dialog box to locate the word or phrase.

You can also display the Find And Replace dialog box by pressing Ctrl+F.

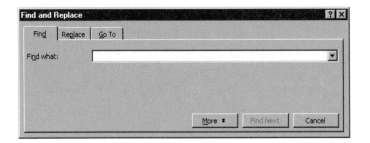

In the Find And Replace dialog box, you can click the More button to display additional search options. These search options allow you to define settings such as whether you are using wildcards or the **Sounds Like** feature.

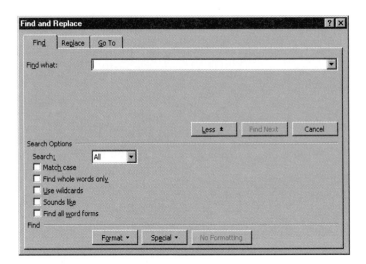

A search string is a group string of characters to be matched in the document when a search is performed.

A **wildcard** character stands for any character that appears in one or more positions within a word or string of text. To use wildcards, in the Find And Replace dialog box, click the More button, and select the Use Wildcards check box. Use the question mark (?) wildcard symbol in a **search string** to represent any character in a single position within the word or text string. For example, the string *h?t* finds *hat*, *hit*, *hot*, and *hut*. Use the asterisk (*) wildcard symbol to represent any string of characters. For example, the string *h*t* finds *hat*, *hurt*, and even *had sent*.

You can use the Sounds Like feature to find words that sound similar to the text string you are searching for but might be spelled differently. For example, when you use the Sounds Like feature for the word *meet*, Word identifies *meet*, *meat*, and *mete* as matching the Sounds Like rule.

In this exercise, you find a string of text within the current document, and you expand the Find And Replace dialog box to display additional search options.

1 Press Ctrl+Home to position the insertion point at the beginning of the document.

2 On the Edit menu, click Find.

The Find And Replace dialog box appears.

3 In the Find What box, type **meetings**, and click the Find Next button.

The word *meetings* at the beginning of the second paragraph is now selected. The Find And Replace dialog box remains unchanged.

4 In the Find And Replace dialog box, click the Find Next button to display the next occurrence of the word *meetings*.

The word *meetings* at the end of the second paragraph is now selected. The Find And Replace dialog box still remains unchanged.

5 Click the Find Next button again.

Word searches again for the word *meetings* and displays a message box indicating that Word has finished searching the document.

6 Click OK.

The message box closes.

7 In the Find And Replace dialog box, click the More button.

The dialog box expands to show the Search Options section.

8 In the Find And Replace dialog box, click the Cancel button.

The dialog box closes.

Keep this file open for the next exercise.

> You don't have to search for full words. You can also search for parts of words or phrases. For example, if you wanted to find the word *envelope*, you could shorten the search string by just searching for *envel* to find all words that have that set of characters in the text.

Using Go To

W2000.3.8

You can also use the Go To tab in the Find And Replace dialog box to move the insertion point to specific text in the document, such as a specific page, section, or heading. To access the Go To tab, on the Edit menu, click Go To.

> To quickly display the Go To section of the Find And Replace dialog box, you can also press F5 or press Ctrl+G.

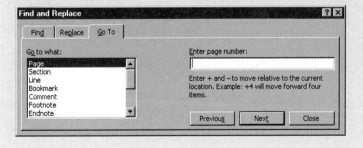

(continued)

continued

In the Go To What list, select the option with which you want to search your document. For example, if you choose Footnote, Word narrows the search to the Footnotes in your document. You can type a plus sign (+) followed by a number and click the Go To button to move forward the designated number of items relative to the current position of the insertion point. For example, if you type a plus sign (+) followed by the number 2 and click the Go To button, the insertion point would move forward two items from where the insertion point was located in the document before you used the Go To button. You can also type a minus sign (-) to move backward the number of items.

To go to a specific page in a document, on the Edit menu, click Go To to display the Go To tab in the Find And Replace dialog box. Select Page in the Go To What list, type the desired page number in the Enter Page Number box, and then click the Go To button.

W2000.1.12

Replacing Specific Text

The Replace command allows you to quickly locate any string of characters, such as a word or phrase. The string of text, when found, can be replaced by a different string using the Find And Replace dialog box.

For example, the Marketing Department is revising a brochure about the organization and services provided by Impact Public Relations. The company used to be commonly referred to as *Impact PR*; however, now the company wants to use the full company name *Impact Public Relations* in all communications. The marketing manager now must find every instance of *Impact PR* in the brochure and change it to *Impact Public Relations*.

You can use Find And Replace in only a portion of a document by selecting text before you begin the replacement.

The marketing manager could scroll through the brochure to visually search for text and replace each instance of *Impact PR* with *Impact Public Relations*, but this task is time consuming and is not a foolproof way to guarantee that all corrections will be made. A better approach is to use Word's feature for replacing specific text.

tip

Most fonts are called **variable-width** fonts because the spaces between characters can be adjusted to accommodate adjoining characters of different widths. For instance, in the word *Wide*, the width of the letter *W* is much greater than the width of the letter *i*. With most fonts, the space before the letter *i* is reduced so that the letter is "tucked in" closer to the letter *W*. When you use variable-width fonts, sentences look more professional when only one space follows a period. (The convention of typing two spaces after a period stems from the use of typewriters to create documents; most typewriters cannot adjust the widths between characters and words.) To make sure that only one space is used at the end of all sentences in a document, you can use Find And Replace. In the Find box, type a period (.) followed by two spaces. In the Replace box, type a period (.) followed by one space. Word searches for all the double spaces after a period and replaces them with a single space.

In this exercise, you find and replace text within the current document.

1 On the Edit menu, click Replace.

The Find And Replace dialog box opens with the Replace tab selected.

Word keeps track of the previous word or phrase that you searched for in case you want to perform the search again. Notice that the Find What box contains the word *meetings*, which you searched for in the previous exercise.

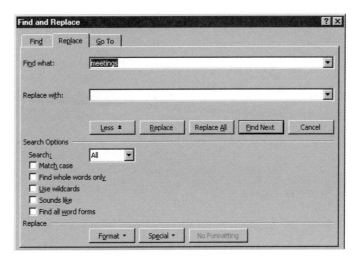

2 Press Delete.

The word *meetings* is removed from the Find What box.

3 In the Find What box, type **Impact PR**.

4 Press the Tab key, or click in the Replace With box, and type **Impact Public Relations**.

5 Click the Find Next button.

The first occurrence of *Impact PR* is selected.

6 Click the Replace button.

The abbreviated company name is replaced with the full company name, and the next occurrence of *Impact PR* is selected.

You can use the Undo command to reverse the previous replacement (when confirming replacements) or to reverse all replacements (if you specified Replace All).

7 Click the Replace All button.

All additional occurrences of *Impact PR* are replaced with *Impact Public Relations* without confirmation, and Word displays a message box indicating that it has completed the search and identifies the number of replacements that were made.

important

Be careful when you use Replace All, because you can accidentally replace things that you didn't intend to. For example, if you are replacing *the* with *a* and you click Replace All, you might also accidentally replace *the* with *a* every time it appears in the middle of a word. For example, *lithe* becomes *lia,* and *weather* becomes *weaar.*

8 In the alert box, click OK.

The alert box closes

9 In the Find And Replace dialog box, click Close.

The Find And Replace dialog box closes.

10 On the Standard toolbar, click the Save button.

Word saves the document.

Keep this file open for the next exercise.

Save

W2000.1.16

Creating AutoCorrect Entries and Exceptions

Word's **AutoCorrect** feature helps eliminate typographical errors in documents. Word uses AutoCorrect to automatically make certain sentence corrections as you type, such as irregular capitalization or commonly mistyped words. AutoCorrect also substitutes certain words or characters when you type. For example, in words like *1st* and *2nd*, AutoCorrect automatically makes the *st* and *nd* superscript (1st, 2nd). When you type fractions by typing a number, typing the slash (/) key, and then typing another number, AutoCorrect "shrinks" the fraction into one character (called a stacked fraction), rather than three characters.

One character   Three characters

$\frac{1}{2}$ 1/2

To open the AutoCorrect dialog box, on the Tools menu, click AutoCorrect.

In the AutoCorrect dialog box, you can view the words and symbols that are automatically replaced. On the AutoCorrect tab of the AutoCorrect dialog box, scroll through the list in the dialog box to display the symbols and words that are automatically replaced.

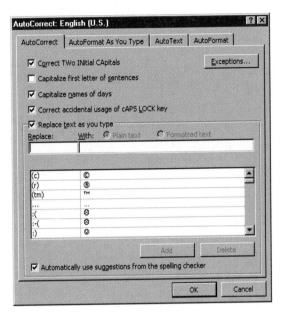

You can also use the AutoCorrect dialog box to create your own AutoCorrect entries, typically to correct an error that you frequently make but that isn't already defined in Word. For example, suppose that you have a habit of inverting the *th* in the word *then* and typing *hten* instead. You could create an AutoCorrect entry to correct this error whenever you type it in a document.

tip

You can use AutoCorrect to create replacement text for a shorthand version that you type. For instance, you can specify that Word replace *IPR* with *Impact Public Relations* whenever you type *IPR*. This approach is similar to AutoText, except you don't need to press F3 to make the replacement. Use AutoCorrect in this way if you're sure that you *always* want to replace a shorthand version of a text string with a lengthier string. If you want *IPR* to remain as an acronym in some locations in a document but want to replace it with *Impact Public Relations* in other locations, create an AutoText entry instead of an AutoCorrect entry.

You might also find that certain acronyms or names require two capital letters at the beginning, such as ULimports. These words can also be added as exceptions to Word's initial capitals AutoCorrect rule.

For words you want uncorrected, such as names, you can use AutoCorrect to create exceptions. AutoCorrect corrects initial caps in words and capitalizes the first letter of sentences. For example, even though Word capitalizes the first letter of sentences, you do not want Word to capitalize the word following an abbreviation when you use the abbreviation within the middle of a sentence. This is considered an **exception**, or an item that Word treats differently than its core rule. Most common abbreviations (such as *dept., Sr., Jr., Assoc., pt., in.*) are already in Word's list of exceptions, but occasionally you might need to specify other exceptions.

You can press Shift+F3 repeatedly to change the case of a word to *title case* (the first letter of every word is capitalized, except for prepositions or articles), all caps, and then all lower case, in that order. You don't need to select the entire word; just click anywhere in the word.

You can also create exceptions by example. For instance, if you type *Our sister organization in San Anselmo, Calif. can also be of service*, Word corrects this as *Our sister organization in San Anselmo, Calif. Can also be of service*, which is not what you want. However, if you correct the sentence by changing *Can* to *can*, Word detects the correction and adds *Calif.* to the list of exceptions. The next time you use the abbreviation *Calif.*, Word does not capitalize the word that follows it.

In this exercise, you create an AutoCorrect entry to replace *htat* with *that*. Then you create an AutoCorrect exception so that Word will not change *ICorrect* to *Icorrect* when you type this text string.

1   Press Ctrl+End, and press Enter twice.

Word positions the insertion point at the end of the document, and then inserts two blank lines.

2   Type **We hope htat you too will take full advantage of these services.**

Word marks *htat* as a potential misspelling but does not correct it.

3   Select the sentence that you just typed, and press Delete.

The sentence is deleted.

4   On the Tools menu, click AutoCorrect.

The AutoCorrect dialog box appears.

5   In the Replace box, type **htat**, and press Tab.

6   In the With box, type **that**.

Word will replace all occurrences of *htat* with *that*.

If Word uses AutoCorrect for a word that you don't want corrected, you can select the corrected word, and then type the original word. Word will not make an auto correction when you select the corrected word and type the original word or letter.

7   Click the Add button, and click OK.

The AutoCorrect dialog box closes.

8   Type **We hope htat you too will take full advantage of these services.**

Word replaces *htat* with *that*.

9 Press Enter twice, type **ICorrect**, and press the Spacebar.

Word makes an auto correction by converting the C in ICorrect to lowercase.

10 On the Tools menu, click AutoCorrect.

The AutoCorrect dialog box appears.

11 Click the Exceptions button, and click the INitial CAps tab.

12 In the Don't Correct box, type **ICorrect**, and click the Add button.

The exception is added.

13 Click OK to close the AutoCorrect Exceptions dialog box, and click OK again to close the AutoCorrect dialog box.

Both dialog boxes close.

14 Select the word *Icorrect*, and type the following:

We also provide a new service called ICorrect. Customers can send their Word documents to us via e-mail, and our expert editors can correct errors and suggest changes.

This time, Word does not change *ICorrect* to *Icorrect*.

15 On the Standard toolbar, click the Save button.

Word saves the document.

Keep this file open for the next exercise.

Notice that *ICorrect* is still underlined in red, even though AutoCorrect did not change the two capitalized letters. The word ICorrect is underlined because it has not been added to Word's dictionary and is unrecognized when Word checks the spelling of the document.

W2000.1.7

You can always tell what color the highlighting will be by looking at the Highlight button. The colored line in the button indicates the currently selected color. If the colored line is white, no highlight color has been selected.

Highlighting Text

You can use Word to highlight text in your document. The Highlight feature works like a highlight color marker that you use on paper. Highlighting text comes in handy when you want to mark text that you are unsure about or if you want to call attention to a particular word or phrase. If you highlight text and later determine that the text needs to be changed, the highlighting can help you remember to make the change before you print or e-mail the document.

The marketing manager at Impact Public Relations is sending out a company memo reminding staff to straighten up their offices because the shareholders will be touring the facilities at the end of the week. She uses the highlighter to highlight the words *"mandatory request per the president"* so all the staff will recognize the importance of the message.

In this exercise, you select text, highlight it in yellow, and then you remove the highlighting.

If you click the Highlight button before you select text, the pointer changes to a highlight marker, indicating that text that you select will be highlighted in the designated color. You can then select the text that you want to highlight. To turn off highlighting, click the Highlight button again.

1   Double-click the word *ICorrect*, which you created when you typed the final paragraph in the previous exercise.

The word is selected.

2   On the Formatting toolbar, click the Highlight down arrow, and click the Yellow square.

The selected text appears highlighted in yellow.

3   Double-click the word *ICorrect*.

The word is selected.

4   Click the Highlight down arrow, and click None.

The highlighting is removed from the selected text.

5   On the Standard toolbar, click the Save button.

Word saves the document.

Keep this file open for the next exercise.

W2000.1.14

Inserting the Date and Time

You can also use Word to insert the current date and time into a document. Occasionally, the Human Resources department of Impact Public Relations sends a document containing amended company policies to all resort employees. The date and time is inserted within the footers of the document so that the employees know that they are reading the most current version of the policies.

Date and time information is available in many different formats and can be inserted as text or as a **field**. A field is a formula that generates specific results within your document. You add the field where you want the information to appear, and the field inserts information when you open the document. For example, if the date or time is inserted as a field, it is updated automatically when a particular action is performed, such as opening, saving, or printing the document.

In this exercise, you insert the current date into the document as text and as a field.

1   Press Ctrl+Home to position the insertion point at the beginning of the document.

2   On the View menu, click Header And Footer.

The Header And Footer toolbar is displayed.

Switch Between Header And Footer

3   On the Header And Footer toolbar, click the Switch Between Header And Footer button.

The view of the document moves to the Footer box on the bottom of the first page.

For more information on Headers and Footers, see Lesson 5, "Changing the Layout of a Document."

You can also insert the date from the Headers And Footers toolbar by clicking the Insert Date button.

Insert Date

4   On the Insert menu, click Date And Time.

The Date And Time dialog box appears, showing all the possible date and time formats in the Available Formats list.

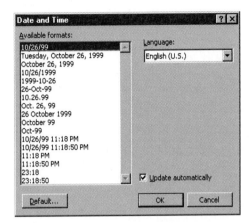

5   Click the third available format (the month that is spelled out, date, and the year), and click OK.

The current date is inserted, and the dialog box closes.

6   Press Tab twice to move to the right edge of the footer, type **Last update on**, and then press the Spacebar.

7   On the Insert menu, click Field.

The Field dialog box appears.

8   Click Date And Time in the Categories list.

The Field Names list displays the options that are available for the Date And Time category.

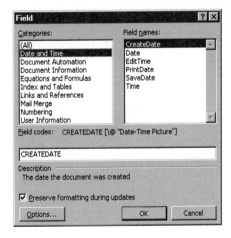

The dates that you insert in steps 5 and 9 show the current date, but only the date field in step 9 is automatically updated each time the document is saved.

9   In the Field Name list, click SaveDate, and click OK.

The date that the document was last saved is inserted on the right side of the footer. Every time this document is saved, the date field is automatically updated.

10   Click the Close button on the Header And Footer toolbar.

Save

11   On the Standard toolbar, click the Save button.

Word saves the document.

Keep this file open for the next exercise.

W2000.1.15

Inserting Special Characters

Special characters are symbols and punctuation marks that do not have a key on most keyboards, such as an em dash (—), an ellipsis (...), a copyright symbol (©), or a trademark (™) symbol. You can insert these special characters by using the Symbol command on the Insert menu. Many symbols also have shortcut keys listed next to them in the dialog box.

The marketing manager at Impact Public Relations is putting together a brochure for a local toy store. Throughout the brochure are listings of various toys. The marketing manager uses Word's special characters to insert the trademark symbol after the product name.

In this exercise, you insert the trademark symbol into the current document.

1   Press Ctrl+End to ensure that the insertion point is at the end of the document.

2   Click to position the insertion point between the *t* and the period in *ICorrect.*

3   On the Insert menu, click Symbol.

The Symbol dialog box appears.

4   Click the Special Characters tab.

The contents of the Special Characters tab appear.

> You can also find many common symbols on the Symbol tab. Click to position the insertion point in the document where you want to insert the symbol, on the Symbol tab, click the symbol, and click Insert. Word inserts the symbol in the document. Click Close to close the Symbol dialog box.

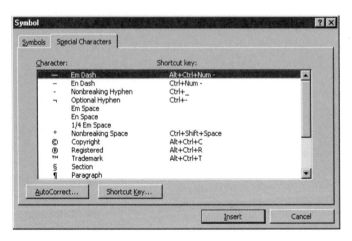

5   Click Trademark, and click the Insert button.

The trademark symbol is inserted in the document at the current position of the insertion point.

6   Click the Close button.

The dialog box closes.

Lesson Wrap-Up

In this lesson, you learned how to use some of Word's editing and proofing tools, such as how to check spelling and grammar in a document; find and replace text; use AutoCorrect; and insert dates, times, and special characters.

If you are continuing to the next lesson:

1   On the Tools menu, click AutoCorrect.

2   Click the Exceptions button, and make sure that the INitial CAps tab is selected.

3   In the list of exceptions, click *ICorrect*, and click the Delete button.

4   Click OK to close the AutoCorrect Exceptions dialog box.

5   In the list of replacements, scroll down until you see the replacement for *htat*, click this line in the list, and click the Delete button.

6   Click OK to close the AutoCorrect dialog box.

Save

7   On the Standard toolbar, click the Save button to save any final changes made to the document that you modified.

8   On the File menu, click Close.

Word saves and closes the file.

If you are not continuing to other lessons:

1   On the Tools menu, click AutoCorrect.

2   Click the Exceptions button, and make sure that the INitial CAps tab is selected.

3   In the list of exceptions, click *Icorrect*, and click the Delete button.

4   Click OK to close the AutoCorrect Exceptions dialog box.

5   In the list of replacements, scroll down until you see the replacement for *htat*, click this line in the list, and click the Delete button.

6   Click OK to close the AutoCorrect dialog box.

Save

7   On the Standard toolbar, click the Save button to save any final changes made to the document that you modified.

8   On the File menu, click Exit.

Word saves the changes to the file.

The file closes and the Word program closes.

Lesson Glossary

AutoCorrect A feature that automatically corrects errors and replaces words or characters as text is typed. Common misspellings or capitalization errors are automatically corrected.

exception An item that Word treats differently than its core rule.

field A formula that generates specific results within your document. You insert a field where you want the information to appear, and the field inserts the information when you open the document.

grammar checking A feature that identifies capitalization and grammatical errors. All questionable phrases and grammatical constructions are marked with a green wavy underline.

search string A group or string of characters to be matched in the document when a search is performed.

Sounds Like A search feature available in the Find dialog box that allows you to find words that sound similar to the text string you are searching for but might be spelled differently.

special characters Symbols and punctuation marks that do not have a key on most keyboards.

spelling checking A feature that identifies incorrectly spelled words and locates occurrences of repeated words. All possible misspellings and repeated words are marked with a red wavy underline.

wildcard A search option available in the Find dialog box that allows you to insert a special character as a placeholder for any other character or characters. The question mark (?) represents a single character, and the asterisk (*) represents multiple characters.

writing style A set of grammatical rules and conventions that determine how a document is checked. You can modify the rules for a writing style on the Spelling & Grammar tab of the Options dialog box.

variable-width The adjustment of spaces between characters that can be adjusted to accommodate adjoining characters of different widths.

Quick Quiz

1   How do you specify a date format when you insert the current date into a document?

2   How do you add an AutoCorrect exception?

3   When searching for a string of text, how can you specify that you want to search for a word that sounds like the one for which you are searching?

4   If you commonly use a word that is interpreted as a spelling error, what command on the shortcut menu allows you to enter this word in the custom dictionary?

5   In a document, what do red and green wavy underlines indicate?

6   How do you replace a text string throughout a document without having to confirm it each time?

7   How can you use the Find And Replace dialog box to display a specific page in the current document?

8   How do you view readability statistics when you check spelling and grammar in a document?

9   How can you view a list of synonyms for a particular word?

10   How would you insert the registered trademark symbol (®) in a document?

important

In the Putting It All Together section below, you must complete Exercise 1 to continue to Exercise 2.

Putting It All Together

Exercise 1: If necessary, start Word. Impact Public Relations has a client who sells fabric and wants to publish an article to help promote sewing. The operations manager at Impact Public Relations has agreed to edit the article.

Open the Ruffles Article 07 document located in the Lesson07 folder in the Word Core Practice folder on your hard disk. Change the writing style of the grammar checker to Formal, and then check the spelling and grammar and correct any errors. Use your judgment about which errors that you want to ignore and which ones you want to change. Then search for the word *material* and replace all instances of the word with *fabric*.

Exercise 2: Add an AutoCorrect entry so that whenever you type *hwen*, it is replaced with the text *when*. To the last sentence in the second paragraph that ends *purchasing your fabric*, add the following text: **Then hwen you place an order, you'll be sure to purchase the correct amount.** Verify that the AutoCorrect entry was added correctly. Insert the date in the bottom footer and align it with the right margin. Save the document as **Ruffles Article 07 Edited**.

LESSON 8

Working with Graphics

After completing this lesson, you will be able to:

✔ *Insert pictures from files.*

✔ *Insert pictures from the Microsoft Clip Gallery.*

✔ *Resize a picture.*

✔ *Create and modify WordArt.*

✔ *Create and modify AutoShapes.*

Documents that contain only text can certainly provide a wealth of information to readers, but they usually aren't very visually interesting. Fortunately Microsoft Word 2000 makes it easy to insert pictures and other graphics into your text documents. A **picture** is any graphical image that is created by another program, captured from a scanner or digital camera, or downloaded from the Web. Pictures include drawings, photographs, and all of the clip art stored in the Microsoft Clip Gallery.

In addition to inserting pictures, you can also create shapes and other graphical objects by using the Drawing toolbar. An **object** can be a curve, a line, an **AutoShape, WordArt,** or a combination of any graphics that you group together so that they can be manipulated as a single unit. An AutoShape is a ready-made shape—such as an arrow, banner, starburst, or flowchart symbol—that you select from the AutoShapes menu on the Drawing toolbar. WordArt is decorative text that you can insert into a Word document. You can also use the Drawing toolbar to change and enhance objects with colors, patterns, borders, and other effects.

In this lesson, you will learn how to insert and edit pictures and graphical objects in a document.

To complete the procedures in this lesson, you will need to use the file Tailspin Toys 08 in the Lesson08 folder in the Word Core Practice folder located on your hard disk.

Sample files for the lesson

For additional information on how to find and open files used in this book, see the "Using the CD-ROM" section at the beginning of this book.

W2000.6.2

Inserting a Picture from a File

You can choose from dozens of programs for creating and editing pictures on your computer. A few examples are Adobe Photoshop, Adobe Illustrator, Microsoft Paint, Paint Shop Pro, and Microsoft PhotoDraw. These and other programs allow you to create, edit, and save pictures. A scanner or **digital camera** is also useful when you want to capture and then store pictures as files on disk. And, of course, millions of picture files are available for downloading on the Web.

In the following exercises, the Standard and Formatting toolbars have been separated. For additional information on how to separate the toolbars see the "Using the CD-ROM" section at the begining of this book.

You can also switch to Print Layout view from the status bar in the bottom of the Word window by clicking the Print Layout View button.

Impact Public Relations has a client who owns a chain of recreational sporting goods stores. The president of the company wants a brochure with picturesque views of mountains, rivers, trails, forests, and so on. The marketing manager, armed with her digital camera, went into the wilderness and took several scenic pictures. She can store the pictures on a disk and later insert them into the brochure.

If you have picture files available on your hard disk, on a floppy disk, or on a CD-ROM, you can insert them easily into your Word documents. A picture is inserted at the location of the insertion point. To work with pictures, you must use Word's Print Layout or Web Layout views; pictures do not appear in Normal view.

In this exercise, you insert a picture into a Word document from a file stored on your hard disk.

Open

1   On the Standard toolbar, click the Open button.

The Open dialog box appears.

2   Click the Look In down arrow, click the icon for your hard disk, double-click the Word Core Practice folder, and then double-click the Lesson08 folder.

3   Double-click the file Tailspin Toys 08.

Word opens the Tailspin Toys 08 document.

4   Click the blank line above the line that reads *Fly up, up, and away*.

5   On the Insert menu, point to Picture, and click From File.

The Insert Picture dialog box appears.

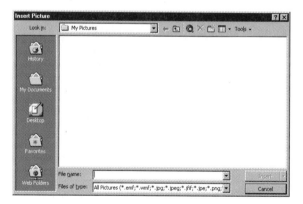

6   Click the Look In down arrow, and navigate to the Lesson08 folder.

Picture files in the folder appear in the Insert Picture dialog box.

Rather than clicking the Insert button, you can double-click the file name in the list to insert the picture.

The picture is inserted where the insertion point was positioned. The blank line that you clicked prior to inserting the picture has already been formatted as a centered paragraph. If the insertion point had been in a paragraph that was left-aligned, the picture would have been inserted along the left margin of the page.

7 Click Balloon, and click the Insert button.

The picture is inserted at the insertion point.

Come Celebrate the
Grand Opening
of Tailspin Toys

Fly up, up, and away.

Entertainment
Prizes
Great Food

8 On the File menu, click Save As, and save the document as **Tailspin Toys 08 Edited**.

Word saves the document.

Keep this file open for the next exercise.

W2000.6.2

You can also use the Clip Gallery to preview and insert sounds and video clips into a document.

To insert a clip art picture, you must use Print Layout View.

Inserting a Picture from the Clip Gallery

Microsoft Office 2000 includes hundreds of ready-made pictures that are available from the Microsoft **Clip Gallery**. Word refers to these pictures as **clip art**. The Clip Gallery includes a wide variety of pictures, from scenic backgrounds to maps, buildings, people, and some photographs that you can insert into any Word document. Depending on how Word was installed on your computer, as many as several hundred or as few as 144 pictures might be installed on your hard disk. Use clip art pictures to add visual excitement to a document, to break up document text, or to help illustrate key points within a document.

The marketing manager at Impact Public Relations created a company memo reminding co-workers of the upcoming holiday office party. She used a picture of snowflakes and a picture of a snowman in the memo to make the appearance of the document more fun. She found these pictures in the Clip Gallery.

Many clip art pictures are stored in the WMF (Windows Metafile) graphic format, which means that you can **ungroup** the image. When you ungroup a clip art picture, each component (or individual part) of the picture is defined as a separate drawing object and can be modified independently. Suppose you insert a WMF picture that shows several balloons and streamers. If you right-click the picture and then click Edit Picture, you can edit different parts of the picture individually. For example, you could delete or move a streamer or change the color of a balloon.

In this exercise, you preview clip art pictures in the Clip Gallery's Insert ClipArt window and then insert a clip art picture into the current document.

1   Press Ctrl+Home.

The insertion point moves to the top of the document.

2   On the Insert menu, point to Picture, and click Clip Art.

The ClipArt window appears.

3   If necessary, click the Pictures tab.

The picture categories appear in the Insert ClipArt window.

You can also access the Insert ClipArt window by clicking the Insert Clip Art button on the Drawing toolbar.

Insert Clip Art

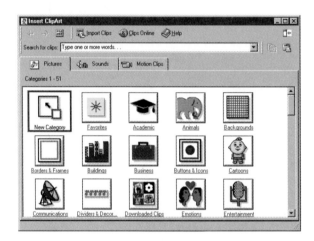

4   Scroll down, and click the Special Occasions picture category.

The Insert ClipArt window displays small versions of the pictures available within the Special Occasions category.

Depending on how Word was installed on your computer, your Insert ClipArt window might display more or fewer pictures than the illustration shown.

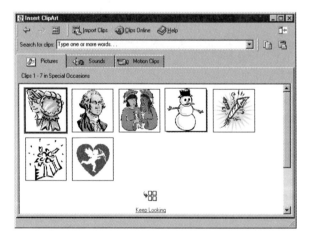

You can also drag a picture from the Clip Gallery into your document.

You can keep the Clip Gallery open after you insert a clip art picture by minimizing the Insert ClipArt window. You can restore the window later if you want to insert other clip art pictures into your documents.

Close

Notice that the text on the invitation is displaced where the picture was inserted and has moved down the page.

Sizing a picture vertically or horizontally can distort it because the original proportions of the picture are changed. To avoid distortion, use the corner sizing handles to resize a picture so that the original proportions are kept intact.

You can learn more about Text Wrapping in Lesson 1, "Using Advanced Paragraph and Picture Formatting," in the Microsoft Word 2000 Step by Step Courseware Expert Skills Student Guide.

5   Click the blue and yellow firecracker picture.

A menu with four buttons appears.

Insert Clip ———

6   Click the Insert Clip button.

7   In the top-right corner of the Insert ClipArt window, click the Close button.

The picture is inserted in the top-left corner of the document.

8   On the Standard toolbar, click the Save button.

Word saves the document.

Keep this file open for the next exercise.

Resizing a Picture

After inserting a picture into a Word document, you can easily increase or decrease the size of the picture. You begin by selecting the picture. When selected, a picture displays eight **sizing handles** (small white or black boxes) around its perimeter.

To resize a picture using the sizing handles, click the picture to select it. You can drag the left or right sizing handles to change the horizontal width of the picture, the top or bottom sizing handles to change the vertical height of the picture, or a corner handle to simultaneously change the width and height.

You can also use the Format Picture dialog box to size a picture to a specific height and width. To size a picture using the Format Picture dialog box, double-click the picture that you want to resize, and click the Size tab, if necessary. Click the Height and Width arrows in the Scale section to the desired percentage.

Often when you insert a picture, you'll discover that text wraps around (or surrounds) the picture in a way that you didn't intend. You can change the text wrapping style by using either the Picture or Drawing toolbar. The Picture toolbar appears whenever you select a picture.

Text Wrapping

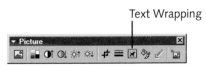

To display the Drawing toolbar, point to Toolbars on the View menu, and click Drawing. To change the text wrapping style, click the Draw button on the Drawing toolbar, point to Text Wrapping, and then click the desired wrapping style on the menu.

The following text wrapping styles are available on the Drawing and Picture toolbars.

You can also change text wrapping by double-clicking the picture and clicking the Layout tab in the Format Picture dialog box. Additional text wrapping styles are available in this dialog box by clicking the Advanced button.

Text Wrapping Style	Button	Effect
Square		Wraps text around all four borders of the picture.
Tight		Wraps text around the picture itself, often within the borders of the picture.
Behind Text		Allows text to be displayed on top of the picture.
In Front of Text		Allows the picture to be displayed on top of text.
Top and Bottom		Allows text to wrap above and below the picture, but not around the left and right borders of the picture.
Through		Wraps text in the same way as the Tight text wrapping style, but also wraps text into any open areas of the graphic.

In this exercise, you reduce the size of the clip art picture by using the sizing handles, and then you change the text wrapping style for the picture.

1   Click the firecracker picture in the top-left corner of the document.

   The picture is selected, and eight, black sizing handles appear around the perimeter of the picture.

2 Position the mouse pointer over the the bottom-right sizing handle until it becomes a diagonal two headed resizing arrow and drag up and to the left until the firecracker is about half its original size, as shown below.

Pictures often look better if you shrink them rather than if you enlarge them. For example, just as photographs will become grainy if they are enlarged, pictures can become blurry if you enlarge them too much beyond their original size.

Text Wrapping

In Front Of Text

3 On the Picture toolbar, click the Text Wrapping button.

A menu of text wrapping styles appears.

4 Click the In Front Of Text button.

The text returns to the top of the document, and the firecracker picture remains in the same position.

5 Click anywhere outside the picture to deselect it.

The top portion of your document should look similar to the illustration below.

You can create the sparkle text effect, as well as other text effects, by selecting the text, clicking Font on the Format menu, clicking the Text Effects tab, and selecting one of the animation effects that appear in the list. These text effects do not appear in a printed document.

Print Preview

Save

6 On the Standard toolbar, click the Print Preview button.

The document appears in the Print Preview window, showing how the document will look when it is printed.

7 On the Print Preview toolbar, click the Close button.

The document returns to Print Layout view.

8 On the Standard toolbar, click the Save button.

Word saves the document.

Keep this file open for the next exercise.

You can select multiple drawing objects or pictures at once and then reposition them or resize them at the same time. To select multiple items, click the Select Objects button on the Drawing toolbar. The mouse pointer changes to a left-pointing arrow. Drag the pointer to draw a box around all the items that you want to select.

The Layout tab of the Format Picture dialog box includes several new options for adjusting the placement of a picture on a page and for controlling the way text wraps around a picture. (Some of these options are available only by clicking the Advanced button on the Layout tab.)

To ensure that a picture moves up or down with the paragraph to which it is anchored, in the Advanced Layout dialog box, select the Move Object With Text check box. To ensure that a picture remains anchored to the same paragraph when you move the paragraph, in the Advanced Layout dialog box, select the Lock Anchor check box.

Repositioning a Picture

The marketing manager at Impact Public Relations is reviewing a brochure layout created by one of her assistants. Inadvertently, the assistant has transposed several pictures. Rather than deleting the current pictures and reinserting them in the appropriate spots, the marketing manager can save time and just drag the pictures to the new locations. You can also attach, or anchor, a picture to a paragraph mark so that if you move the paragraph, the picture automatically moves with it. Additionally, you can move or "nudge" pictures in small increments by selecting the picture and pressing the arrow keys. If you want to move an item only horizontally or vertically, press Shift as you drag.

To position a picture in relation to the page, a paragraph, or another anchor, select the item that you want to reposition. On the Format menu, click Picture. In the Format dialog box, click the Layout tab, and click the Advanced button. You can use this method to position other objects, including WordArt and AutoShapes.

In the Advanced Layout dialog box, click the Picture Position tab, and select the options that you want for the horizontal and vertical positioning. For example, you can align the picture horizontally relative to the margin, the page, the column, or a character. You can also specify a precise numeric position for the picture relative to the page, the paragraph, and so on.

W2000.6.2

Creating WordArt

You can create decorative text effects with WordArt—a ready-made collection of text designs—called WordArt styles. To create WordArt, you first select one of the text styles, and then you type the text that you want to appear in that style. When you create WordArt text, the text is inserted into your document as an object. The following figure shows a WordArt object that was created for the text *Welcome to LMR*.

When you click a WordArt object, the WordArt toolbar appears.

You can use the WordArt toolbar to modify the appearance of the WordArt object. The following table explains the buttons that appear on the WordArt toolbar.

Description	Button	Used to
Insert WordArt		Insert a new WordArt object into a document.
Edit Text	Edit Text...	Change the font, font size, and font style for the WordArt text, or enter different text.
WordArt Gallery		Change the text to a different ready-made WordArt style.
Format WordArt		Change the fill colors, wrapping style, object size, and other formatting attributes. When you click the Format WordArt button, a dialog box appears and provides different formatting tabs. Most of the formatting changes you can make in this dialog box can be made more easily by using the Drawing toolbar or by resizing the object using the sizing handles around the WordArt object.
WordArt Shape	Abc	Change the shape that the WordArt text forms. For example, you can change the shape to form a ring or a wave, or to slant the text up or down.
Free Rotate		Rotate the WordArt object in any direction. When you click the Free Rotate button, the WordArt object sizing handles change to rotate handles (small green circles). You can drag one of the rotate handles to rotate the object in any direction and to any angle.
Text Wrapping		Change the way text wraps around the WordArt object.
Same Letter Heights	Aa	Convert all text to the same height. For example, if you typed the WordArt text with mixed uppercase and lowercase letters, the WordArt Same Letter Heights button, when clicked, would convert all letters to the same height as the uppercase letters.
WordArt Vertical Text	Ab bↄ	Display the text vertically, instead of horizontally.
WordArt Alignment		Change the text alignment (right, left, center, and so on) when the WordArt text is on multiple lines.
WordArt Character Spacing	AV	Change (expand or condense) the spacing between text characters.

You can also use the Drawing toolbar to change WordArt text effects. For example, you can change the fill colors that appear in the text characters, create a text shadow or change the text to appear with a 3-D effect.

In this exercise, you create a WordArt object to replace the title lines in the Tailspin Toys 08 Edited document. You also change several WordArt settings to enhance the appearance of the WordArt object.

1   Select the three heading lines (*Come Celebrate the Grand Opening of Tailspin Toys*) at the top of the document, and press Delete.

The header lines are removed.

2   On the View menu, point to Toolbars, and click Drawing, if necessary.

The Drawing toolbar appears along the bottom of the window.

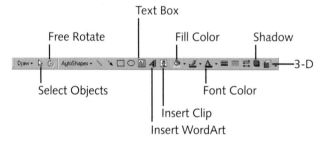

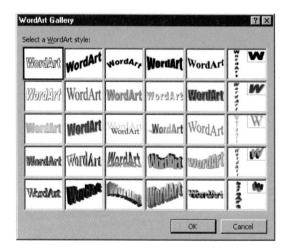

Insert WordArt

3   On the Drawing toolbar, click the Insert WordArt button.

The WordArt Gallery dialog box appears.

The WordArt object you choose is displayed in your document in the colors shown in the WordArt Gallery dialog box. You'll learn how to change the colors of a WordArt object later in this exercise.

4   Click the gold-colored WordArt style in the first column of the third row, and click OK.

The Edit WordArt Text dialog box appears.

Notice that the toolbar includes the buttons to change the formatting of the WordArt text to bold or italics.

5   Type **Come Celebrate the**, and press Enter.

The first line of WordArt text is entered.

6   Type **Grand Opening of**, and press Enter.

The second line of WordArt text is entered.

7   Type **Tailspin Toys**, click the Size down arrow, click 24, and then click OK.

The WordArt object is inserted in the document, with text sized at 24 points, and the WordArt toolbar appears.

Text Wrapping

8   On the WordArt toolbar, click the Text Wrapping button, and click Top And Bottom.

Word wraps text and objects above and below the WordArt object.

Move Pointer

9   Position the mouse pointer over the WordArt object until the move pointer appears, and then drag the WordArt object so that it is in the position shown in the following illustration.

WordArt Shape

Position the mouse pointer over a
WordArt shape to view its name.

10   On the WordArt toolbar, click the WordArt Shape button.

A menu of WordArt shapes appears.

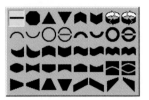

Wave 1

Fill Color

11   Click the Wave1 shape (the fifth shape in the third row).

The WordArt object appears in the wave shape.

12   On the Drawing toolbar, click the Fill Color down arrow.

A color palette appears.

13   On the color palette, click Fill Effects.

The Fill Effects dialog box appears.

Notice that the current fill effect is a
two-color gradient.

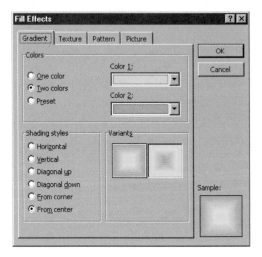

14   Click the Color 2 down arrow, and click the Blue square (second row, sixth square).

15   Click OK.

The WordArt text appears with the new gradient colors.

16 Click an empty area of the document.

The WordArt object is deselected, and the WordArt toolbar is removed from view. The top portion of your document should look similar to the following illustration.

Save

17 On the Standard toolbar, click the Save button.

Word saves the document.

Keep this file open for the next exercise.

W2000.6.1

Drawing a Shape

Word comes with a set of ready-made AutoShapes that you can insert into a document. AutoShapes include complex shapes, block arrows, flowchart symbols, stars and banners, and callout balloons (much like the text balloons that appear in comic strips) that you can select to insert in a document. When you select an AutoShape, Word inserts the shape into your document, saving you the time and effort of creating the shape on your own.

You can also use the Drawing toolbar to draw basic shapes, such as rectangles, circles, and lines. After you've inserted an AutoShape or drawn a **shape** in a document, you can use the Drawing toolbar to change the characteristics of the shape, such as resizing, rotating, or flipping the shape, or changing its fill color. In addition, you can combine and group different shapes to make a more complex design.

After you've created an AutoShape, you can resize the object using the sizing handles. Additionally, some AutoShape objects appear with yellow diamonds on the drawing that allow you to change the internal shape of the object.

For example, if you choose the AutoShape Up Ribbon banner, yellow diamonds appear above and below the ribbon. You can click the yellow diamond to change the dimensions of the banner.

AutoShapes are inserted with the In Front Of Text wrapping style applied. To change the text wrapping style, on the Drawing toolbar, click the Draw button, point to Text Wrapping, and then click the desired option.

In this exercise, you insert two AutoShapes into the current document, add fill colors to both shapes, and rotate one of the shapes.

1   Scroll down until you can see the lines *Entertainment*, *Prizes*, and *Great Food*.

2   On the Drawing toolbar, click the AutoShapes button.

The AutoShapes menu appears.

3   Point to Stars And Banners.

The Stars And Banners menu appears.

Position the mouse pointer over an AutoShape to view its name.

4   Click the Explosion 2 button (the second AutoShape in the first row).

Explosion 2

5   Drag the mouse pointer so that the explosion AutoShape is drawn at the approximate size and location of the one shown below.

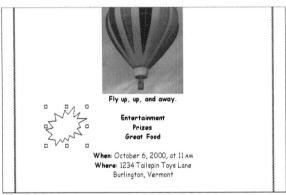

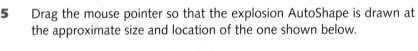

6   Make sure that the shape is still selected, and on the Drawing toolbar, click the Fill Color down arrow.

Fill Color

A color palette appears.

7   In the color palette, click the Light Orange square (third row, second square).

The AutoShape is filled with the selected color.

8   Click anywhere outside the shape.

The sizing handles no longer appear around the shape.

You don't need to deselect a shape in order to select another shape on the Drawing toolbar. Word will automatically deselect the current shape when you select and insert another shape.

9   On the Drawing toolbar, click the AutoShapes button.

The AutoShapes menu appears.

10 Point to Stars And Banners.

The Stars And Banners menu appears.

Curved Down Ribbon

11 Click the Curved Down Ribbon button (the fourth AutoShape in the third row).

The mouse pointer changes to a crosshairs pointer.

12 Drag the mouse pointer so that the ribbon is drawn at the approximate size and location as the one shown below.

13 Make sure that the ribbon shape is still selected, and on the Drawing toolbar, click the Fill Color down arrow.

A color palette appears.

14 On the color palette, click the Dark Blue square (first row, sixth square).

Free Rotate

15 On the Drawing toolbar, click the Free Rotate button.

Word replaces the sizing handles with rotate handles (small green circles).

You can rotate shapes and AutoShapes, but you can't rotate pictures.

16 Click the top-left rotate handle and drag it up until the ribbon is at the approximate angle of the one shown below.

17 Click anywhere outside the shape.

The sizing handles no longer appear around the shape.

Save

18 On the Standard toolbar, click the Save button.

Word saves the document.

Lesson Wrap-Up

In this lesson you learned how to insert and resize pictures from a file and from the Clip Gallery. You also learned how to use WordArt and AutoShapes to insert graphical objects, how to change the fill color, and how to rotate shapes.

If you are continuing to other lessons:

●   On the File menu, click Close. If Word prompts you to save any changes, click No.

   Word saves and closes the file.

If you are not continuing to other lessons:

●   On the File menu, click Exit. If Word prompts you to save any changes, click No.

   The file closes and the Word program closes.

Lesson Glossary

AutoShape A preset shape that comes with Word, such as an arrow, banner, or flowchart, that is inserted in the document.

clip art Picture files that are available from the Microsoft Clip Gallery and can be inserted into Word documents.

Clip Gallery The Microsoft Office program that you use to find, select, and insert clip art pictures.

digital camera A camera that allows you to take pictures and download them as picture files stored on a disk.

object A graphical shape or design, including AutoShapes and WordArt, that you can insert and modify in a Word document.

picture Any image that has been created by a program other than Word, or has been downloaded from a camera, scanner, or Web site and saved to a disk.

shape A drawing created using the mouse pointer and a button on the Drawing toolbar or the AutoShapes menu.

sizing handles Small white or black squares located in the corners and on the sides of a picture or an object and used for diagonal, vertical, or horizontal resizing.

ungroup To separate a graphic into its individual graphical elements, which can then be edited independently.

WordArt Ready-made designs that you can use to create decorative and colorful text.

Quick Quiz

1   How do you access the AutoShapes menu?

2   How do you rotate an AutoShape?

3   Identify two methods that you can use to resize a picture.

4   From the Insert Clip Art dialog box, what two ways can you use to insert a picture?

5   How do you change the shape of WordArt text?

6   How do you change the text size in a WordArt object?

7   When you select a picture, small boxes surround the perimeter. What are these boxes used for?

8   What menu command do you use to insert a picture that exists in another file and isn't a clip art picture?

9   Which command do you use to insert a clip art picture?

important

In the Putting It All Together section below, you must complete Exercise 1 before continuing to Exercise 2.

Putting It All Together

Exercise 1: Open a new blank document and create an invitation for the grand opening of a coffee house. Type the following text in the invitation, except insert a WordArt object for the first three lines. Format the WordArt object as desired, and position it near the center at the top of the document, with the address and other invitation information below the WordArt object. Use the Clip Gallery to add a clip art picture related to coffee or a bakery, and place the picture below the invitation.

> You're invited to celebrate
> The grand opening of
> Kenya Coffee Company & Bakery
> 5678 Washington Street, Burlington, Vermont
> On Saturday, November 06, 2001, beginning at 6:30 p.m.
> Entertainment and dinner provided.

Exercise 2: Insert two five-point stars (AutoShapes) to the right and left of the address, and fill both stars with a two-color gradient. Rotate both stars about 30 degrees . Add a shadow effect to both stars (hint: use the Drawing toolbar). Save the document as Coffee House Opening.

LESSON 9

Working with Columns

After completing this lesson, you will be able to:

✔ *Create columns.*

✔ *Adjust column width.*

✔ *Adjust column spacing.*

✔ *Insert a column break.*

✔ *Insert a vertical line between columns.*

Open a dictionary, a newspaper, or an issue of your favorite magazine, and you'll usually see text displayed in columns. In word processing, **columns** are two or more blocks of text on a page in which text flows to the top of the next column when the first column is filled. (Columns can also contain pictures and objects.) Numerous readability studies show that people are more likely to read text carefully when the widths of lines are short. That's why most newspapers and magazines format text into columns that are usually no more than three inches wide.

You can use Microsoft Word 2000 to easily format text into columns. Although columns aren't always appropriate (you probably wouldn't use them in letters, memos, or many business reports), they work well for newsletters, brochures, indexes, and lists. At times, columns can even help to make a document shorter, typically when most lines of text are short. For example, if you typed the names of all the glossary terms in this book and pressed Enter after each entry, you would have dozens of pages of text, but a lot of empty space on the right side of the document. If you typed the terms using two or three columns per page, the glossary would occupy far fewer pages.

Depending on how margins are set in a Word document, you can create up to 12 columns per page, although you'll rarely need more than four or five columns per page. After you define columns in a document and type text so that it flows into the columns, you'll often discover that you can improve formatting by manually changing where some columns break at the bottom, especially when a column ends in the middle of a sentence. You might also want to customize columns by changing the width, length, or spacing between the columns. You can perform all of these column formatting tasks in Word. You can even add a vertical line between columns to enhance your document's appearance.

In this lesson, you will learn how to convert the text in a brochure to columns and adjust the formatting for different sections of the brochure.

**Sample files
for the lesson**

For additional information on how
to find and open files used in this
book, see the "Using the CD-ROM"
section at the beginning of this book.

W2000.3.12

To complete the procedures in this lesson, you will need to use the file Brochure 09 in the Lesson09 folder in the Word Core Practice folder located on your hard disk. This document was created to explain the services provided by Impact Public Relations.

Creating Columns

Before you begin modifying a document to create columns, it's important to think about how you want the columns to look on the page, how many columns you want, and how you want them to be formatted. The following is a list of items that you should consider when using columns.

- The width of the page minus the left and right margins.

   If the right and left page margins are two inches each, the width of the document becomes much smaller. Remember that you'll also have to include space between the columns. The wider you want the page to be, the smaller the page margins should become to accommodate the text and columns.

- The number of columns that you want to appear across the page.

   Most documents that use columns have between two and three columns per page. The more columns you have on one page, the narrower the columns become. Narrower columns increase the number of hyphenated words and make the document harder to read.

- The length of each column.

   The length of each column determines how far the text extends to the bottom of the page.

- The amount of space between columns.

   Standard space between columns is .5 inches. If you have less space between the columns, the page becomes difficult to read. The greater the space between the columns, the smaller the columns become, and again, the harder the document is to read.

To arrange text into more than six columns, you must use the Columns dialog box. On the Format menu, click Columns, and type the number of columns that you want.

You can quickly create columns of equal width by using the Columns button on the Standard toolbar. When you click the Columns button, Word displays a graphical menu that you can use to specify the number of columns you want. You can also use the Columns dialog box to create columns of equal or unequal width, or you can customize each column with a specific column measurement. After you define the column formatting, you can modify the columns using either the Columns dialog box or the ruler. If you define columns in an existing document but don't select any text, Word flows the entire document into columns using the formatting that you've specified.

In the following exercises, the Standard and Formatting toolbars have been separated. For additional information on how to separate the toolbars see the "Using the CD-ROM" section at the beginning of this book.

To create customized columns using the Columns dialog box, type the desired number of columns in the Number Of Columns box, clear the Equal Column Width check box, and then type the desired measurements in the Width boxes. (You'll customize column widths in a later exercise.)

If you want only certain sections of a document to be formatted into columns, you first select the text that you want formatted into columns and then apply column formatting to the selection. Word automatically inserts section breaks at the beginning and end of the selected text and flows the text into columns. In Word, a **section break** is a portion of a document that can have its own page formatting, independent of the formatting in other sections of the same document.

To create columns of equal width, select the text that is to be formatted into columns. On the Standard toolbar, click the Columns button to display the Columns menu, and click the number of columns you want.

You can also use Word to create columns of unequal width. You might want to do this to create a unique apperance or to accomodate different types of text (for example, a list of topics in a narrow column and topic descriptions in a wider column).

To create columns of unequal length, select the text to be formatted and on the Format menu, click Columns to display the Columns dialog box. To create two columns of unequal width, in the Presets section, click Left to make the left column narrower, or click Right to make the right column narrower.

The marketing manager at Impact Public Relations decided that she wants to reformat a brochure that describes the services that the company provides. Specifically she wants the text to appear in columns.

In this exercise, you format the entire Impact Public Relations brochure into columns by using the Columns button, and then you format a selection of text into uneven columns by using the Columns dialog box.

Open

1 On the Standard toolbar, click the Open button.

The Open dialog box appears.

2 Click the Look In down arrow, navigate to the Word Core Practice folder on your hard disk, and then double-click the Lesson09 folder.

3 Double-click the file Brochure 09.

The file Brochure 09 appears in Word, and the Open dialog box closes.

4 On the Standard toolbar, click the Show/Hide ¶ button.

Formatting characters appear in the document.

¶

Show/Hide ¶

To learn more about formatting marks see Lesson 5, "Changing the Layout of a Document."

Columns

5   On the Standard toolbar, click the Columns button.

The Columns menu appears. Unlike most menus, the Columns menu is a graphical representation that you can use to specify the number of columns for a document or section of a document.

You aren't limited to four columns, as the Columns menu seems to indicate. To create more than four columns, drag to the right on the Columns menu to expand the menu to up to six columns and select the desired number of columns you want.

6   Click the third column in the menu.

The text in the entire document is arranged into three columns. The WordArt object appears over some of the text at the top of the page.

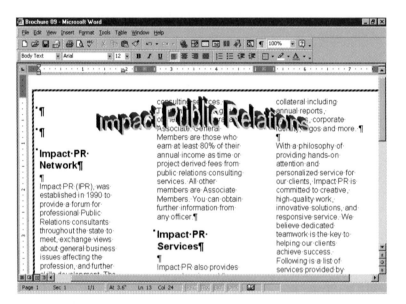

Undo

7   On the Standard toolbar, click the Undo button.

The document returns to its original layout.

8   Position the insertion point to the left of the paragraph mark under the subheading *Impact PR Network*.

To select large blocks of text, click to position the insertion point at the beginning of the text, hold down the Shift key, and then click to the right of the last word that you want to select.

9   Select the paragraph mark and all the text under the *Impact PR Network* subheading. Be sure to select the last paragraph mark in this section, but do not select the subheading *Impact PR Services* or any text under this heading.

Columns

10   On the Standard toolbar, click the Columns button, and in the Columns menu, click the second column.

The selected text is formatted into two columns.

11 Click anywhere in the document to deselect the text.

12 On the Standard toolbar, click the Zoom down arrow, and click Whole Page.

Zoom

13 Select all the text under the subheading *Impact PR Services*, but do not select the subheading.

Make sure that you move the insertion point to the end of the document on the second page, *not* to the end of the first page.

14 On the Format menu, click Columns.

The Columns dialog box appears.

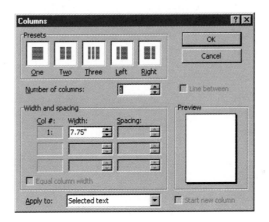

15 In the Presets section, click Right, and click OK.

The selection of text is formatted into two columns, and the left column is wider than the right column.

16 Click anywhere in the document to deselect the text.

The document should look similar to the following illustration.

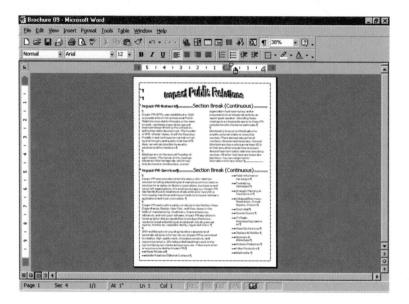

Zoom

17 On the Standard toolbar, click the Zoom down arrow, and click 75%.

The document layout appears at 75 percent of actual size.

> The zoom percentage that appears in the Zoom box can vary depending on the size of your monitor and the number and arrangement of toolbars that are open.

18 On the File menu, click Save As, and save the document in the Lesson09 folder as **Brochure 09 Edited**.

Word saves the document.

Keep this file open for the next exercies.

W2000.3.13

Specifying Column Width

In the previous exercise, you saw how to use the Presets section of the Columns dialog box to create columns of unequal widths. You can also modify the widths of columns using either the ruler or width settings in the Columns dialog box. Depending on how wide or narrow you make the columns, the space between the columns might automatically become wider or narrower.

For example, if you specify in the Columns dialog box that you want five columns, Word automatically formats the columns with equal width and spacing. If you make one of the columns wider in the Width box, all the subsequent column widths become narrower to accommodate the wider column. If you want to customize column widths, you should check the Preview area in the Columns dialog box as you change the settings to see how the other columns are affected by the modifications.

Move Column marker

> You can also use the up and down arrows to the right of the Width box to change the column width in increments of .5 inch.

In this exercise, you customize column widths using both the Columns dialog box and the ruler.

1 Click anywhere under the subheading *Impact PR Services*.

2 On the Format menu, click Columns.

The Columns dialog box appears.

3 In the Width box for the first column, select the contents, type **4.5**, and press Tab.

The width for column 2 automatically changes to 2.5 inches to accommodate the available space for this column after the left and right margin widths, the column width for column 1, and the space between columns have been calculated.

4 Click OK.

The column widths are adjusted based on the measurement that you entered.

5 On the ruler, position the mouse pointer on the Move Column marker until the pointer turns to a double-headed arrow. Hold down the Alt key, and drag the marker to the left so the left column is 4.25 inches wide (at which point the right column will be 2.75 inches wide).

It isn't necessary to hold down the Alt key when you drag the Move Column marker; however, doing so allows you to view the measurements for the column widths so that you can be more precise.

6 Release the Alt key.

The column widths are adjusted.

7 On the Standard toolbar, click the Save button.

Word saves the document.

Keep this file open for the next lesson.

Save

Adjusting Column Spacing

W2000.3.13

The measurements in the Spacing boxes identify the blank space that appears *after* each column. Make sure to look in the Preview area to see how the modifications affect other columns.

If you want to change the spacing between columns, you can use the ruler or the Columns dialog box to adjust the spacing. If you use the Columns dialog box, make sure to preview how the changes affect the columns.

For example, while creating the brochure, the marketing manager specifies in the Columns dialog box that she wants two columns. Word displays a preview of the columns, both set to 3.5 inches wide. The spacing between columns is set to .5 inch. The marketing manager decides to do some experimenting and sets the spacing to 2.5 inches; however, when she does this, the first column's width automatically changes to 1.5 inches, and the second column's width remains at 3.5 inches. Dissatisfied with the results, the manager sets the second column's width to 1.5 inches, which automatically changes the first column's width to 2.5 inches. She likes the preview, so she applies the settings to the brochure.

To change column spacing using the ruler, click anywhere in the section that contains the columns that you want to modify. The ruler displays the Move Column markers. Position the mouse pointer on the right edge of the Move Column marker until you see the ScreenTip *Left Margin*, and drag the marker to the new position.

In this exercise, you change the spacing between columns by using the Columns dialog box.

1   Click anywhere in the section under the sub heading *Impact PR Network*.

2   On the Format menu, click Columns.

The Columns dialog box appears.

3   Clear the Equal Column Width check box, if necessary.

4   Select the measurement in the Spacing box for column 1, type **.1**, and press Tab.

The width of the second column changes to 3.9 inches.

5   Select the measurement in the Width box for the first column, type **3.7**, and press Tab.

The width of both columns is adjusted to 3.7 inches.

6   Click OK.

The Columns dialog box closes, and the spacing between the columns changes.

Zoom

7   On the Standard toolbar, click the Zoom down arrow, and click Whole Page.

The document layout is displayed as an entire page on your screen.

8   Click anywhere in the two-column section under the subheading *Impact PR Services*.

9   On the Format menu, click Columns.

The Columns dialog box appears.

10 Select the measurement in the Spacing box, type **.1**, and press Tab.

The width of the second column changes to 3.15 inches.

11 Click OK.

The Columns dialog box closes, and the spacing between the columns changes.

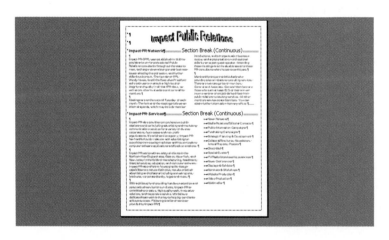

Zoom

Save

12 Click the Zoom down arrow, and click 75%.

The document appears at 75 percent of actual size.

13 On the Standard toolbar, click the Save button.

Keep this file open for the next exercise.

Inserting a Column Break

You can also insert a manual column break by pressing Ctrl+Shift+Enter.

When text in a column reaches either the bottom margin of a page or the next section break, the text flows into the next column on that page or sections. When the text reaches the bottom of the last column on a page, the text flows into the first column on the next page. You can override an automatic **column break** that Word creates by inserting a manual column break.

To insert a manual column break, position the insertion point at the location where you want to insert the break. On the Insert menu, click Break. In the Break dialog box, click the Column Break option, and click OK.

Show/Hide ¶

To delete a column break, make sure the Show/Hide ¶ button is selected on the Standard toolbar, click the Column Break marker, and press Delete.

In this exercise, you create a column break in the second column to view the results, and then you delete the column break.

1 In the last section, click to position the insertion point at the beginning of the third paragraph (which begins *With a philosophy...*).

2 On the Insert menu, click Break.

The Break dialog box appears.

3   Click the Column Break option, and click OK.

The first column ends at the location of the column break.

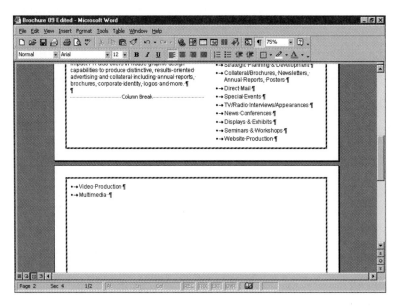

4   Click the Column Break marker, and press Delete.

The column break is removed, and the columns are formatted the way they were before you inserted the column break.

Save

5   On the Standard toolbar, click the Save button.

Word saves the document.

Keep this file open for the next exercise.

Inserting Vertical Lines Between Columns

If you review the column formatting in magazines and newspapers, you'll often notice that columns are separated with a vertical line as well as column spacing. The vertical lines help the reader to distinguish between columns and add a clean, attractive appearance to the page.

You can easily add a vertical line between columns by using the Format Columns dialog box. Click anywhere in the section that contains the columns, and display the Format Columns dialog box. Select the Line Between check box, and click OK. The line that appears between columns will be the complete length of the longest column. If you want to select multiple sections so that you can add vertical lines to all sections, you can do so *only* if all of the sections have the identical column formatting. Because section breaks usually separate sections that have different column formatting, this usually isn't a practical alternative. Instead, you should specify vertical lines for one section at a time.

If you want to control the length and width of the vertical lines that appear between columns, you can use the Drawing toolbar to manually draw lines between columns. However, if you change the widths or lengths of any columns, the manually drawn lines do not change their position. By contrast, when you use the Format Columns dialog box to insert vertical lines between columns, the location and length of the lines are

important

In the Putting It All Together section below, you must complete Exercise 1 to continue to Exercise 2.

Putting It All Together

Exercise 1: Open the Industries Services 09 document in the Lesson09 folder. Format the first portion of the document to two columns of equal width, excluding the title at the beginning and the last section (the part under the subheading *We Know Your Message*). Save the document as **Industries Services Edited.**

Exercise 2: Using the file Industries Services 09 Edited, adjust the widths of the columns that you just created so that the left column is about twice as wide as the right column (4 inches for the first column and 2 inches for the second), and change the spacing between the two columns to .1. Format the final section of the document into four columns excluding the subtitle from the columns, and change the spacing between the four columns to .1. Insert vertical lines between all columns.

LESSON 10

Working with Tables

After completing this lesson, you will be able to:

✔ *Insert a table.*

✔ *Navigate and select cells within a table.*

✔ *Merge table cells.*

✔ *Insert and delete columns and rows.*

✔ *Resize a table.*

✔ *Add shading to a table.*

✔ *Modify table borders.*

Tables provide a convenient way to group, organize, and format similar data. You see and use tables frequently in your daily routine. For instance, a wall calendar is a table that contains headings in the top row for the names of the days of the week. Each additional row shows the days for one week. An invoice is another example of a commonly used table. The top row of the invoice typically displays headings, such as *Description, Quantity,* and *Total.* Each subsequent row can be used to fill in information about a particular product that is purchased. Throughout this course, you've learned how to use Microsoft Word 2000 to format text and graphics in numerous ways, so it probably won't come as a surprise to learn that Word also provides a variety of techniques for creating and formatting tables.

In Word, a **table** is a structure made up of rectangular boxes called cells, which are arranged in columns and rows. A **cell** is the intersection of a row and column and is used to store and format text, a numeric value, or a graphic. A **column** is the vertical arrangement of text or numbers in a table. A **row** is the horizontal arrangement of text or numbers in a table.

Word allows you to create a table in four ways:

■ You can use the mouse pointer to draw the rows, columns, and cells in the format you want.

■ On the Standard toolbar, you can click the Table button to specify the number of columns and rows that you want in your table.

■ You can use the Insert Table dialog box to specify the number of columns and rows for your table, along with other table formatting.

■ You can convert existing text to a table.

In the following exercises, the Standard and Formatting toolbars have been separated. For additional information on how to separate the toolbars, see the "Using the CD-ROM" section at the beginning of this book.

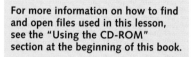

Sample files for the lesson

For more information on how to find and open files used in this lesson, see the "Using the CD-ROM" section at the beginning of this book.

W2000.5.1
W2000.5.3

The first time you insert a table using the Tables And Borders button, the Office Assistant might appear. If you want to use the Office Assistant, click Show Me. If not, click Cancel.

New!

You can now create nested tables (tables within a table) in Word 2000. You create a nested table in the same way you create a table, except that the insertion point is positioned within an existing table cell when you create the new, nested table.

Show/Hide ¶

New Blank Document

After you've created a table, you can continue to modify its structure by combining cells, inserting and deleting columns or rows, resizing rows and columns, or applying formatting to the entire table or to selected rows, columns, or cells. You use Formatting options to change the way borders appear around individual cells, rows, and columns, or the entire table. You can also shade parts of a table with different colors or patterns.

In this lesson, you will learn how to insert a table into a document, navigate within a table, merge table cells, insert and delete columns and rows, change cell formatting, and add shading and borders to a table.

To complete the procedures in this lesson, you will need to use the file Salary Survey 10 in the Lesson10 folder in the Word Core Practice folder located on your hard disk. This document reports the results of a national survey administered to public relations consultants throughout the United States.

Inserting a Table

One way to create a table is to draw it. When you click the Tables And Borders button on the Standard toolbar, the Tables And Borders toolbar appears, and the mouse pointer turns into a pencil. You then use the pencil to draw the borders for cells, rows, and columns—just as if you were drawing a table on a sheet of paper.

The quickest way to create a table is to click the Insert Table button. A graphical menu then appears. The menu is a grid that you use to specify the number of rows and columns for the table. Although this approach is quick, it does not allow you to define any formatting—such as the width of columns—although you can do so later. If you want to specify column width or other table formatting, you can use the Insert Table dialog box to define the table. You open the Insert Table dialog box by pointing to Insert on the Table menu and clicking Insert.

Each cell contains an end-of-cell mark and each row contains an end-of-row mark. To view these **end marks** in a table, on the Standard toolbar, click the Show/Hide ¶ button. End marks appear only on the screen and not on the printed page. An end mark looks like a circle with four small marks extending out of it.

In this exercise, you create tables by using the Insert Table button, the Tables And Borders button, and the Insert Table dialog box.

1   If necessary, on the Standard toolbar, click the New Blank Document button.

Insert Table

You can use the Insert Table button to create a table of 13 rows by 8 columns or larger. The row and column limit depends on the size of your computer screen and its screen resolution.

2   On the Standard toolbar, click the Insert Table button.

The Insert Table menu appears.

3   Drag the mouse pointer to the cell in the third column of the third row, and release the mouse button.

An empty table with three columns and three rows appears in the document window.

4   Press the Down arrow key three times until the insertion point is no longer in the table, and press Enter.

A blank line is inserted after the table.

Tables And Borders

You can drag the Tables And Borders toolbar to the top or bottom corner of your screen if it is in your way, or you can close it.

In Print Layout view, you can use the rulers along the top and left side of the document as guides for drawing the table height and width.

5   On the Standard toolbar, click the Tables And Borders button.

The mouse pointer turns into a pencil, and the Tables And Borders toolbar appears.

6   Under the table you just created, align the pencil at the left margin, and drag down and to the right until you have created a box about 2.5 inches wide by 3.5 inches high.

The outside borders of the table are created.

7   Position the pencil along the left border of the table about 0.5 inch from the top border of the table.

8   Drag the pencil straight across to the right border of the table and release the mouse button.

The first row of the table is created.

9   Repeat steps 7 and 8 to create two more horizontal lines under the line that you just created, spacing them about 0.5 inch apart, as shown in the following illustration.

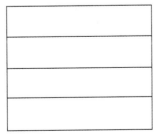

10   Position the pencil on the line that forms the bottom of the first row, about 1 inch from the left border of the table, and drag the pencil straight down to the bottom border of the table.

The first column is created, but it does not include the first row.

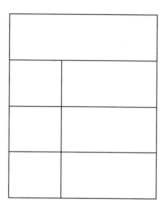

If you don't like the placement of one or more lines in the table, on the Tables And Borders toolbar, click the Eraser button, and drag the mouse pointer across any line that you want to erase.

Eraser

Distribute Rows Evenly

11   Position the pencil on the line that forms the bottom of the first row, about 1 inch to the right of the vertical line that you just created, and then drag the pencil straight down until the pencil reaches the bottom of the second row.

12   On the Tables And Borders toolbar, click the Distribute Rows Evenly button.

The rows in the table are evenly spaced.

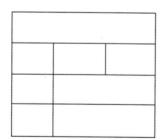

You can also use the Distribute Columns Evenly button if your columns are uneven. If you use the Distribute Columns Evenly button in this exercise, the columns will shift. On the Standard toolbar, you can click the Undo button to return the columns to their original positions.

Draw Table

13   On the Tables And Borders toolbar, click the Draw Table button, and on the Standard toolbar, click the Tables And Borders button.

The pointer changes back to the insertion point, and the Tables And Borders toolbar no longer appears.

14   Press Ctrl+End, and press Enter.

The insertion point moves to the end of the document, and a blank line is inserted after the table.

15 On the Table menu, point to Insert, and click Table.

The Insert Table dialog box appears.

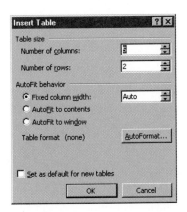

16 In the Number Of Columns box, type **3**, press Tab, and in the Number Of Rows box, type **4**.

17 Click OK.

The Insert Table dialog box closes, and the table is inserted into the document.

18 On the File menu, click Save As, and save the file as **Table Create 10**.

Word saves the document.

Keep this file open for the next exercise.

Moving Around and Selecting Cells in a Table

You need to be able to move from cell to cell to enter text into a table. You can use a variety of methods to move around in a table, such as pressing the arrow keys, clicking the mouse, or pressing the Tab key.

If you're using the mouse, you can click in the desired cell to position the insertion point in the cell. If you're using the keyboard, there are a number of keyboard combinations that you can use to maneuver around and position the insertion point.

The following table explains the keys you can use to navigate throughout a table.

Notice the use of various key combinations, such as Shift+Tab, that help you move through the document. You can learn more about key combinations in Lesson 2, "Editing a Document."

Use these keys	To move
Tab	To the next cell or to add a new row if the insertion point is in the bottom-right cell of the table. Pressing Tab also selects the next cell's data.
Shift+Tab	To the previous cell.
Up arrow key	To the previous row.
Down arrow key	To the next row.
Left arrow key	To the previous character.
Right arrow key	To the next character.
Alt+Home	To the first cell in the row.
Alt+End	To the last cell in the row.
Alt+Page Up	To the first cell in the column.
Alt+Page Down	To the last cell in the column.

If you want to format a particular cell, column, or row, by changing the font of text in cells, adding italics to cell content, or adding shading to cells, for example, you must select the portion of the table that you want to change. Using the keyboard or the mouse, you can make the following selections.

To select	Do this
The entire table	Press Alt+5 (use the numeric keypad with the Num Lock button off) or click the table move handle.
Successive cells	Press Shift+arrow key, or drag the pointer over the cells.
A row	Click the selection area to the left of the row.
A column	Click the top of the column when the down-pointing arrow appears.
Multiple rows	Click the selection bar to the left of the first row that you want to select, and then drag up or down.
Multiple columns	Click the top of the first column that you want to select when the down-pointing arrow appears, and then drag to the right or left.
A cell	Click the bottom-left corner of the cell when the cell selection pointer (diagonal arrow) appears.

New!

The table move handle is a square containing two arrows that are crossed and is located just outside the top-left corner of the table. You can click the table move handle to select the entire table or drag the handle to move the table.

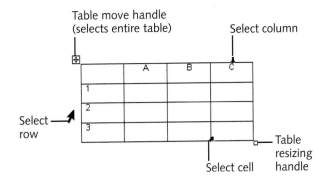

Table Move Handle

The following illustration shows where you click to select the entire table, individual rows, columns, or a cell.

In this exercise, you insert text into a table and practice maneuvering around. Then you select areas of the table and format the text in the cells.

1   Click in the top-left cell of the third table that you created in the previous exercise, if necessary. This is the table with three columns and four rows.

2   Type **Zip Code**, and press Tab.

The text is entered in the cell, and the insertion point moves to the next cell in the row.

3   Type **State**, and press Tab.

4   Type **Salary**, press the Down arrow key, and then hold down the Shift key while you press Tab twice.

The insertion point moves to the last cell of the second row and then moves backward to the first cell in the row.

5   Type the following, pressing Tab after each entry to move from cell to cell.

01*

MA

$51,920

The numbers in the second row are entered, and the insertion point is in the last cell of the row.

You can also convert existing text to a table. The text that is to appear in each cell must be separated by paragraph marks, tabs, commas, or any punctuation that you specify (such as a dash or colon). This punctuation indicates where a new cell's contents begin. To convert text to a table, select the text that is to be converted, on the Table menu, point to Convert, and then click Text To Table.

6   Press Tab to move to the first cell in the next row, and type the following, pressing Tab after each entry to move from cell to cell. Do not press Tab after you enter **$59,300**.

03*

NH

$59,300

The numbers in the third row are entered, and the insertion point is in the last cell of the row.

7   Press Alt+Page Down.

The insertion point moves to the last cell in the column.

8   Press Alt+Home.

The insertion point moves to the first cell in the row.

9 Type the following, pressing Tab after each entry to move from cell to cell.

06***

CT

$50,000

Your table should match the following illustration.

Zip Code	State	Salary
01***	MA	$51,920
03***	NH	$59,300
06***	CT	$50,000

10 Press the Down arrow key.

The insertion point is no longer in the table.

11 Click the selection area to the left of the first row in the table.

The first row of the table is selected.

Bold

12 On the Formatting toolbar, click the Bold button.

The text in the first row is formatted in Bold.

13 Click the last cell in the second row, hold down Shift, and press the Down arrow key twice.

The last cells for the three rows are selected.

Align Right

14 On the Formatting toolbar, click the Align Right button, and click outside the table to deselect the cells.

The text in the cells are aligned along the right edge of the cells.

Zip Code	**State**	**Salary**
01***	MA	$51,920
03***	NH	$59,300
06***	CT	$50,000

Save

15 On the Standard toolbar, click the Save button.

Word saves the document.

16 On the File menu, click Close.

The document closes.

W2000.5.4

Merging Table Cells

After you've created a table, you might determine that some of the table data doesn't fit neatly within the row-and-column format that you've defined. For instance, if you created a four-column table in which each column contains monthly sales information for the current quarter, the first row of your table might contain the title of the table, while the last row might contain a grand total and a label for the total.

Current Quarter Monthly Sales			
January	February	March	April
$31,900	$45,800	$29,600	$52,300
Grand Total:	$159,600		

The title row would be much easier to format if the title is contained in one long cell that spanned the width of the table, rather than four smaller cells in the row. The grand total row would be easier to format if it contained two cells—one for the label and one for the total itself.

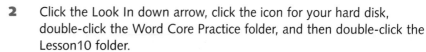

Current Quarter Monthly Sales			
January	February	March	April
$31,900	$45,800	$29,600	$52,300
Grand Total:	$159,600		

You can use Word to **merge cells** for this kind of table formatting. Merging cells is the process of joining multiple cells into one larger cell. You can merge multiple cells in a row into a single cell, or you can merge multiple cells in a column to form a single cell. You can even select multiple cells in multiple columns and merge them into one cell. All of these merging tasks use the Merge Cells command on the Table menu. To merge cells, select the cells that you want to merge, and on the Table menu, click Merge Cells.

In this exercise, you merge cells to create table headers.

1 On the Standard toolbar, click the Open button.

The Open dialog box appears.

Open

2 Click the Look In down arrow, click the icon for your hard disk, double-click the Word Core Practice folder, and then double-click the Lesson10 folder.

The contents of the Lesson10 folder appear in the Open dialog box.

3 Click the file Salary Survey 10, and click the Open button.

The file Salary Survey 10 appears in Word, and the Open dialog box closes.

> You can tell when the pointer is in the selection area because it changes to a right-pointing arrow.

4 Click the selection area to the left of the first row in the table.

The first row of the table is selected.

5 On the Table menu, click Merge Cells.

The first row is no longer divided into eight cells. The text in the first cell is spread across the row, and the row height decreases.

> You can also merge cells by selecting a row or column, right-clicking, and on the shortcut menu that appears, clicking Merge Cells.

6 Scroll down to the row that contains the subheading *Years of Experience*, and select the entire row.

7 On the Table menu, click Merge Cells.

The row is no longer divided into eight cells. The text in the row is spread across the row, and the row height decreases.

8 Select the next row, which contains the text *(in Public Relations field)*.

9 On the Table menu, click Merge Cells.

The selected cells are merged together.

> You can also split cells. When you split a cell, you divide the cell into more columns or rows. Select the cells to be split, and on the Table menu, click Split Cells. In the Split Cells dialog box, choose how many columns or rows you want to insert into the cell.

Merge Cells

Another way to merge cells is to select the cells, and on the Tables And Borders toolbar, click the Merge Cells button. You can display the Tables And Borders toolbar by clicking the Tables And Borders button on the Standard toolbar or by pointing to Toolbars on the View menu and clicking Tables And Borders.

10   Select both of the rows that you have just merged—*Years of Experience* and *(in Public Relations field)*—and on the Table menu, click Merge Cells.

The two rows are merged into one row.

Years of Experience (in public relations field)							
Less than 2 years	37	37,940	—	29,950	35,000	43,250	—
2-5 years	164	41,650	31,320	35,000	40,000	46,500	55,000
6-10 years	171	49,810	35,520	41,000	48,000	56,000	69,000
11 years or more	202	53,960	39,040	45,000	52,880	61,750	71,640

11   On the Standard toolbar, click the Show/Hide ¶ button.

Formatting marks appear throughout the table.

You can learn more about formatting marks in Lesson 5, "Changing the Layout of a Document."

12   Delete the paragraph mark at the end of the text *Years of Experience*, and press the Spacebar.

The line *in Public Relations field* moves alongside the line *Years of Experience* and a space is inserted between the text.

Show/Hide ¶

13   On the Standard toolbar, click the Show/Hide ¶ button.

The formatting marks no longer appear.

14   On the File menu, click Save As, and save the document as **Salary Survey 10 Edited**.

Word saves the document.

Keep this file open for the next exercise.

Inserting and Deleting Columns and Rows

W2000.5.3

After you create a table, you might need to add new columns and rows or delete unwanted columns and rows. For instance, you might decide to add a heading row that you didn't originally plan for, or you might realize that you need to create a column at the end of the table to contain a total for each row. You can use the Table menu to easily add or delete columns and rows.

To insert columns or rows into a table, position the insertion point inside a cell that is above or below the area where you want to insert a row or column. On the Table menu, point to Insert, and click one of the options, depending on whether you want to insert a column or row, and where you want that column or row inserted. You can also select multiple rows or columns to indicate that you want to insert this number of rows or columns at the indicated location.

If you select a row or column, and then press the Delete key, Word will delete the contents of the row or column, but will not delete the row or column itself.

For example, if you select Columns To The Left, Word inserts the number of columns that you selected to the left of the insertion point. If you choose Row Above, Word inserts the number of rows that you selected above the insertion point. To delete columns or rows from a table, select the columns or rows to be deleted. On the Table menu, point to Delete, and click Columns or Rows, as desired.

In this exercise, you add a new row to the table and delete an unwanted row.

1 Scroll to the top portion of the table, and click the cell that contains the text *Entry*, under the subheading *Employment Level*.

2 On the Table menu, point to Insert, and click Rows Above.

A row is inserted into the table.

3 Click the first cell in the new row and type the following text, pressing Tab after each entry.

Internship

15

15,000

8,000

12,000

15,500

18,000

21,000

The cells in the row are filled in.

4 Select the blank row above the row with the subheading *Employment Level*.

5 On the Table menu, point to Delete, and click Rows.

The row is deleted.

6 Continue selecting and deleting all the blank rows in the table.

The table should now look similar to the following illustration.

> You can also insert a row or column by first selecting the row or column, right-clicking the selected row or column, and then clicking the desired command on the shortcut menu that appears. You can use this same technique to insert multiple rows or columns.

> You can select and delete multiple columns or rows that adjoin one another, but you cannot select multiple non-adjoining rows or columns at one time.

1998 UNITED STATES SALARY SURVEY *(By selected groupings)*

Grouping	Base	Mean	10%	25%	50%	75%	90%
Total	578	$48,250	$33,000	$38,500	$46,500	$55,000	$68,000
Employment Level							
Internship	15	15,000	8,000	12,000	15,500	18,000	21,000
Entry	52	36,100	28,600	31,800	35,500	39,000	44,800
Mid-Level, Non-supervisory	207	42,410	31,500	35,000	41,300	48,350	54,650
Mid-Level, Supervisory	57	47,730	35,000	39,930	48,000	52,970	59,200
Senior-Level, Non-supervisory	186	55,500	42,000	46,000	54,510	62,800	72,000
Senior-Level, Supervisory	64	55,900	39,940	46,000	55,000	65,000	71,920
Education Level							
Bachelor's Degree	358	47,300	32,500	37,650	44,260	54,940	65,000
Master's Degree	148	49,460	35,000	38,700	50,000	56,000	68,600
Doctorate	16	59,480	—	—	59,000	—	—
Sex							
Female	396	47,540	33,000	38,000	45,330	55,000	63,640
Male	180	49,690	33,800	39,000	49,500	58,000	70,000
Age							
20-29	82	37,800	28,200	33,100	36,070	41,510	49,600
30-39	178	47,290	32,930	38,890	46,000	53,040	63,620
40-49	200	50,440	35,000	41,550	49,050	58,000	69,300
50 years and over	114	52,950	35,000	43,250	52,000	61,900	71,480
Years of Experience (in public relations field)							
Less than 2 years	37	37,940	—	29,950	35,000	43,250	—
2-5 years	164	41,650	31,320	35,000	40,000	46,500	55,000
6-10 years	171	49,810	35,520	41,000	48,000	56,000	69,000
11 years or more	202	53,960	39,040	45,000	52,880	61,750	71,640

Save

7 On the Standard toolbar, click the Save button.

Word saves the document.

Keep this file open for the next exercise.

W2000.5.4

The table resize handle is new in Word 2000. The table resize handle is the small square that appears outside the bottom-right corner of the table when you position the pointer over the table.

□

Table Resize Handle

You can change the horizontal and vertical alignment of text in a selected table cell. On the Tables And Borders toolbar, click the Align down arrow and click the desired alignment option, such as Align Bottom Center or Align Top Right.

Align

If you want to apply a unique format to a table, you can use the AutoFormat feature. AutoFormats are preformatted table designs that vary in color and border style. To apply an AutoFormat, click anywhere in the table, on the Table menu, click Table AutoFormat, click an AutoFormat in the Formats list, and then click OK.

Table Move Handle

Center

Resizing a Table

When you are entering text or other values into cells, you might notice that some cell entries wrap to two or more lines because they do not fit on one line within a cell. If you don't want the content of a cell to wrap, you can widen the column that the cell is in so that the text or number fits on one line. Similarly, you can narrow the width of a column if you discover that all the values in the column are much smaller than the current column width. You can even change the height of a row, especially if you want to make the row higher to call attention to it.

Word lets you resize a table in many ways. You can resize the entire table by positioning the mouse pointer over the table resize handle and then dragging the mouse pointer to make the table larger or smaller. You can also adjust the size of a column or row by dragging vertical or horizontal borders in the appropriate direction, which resizes the table as well.

To resize a column or row, position the pointer on a horizontal or vertical border anywhere in the table and wait until the resizing pointer (a double-headed arrow) appears. Drag the mouse pointer in the desired direction to resize the column or row.

Row resize pointer

50 years and over	114	52,950	35,000	43,250	52,000	61,980	71,480
Years of Experience (in public relations field)							
Less than 2 years	37	37,940	—	29,950	35,000	43,250	—
2-5 years	164	41,650	31,320	35,000	40,000	46,500	55,000
6-10 years	171	49,810	35,520	41,000	48,000	56,000	69,000
11 years or more	202	53,960	39,040	45,000	52,880	61,750	71,640

Column resize pointer   Table resize handle

In this exercise, you resize a table, change the row height, and change the column width.

1 Press Ctrl+End to move the insertion point to the end of the document, where you'll find the table labeled *Median Salary by One-Digit Zip Codes*.

2 Position the insertion point over the table until the table resize handle appears outside the bottom-right corner of the table.

3 Drag the table resize handle to the left about an inch.

The table becomes narrower.

4 Position the insertion point over the table until the table move handle appears outside the top-left corner.

5 Click the table move handle, on the Formatting toolbar, click the Center button, and then click outside the table to deselect it.

The entire table is selected, centered on the page, and then deselected.

Row Resize

New!

The ability to adjust a row's height directly within a table is new in Word 2000.

Center

> When you click outside the table to deselect it, you should avoid clicking to the left of the table in the selection bar; otherwise, you'll select a row, and the table won't be completely deselected.

Column Resize

6 Position the insertion point on the horizontal line below the text *Median Salary by One-Digit Zip Codes*.

The insertion point turns into a resizing pointer.

7 Drag the line down about .25 inches.

The height of the top row increases.

8 Position the insertion point on the horizontal line below the text *Zip Code* and *Salary* so that the row resizing pointer appears, and drag the line down about .25 inches.

The height of the row increases.

9 Click anywhere in the text of the first row, and on the Formatting toolbar, click the Center button.

The text is centered.

10 Select the second row, and on the Formatting toolbar, click the Center button, and then click outside the table to deselect the row.

The text in both columns of the second row is centered.

11 Position the insertion point on the vertical line in the center of the table, and drag the line to the left until the first column is about 1 inch wide.

The insertion point turns into a resizing pointer, the width of the left column decreases, and the width of the right column increases.

12 Position the insertion point on the vertical line at the right border of the table so that the column resizing pointer appears, and drag the line about 3.5 inches to the left.

The width of the right column decreases. The table should now look similar to the following illustration.

Median Salary by One-Digit Zip Codes	
Zip code	**Salary**
0****	$52,000
1****	49,150
2****	44,550
3****	47,200
4****	39,400
5****	40,880
6****	43,030
7****	46,000
8****	43,000
9****	54,250

Save

13 On the Standard toolbar, click the Save button.

Word saves the document.

Keep this file open for the next exercise.

W2000.5.2

Adding Shading to a Table

In Lesson 4, "Formatting Text," you learned how to add shading to a paragraph to call attention to it or simply to make it more attractive. Similarly, you can add shading to all or parts of a table to emphasize a portion of the table or to give the appearance of different sections in the table. Shading can also help call attention to special titles or headings.

The marketing manager at Impact Public Relations is putting together the company's annual report. A page of the report consists of four tables, each detailing quarterly summaries of the company's expenses. To separate the tables from one another, the marketing manager shades each table with a different color. Not only are the tables easy to distinguish on paper, but also when the shareholders need to review the annual report, the marketing manager can have them direct their attention to a specific colored table to find the information.

In this exercise, you add shading to the introductory paragraph and the table.

1   Select the first row in the table with the text *Median Salary by One-Digit Zip Codes*.

Tables And Borders

2   On the Standard toolbar, click the Tables And Borders button.

The Tables And Borders toolbar appears.

3   Click the Shading Color down arrow.

The Shading Color palette appears.

Shading Color

4   Click the Light Green color square (fifth row, fourth square), and click outside the table to deselect it.

The first row of the table is now shaded in light green.

> If the shade that you pick is dark, Word automatically converts the text to white.

5   Select all rows except the first row.

6   Click the Shading Color down arrow.

7   On the color palette, click the Tan square (last row, second square), and click outside the table to deselect it.

The rest of the table is now shaded in tan.

Keep this file open for the next exercise.

> When you print a shade, the printer creates the shade by applying dots of color at varying densities, depending on the shading percentage that you specify. For example, a 5 percent shade has fewer dots of color than a 65 percent shade. Word can also arrange these dots of color into different patterns, such as vertical, horizontal, and diagonal lines; grids; and trellises. Before selecting a pattern, on the Shading tab, in the Fill section, you must select No Fill.

Median Salary by One-Digit Zip Codes	
Zip code	Salary
0****	$52,000
1****	49,150
2****	44,550
3****	47,200
4****	39,400
5****	40,880
6****	43,030
7****	46,000
8****	43,000
9****	54,250

W2000.5.2

Modifying Table Borders

Just as you can modify paragraph borders, you can also modify table borders. You can change the border around an entire table or around selected cells within a table. You can use the buttons on the Tables And Borders toolbar to modify the table borders, or you can use the Borders And Shading dialog box.

The marketing manager at Impact Public Relations is reviewing the final layout for the company's annual report. At the last minute, she decided that the existing table borders needed to be changed. She can use Word to change the borders without having to rewrite or re-create the table structure and data.

In this exercise, you use the Tables And Borders toolbar to modify the table borders.

1 Position the insertion point over the table with the title *Median Salary by One-Digit Zip Codes* until the table move handle appears outside the top-left corner.

Table Move Handle

2 Click the table move handle to select the entire table.

3 If necessary, on the Standard toolbar, click the Tables And Borders button to display the Tables And Borders toolbar.

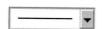

Tables And Borders

4 On the Tables And Borders toolbar, click the Line Style down arrow.

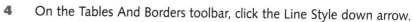

Line Style

5 Scroll through the list of line styles until you see a line that is similar to the selected line style in the following illustration, and click the line.

By default, tables have a black 0.5 point, single, solid-line border that is printed when the table is printed. Even if you remove all or some borders from a table, you can still display grid lines that form the cell boundaries and help you see the intersections of rows and columns. On the Table menu, click Show Gridlines. These gridlines are visible on the screen, but they are not printed.

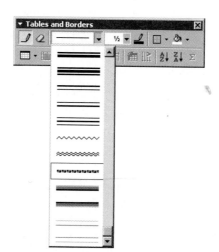

Border Color

6 On the Tables And Borders toolbar, click the Border Color button.

A color palette appears.

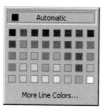

7 Click the Green color square (second row, fourth square).

Outside Border

8 On the Tables And Borders toolbar, click the Border down arrow, and click the Outside Border button.

The green line style is applied to the outside border of the table.

9 Select the first row of the table, and on the Tables And Borders toolbar, click the Outside Border button.

The green line style is applied to the bottom border of the first row.

10 Select the second row of the table, and click the Outside Border button again.

The green line style is applied to the bottom border of the second row.

11 With the second row still selected, click the Border down arrow, and click the Inside Border button.

The green line style is applied to the inside borders of the second row.

Inside Border

12 Click the Inside Border button again.

13 Select all rows except the first two rows.

14 On the Tables And Borders toolbar, click the Line Style down arrow, and click the dash-dot-dot line style.

Notice that the Inside Border button is now displayed on the Tables And Borders toolbar instead of the Outside Border button. The inside border in the first row is removed.

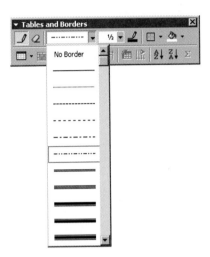

15 On the Tables And Borders toolbar, click the Inside Border button.

The dash-dot-dot line style is applied to the inside borders of the table.

16 On the Tables And Borders toolbar, click the Line Style down arrow, and click the three-line style.

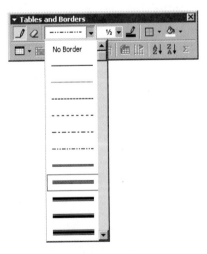

Inside Vertical Border

17 On the Tables And Borders toolbar, click the Border down arrow, and click the Inside Vertical Border button.

The three-line style is now applied to the line between the two columns.

Save

18 Click outside the table to deselect it, and on the Standard toolbar, click Save.

Word saves the document.

The table should look similar to the following illustration.

Median Salary by One-Digit Zip Codes	
Zip code	Salary
0****	$52,000
1****	49,150
2****	44,550
3****	47,200
4****	39,400
5****	40,880
6****	43,030
7****	46,000
8****	43,000
9****	54,250

W2000.5.5

Rotating Text in a Table

In Word, you can change the orientation or direction in which text appears within a cell. By default, Word aligns text horizontally in table cells. You can change the text orientation so that the text is displayed vertically, reading up or down. This approach is useful if the first row of your table contains column labels and the label text is much longer than the content of the columns themselves. By changing the text orientation of the labels, you can avoid the need to widen the columns of the table.

Left to right	Top to bottom	Bottom to top

Change Text Direction

To change the orientation of text in a table, click the cell containing the text that you want to rotate. On the Format menu, point to Text Direction, and click the desired orientation. Alternatively, on the Tables And Borders toolbar, you can click the Change Text Direction button.

Lesson Wrap-Up

In this lesson, you learned how to work with Word's features for creating, modifying, and formatting tables. You created tables and learned to modify them by inserting, merging, and deleting cells, columns, and rows. In addition, you learned how to resize a table; add shading to selected cells, rows, and columns; and how to modify table borders.

If you are continuing to other lessons:

- On the File menu, click Close to close the file. If you are prompted to save changes, click No.
  The file closes and the Word program closes.

If you are not continuing to other lessons:

1   On the File menu, click Close to close the file. If you are prompted to save changes, click No.
    The file closes.

2   On the File menu, click Exit.
    The Word program closes.

Lesson Glossary

cell   The intersection of a row and column in a table. The cell is displayed as a small rectangular box in which text or numbers can be typed. A cell can also contain a graphic.

column   The vertical arrangement of text or numbers in a table.

end marks   Characters called end-of-cell and end-of-row marks that appear on screen when the Show/Hide ¶ button is selected and cannot be printed. An end mark looks like a circle with four small marks extending out of the circle.

merge cells   The process of joining multiple cells into one larger cell.

row   The horizontal arrangement of text or numbers in a table.

table   A data structure that is made up of rectangular boxes called cells, which are arranged in columns and rows.

Quick Quiz

1   How can you select an entire table without having to drag the mouse pointer across the entire table?

2   How do you delete a column from a table?

3   How do you remove shading from a table?

4   What are the maximum number of rows and columns that you can create using the Insert Table button?

5   When using the Change Text Direction button on the Tables And Borders toolbar to change the orientation of text in the current table cell, how do you specify the desired text direction?

6   What are three ways in which you can insert a table into a document?

7   What two methods can you use to resize a table?

8   What keyboard shortcuts can you use to move the insertion point to the first cell in the table?

important

In the Putting It All Together section below, you must complete Exercise 1 to continue to Exercise 2.

Putting It All Together

Exercise 1: If necessary, start Word. Create a new blank document, and create a table that is four rows by three columns. Adjust the size of the table so it is approximately 4 inches wide and 3 inches high, and then distribute the rows and columns evenly. Delete the last column.

Exercise 2: Merge the cells in the first row of the table that you created in Exercise 1, type the heading **Clients by Industry**, and then narrow the first row to about .75 inches. Format the heading so that it is centered and bold with a 20-point Arial font. Then add black shading to the row. Change the outside border and the line between the columns to a double-line border. Save the table as **Table Practice 10** in the Lesson10 folder.

LESSON 11

Word and the Web

After completing this lesson, you will be able to:

✔ *Insert a hyperlink to a Web page.*

✔ *Send a document as an e-mail message attachment.*

✔ *View a document in Web Page Preview.*

✔ *Save a Word document as a Web page.*

Most documents that people create for business and personal use are composed chiefly of text—with some graphics added to provide visual information and attractive effects. For years, Word has been and continues to be the most popular software tool for creating these documents.

However, in recent years, a different type of document has been growing in popularity and use. As the **Internet** continues to grow in popularity, an ever-increasing number of people want to create documents that can be viewed on the **Web**—the term used to describe the technology that delivers text, graphics, sound, and even video on the Internet. Although these multimedia capabilities are widely used by Web sites around the world, most Web documents continue to be composed chiefly of text and graphics.

It makes sense, then, to use Microsoft Word 2000 to create Web documents. In previous versions of Word, you could convert your Word documents to Web documents, called **Web pages**. Web documents use a coding system called **HTML** (Hypertext Markup Language) to format text and graphics on screen. The text and graphic formatting system that Word uses to display and print documents is much more sophisticated. Consequently, with these earlier versions, Word had to convert much of the complex text and graphic formatting in Word documents into more basic HTML formatting. Web pages that originated as Word documents often looked nothing like the original documents.

Fortunately, HTML formatting has evolved rapidly in recent years, and so has Word. With Word 2000, you can save your Word documents as Web pages with little or no loss in formatting. And Word has many additional features that make it a useful tool when you work with the Web. For example, you can insert a **hyperlink** in your Word documents. When readers open your Word document and click the hyperlink, their **Web browser** (such as Microsoft Internet Explorer) opens, and a page on a Web site appears in the Web browser. You can even send your Word documents as **e-mail** messages—without having to quit Word to do so.

In this lesson, you will learn how to use these and other Web features that Word provides. You will learn how to save a Word document as a Web page, how to add hyperlinks to your Word documents, and how to send a Word document as an e-mail **attachment** or as an e-mail message itself.

To complete the procedures in this lesson, you will need to use the file Brochure 11 in the Lesson11 folder in the Word Core Practice folder located on your hard disk. This document publicizes the services of Impact Public Relations. You will insert hyperlinks into the document, and you'll attach the document to an e-mail message and send it to a prospective client. Because the Webmaster of the company wants to post the brochure on the company's Web page, you'll also save the brochure as an HTML (Web) document.

Sample files for the lesson

For additional information on how to find and open files used in this book, see the "Using the CD-ROM" section at the beginning of this book.

W2000.4.8

Inserting a Hyperlink to a Web Page

When you type a **Web address** directly into a document, Word automatically converts the address to a hyperlink. A hyperlink is underlined and colored blue. For example, if you type *www.microsoft.com*, and then press Enter, the text is underlined, colored blue, and converted to a hyperlink.

To create a hyperlink for a Web address, you type the Web address in the Word document. Word recognizes only Web addresses that begin with *www* or *http://*. Word displays the Web address as a link after you press Enter or the Spacebar following the address.

Word also lets you designate a string of text (such as a word, several words, or a sentence), instead of the complete Web address, as a hyperlink. For instance, suppose you type the following sentence in a Word document:

> *Click here for more information.*

If you want to type a Web address in a document but don't want it to be a hyperlink, you can remove a hyperlink without changing your computer's settings. Position the insertion point just after the Web address and press Backspace. Or select the hyperlink, click the Insert Hyperlink button on the Standard toolbar, and then click the Remove Hyperlink button in the Insert Hyperlink dialog box.

You could then select the words *Click here* and assign a Web address to the selected text. When a person opens and displays the Word document and then clicks anywhere on the words *Click here* (which will appear underlined and in blue like any other hyperlink), his or her Web browser opens and the Web page for the link appears. This approach is especially useful if the Web address for the hyperlink is lengthy. For instance, it is more readable to type *Click here* as the hyperlink text rather than *http://mspress.microsoft.com/mspress/products/1349/default1.htm*.

After inserting a hyperlink into a Word document, it's important to test the link to verify that you typed the address correctly and to make sure that the hyperlink is linked to the correct Web page. To test a hyperlink, verify that you are currently connected to the Internet, and then click the hyperlink. If the hyperlink is correctly linked, the Web page for the link should appear.

To create a hyperlink for selected words, type and select the text that you want to use as the hyperlink. On the Standard toolbar, click the Insert Hyperlink button to display the Insert Hyperlink dialog box. In the Type The File Or Web Page Name box, type the Web address that you want to link the text to, or click an address in the list. You can use this same approach to create a hyperlink for a picture or other object. You simply select the picture or object instead of selecting text.

Insert Hyperlink

For additional information on ScreenTips, see Lesson 1, "Getting Started with Word."

In the following exercises, the Standard and Formatting toolbars have been separated. For additional information on how to separate the toolbars, see the "Using the CD-ROM" section at the beginning of this book.

tip
When you rest the mouse pointer over a hyperlink, a ScreenTip appears. The ScreenTip usually displays the address associated with the hyperlink. Word inserts the target address as the hyperlink's ScreenTip; however, you can customize a hyperlink ScreenTip from the Insert Hyperlink dialog box. To customize a ScreenTip, select the hyperlink and click the Insert Hyperlink button. In the Insert Hyperlink dialog box, click the ScreenTip button to display the Set Hyperlink ScreenTip dialog box. Type the desired ScreenTip text, and click OK.

In this exercise, you create two hyperlinks—first by typing a Web address and then by defining a string of text as a hyperlink.

Open

1   On the Standard toolbar, click the Open button.

The Open dialog box appears.

2   Click the Look In down arrow, click the icon for your hard disk, double-click the Word Core Practice folder, and then double-click the Lesson11 folder.

The contents of the Lesson11 folder appear in the Open dialog box.

3   Double-click the file Brochure 11.

The Open dialog box closes, and the file Brochure 11 appears in the Word window.

4   Click to position the insertion point at the end of the third paragraph (the last paragraph in the first section), after the period in the sentence ending *Associate Members*.

If you do not want Word to automatically create a hyperlink every time you type a Web address, click AutoCorrect on the Tools menu, and then click the AutoFormat As You Type tab. In the Replace As You Type section, clear the check box labeled Internet And Network Paths With Hyperlinks.

5   Press the Spacebar, and type **For more information, see www.microsoft.com**, and then press the Spacebar again.

The Web address is underlined and colored blue, and it is converted to a hyperlink.

Impact Public Relations (IPR) was established in 1990 to provide a forum for professional Public Relations consultants throughout the state to meet, exchange views about general business issues affecting the profession, and further skills development. IPR provides invaluable services to all its members.

Meetings are on the second Tuesday of each month. The format of the meetings follows an informal agenda, which may include member introductions, a short organization business review, and a presentation on professional skills by an expert guest speaker. Attending

Impact Public Relations Services

IPR also provides comprehensive public relations services, including advertising and marketing communications services for a variety of diverse corporations, businesses, and non-profit organizations. It is a full service agency; IPR has

these meetings is an invaluable asset to those PR consultants who choose to participate.

Membership is open to individuals who provide personal relations consulting services. There are two categories of members: General and Associate. General Members are those who earn at least 80 percent of their annual income as time or project-derived fees from public relations consulting services. All other members are Associate Members. For more information, see www.microsoft.com

- News Releases
- Media Relations/Editorial Contacts
- Public Information Campaigns
- Fundraising Campaigns

Hyperlink

6 Click the hyperlink *www.microsoft.com* to test it.

Your Web browser starts, and the specified Web page opens.

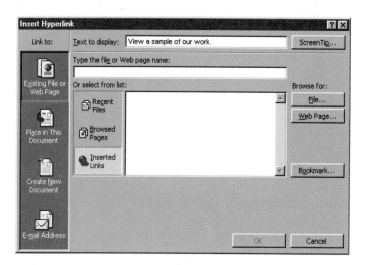

Close

7 Click the Close button in the top-right corner of your Web browser.

The Web browser closes, the Word document reappears, and the color of the visited hyperlink changes.

8 Press Ctrl+End.

The insertion point moves to the end of the document.

Insert Hyperlink

9 Select the text *View a sample of our work.*, and on the Standard toolbar, click the Insert Hyperlink button.

The Insert Hyperlink dialog box appears, and the text that you selected now appears in the Text To Display box.

In the Insert Hyperlink dialog box, a list appears that shows links to recently accessed files, recently browsed Web pages, or recently inserted links. The information displayed in the list varies depending on which option is selected just to the left of the list. Also, the contents of the list vary from computer to computer depending on the files, Web pages, or inserted links used recently on the computer.

Normally you don't have to type *http://*. Word inserts the characters *http://* at the beginning of Web addresses. Because the Web address used in this example does not include *www*, Word doesn't recognize it as a Web address and doesn't automatically insert *http://*.

The Insert Hyperlink dialog box closes, and the selected text is underlined and colored blue, indicating that it is linked to the Web page that you specified.

10 In the Type The File Or Web Page Name box, type **http://mspress.microsoft.com/mspress/products/1349/default1.htm**, and click OK.

11 Click the hyperlink *View a sample of our work* to test it.

The Web browser starts, and the Web page for Lakewood Mountains Resort opens.

12 Click the Close button in the top-right corner of your Web browser.

The Web browser closes, and the Word document reappears. (You might have to click the Brochure 11 button on the taskbar to return to the Word document.)

13 On the File menu, click Save As, and save the document as **Brochure 11 Edited** in the Lesson11 folder.

Word saves the document.

Keep this file open for the next exercise.

Inserting a Hyperlink to a File

You can also create a hyperlink that, when clicked, displays an existing file or a specific location within a file. When a hyperlink is linked to a file, clicking the link opens the file to which the object or text is linked. When a hyperlink is linked to a specific location within a file, clicking the hyperlink opens and displays the target file, and the insertion point appears at the location defined by the link. These types of hyperlinks are useful in documents that refer to information contained in other files. For example, the marketing manager at Lakewood Mountains Resort inserts hyperlinks to several files mentioned in a document analyzing the effectiveness of different marketing materials. All of these files are stored on the resort's network server. The marketing manager distributes the document electronically, and recipients can click the hyperlinks to view the marketing materials being discussed.

To link to an existing file:

1 Select the text that you want as the hyperlink, and click the Insert Hyperlink button.

2 In the Insert Hyperlink dialog box in the Link To Places Bar along the left side of the dialog box, click Existing File Or Web Page, and then in the Browse For section, click the File button.

3 Locate and select the file that you want to link to, and then click OK twice.

When you link to a specific location within an existing file, you must first insert a **bookmark** in the desired location of the target document. The bookmark identifies the location to which you want to link.

To insert a bookmark:

1 On the Insert menu click Bookmark , type the name of the bookmark, and click the Add button.

2 Open the file that will contain the hyperlink, select the text that you want to use as the hyperlink, and click the Insert Hyperlink button.

3 In the Insert Hyperlink dialog box under Link To, click Existing File Or Web Page, and then in the Browse For section, click the File button.

4 Locate and select the target file to which you want to link. Click the Bookmark button, and then select the desired bookmark.

You can use this approach to link to a different part of the same document, which can be helpful to your readers if the document contains several pages. Instead of scrolling through the document to locate particular text, your readers can click the hyperlink to move to the specified location instantly.

You can also create a hyperlink that links to a new file that you haven't created yet. In the Link To Places Bar along the left side of the Insert Hyperlink dialog box, click Create New Document to link to a file that you haven't yet created. After you specify a name for the new file, the file is created for you. You can then open the file for editing immediately or come back to it later.

A bookmark is a link to a Web page or other URL that you have stored in a file. You can use the bookmark to return to the Web page later, rather than having to type the Web page address.

Sending a Document as an E-mail Message Attachment

Documents can be easily sent via e-mail from within Word. E-mail is an abbreviated term for electronic mail. By using an e-mail program (such as Microsoft Outlook or Microsoft Outlook Express), you can send an electronic message or document to another person over the Internet. The recipient must also have an e-mail program as well as an e-mail address (a unique e-mail identifier). You can send a document as an attachment to an e-mail message, or Word can convert the document into a format that e-mail programs can read, in which case the document becomes the body of the e-mail message. An attachment is a file that can be sent as part of an e-mail message. When a recipient receives the e-mail message, he or she can open and view the attached file in Word.

To send a document as an attachment to an e-mail message, open the document that you want to send and, if necessary, connect to the Internet. On the File menu, point to Send To, and click Mail Recipient (As Attachment). By clicking Mail Recipient, Outlook, Outlook Express, or the default e-mail program on your computer opens. Type the name of the recipient in the To box, type a message in the message box, and then click the Send button.

You can also send a Word document as the content of an e-mail message, rather than as an attachment. To do this, open the document that you want to send, and on the Standard toolbar, click the E-mail button. Word converts the document into an e-mail message, which is coded in HTML. A message window appears so that you can address and send the e-mail.

The recipient does not have to open an attachment to read the e-mail message; however, if the document that you sent has formatting that can't be converted to HTML, the recipient's document might not look the way you had intended. For this reason, it is a good idea to send documents as attachments so that formatting is not lost in the conversion. If you attempt to send a Word document as an e-mail message and the document contains characters that cannot be converted to HTML, Word displays a dialog box asking you to specify the **character set** (all the alphabetic, numeric, and special characters that are available to a particular program or feature) to use when the message is sent.

You can create a hyperlink to an e-mail address. When you click a hyperlink to an e-mail address, the Web browser creates an e-mail message with the correct e-mail address in the To box. You must have an e-mail program installed to send a message using this type of hyperlink. To create a hyperlink to an e-mail address, type the e-mail address in the document, and then press Enter or the Spacebar. Word converts the address you typed to a hyperlink. For example, if you type *someone@microsoft.com* and press the Spacebar, Word creates the hyperlink.

E-mail

If you click the E-mail button and then decide that you don't want to send the Word document as an e-mail message, click the E-mail button again to remove the message window.

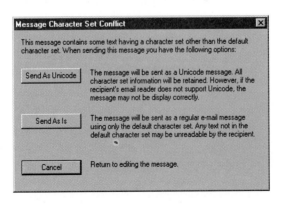

You can send a Word document without having to attach it. Word converts the document into an HTML e-mail message when you click the E-mail button on the Standard toolbar.

The marketing manager at Impact Public Relations decided to send the Impact Public Relations brochure to some prospective clients as an attachment to an e-mail message.

In this exercise, you send the brochure as an attachment to an e-mail message.

1 On the File menu, point to Send To, and click Mail Recipient (As Attachment).

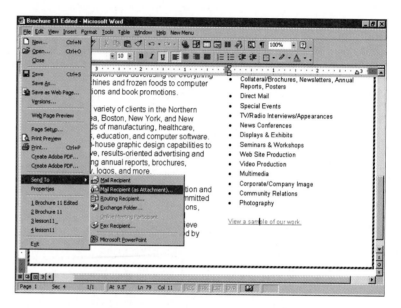

Your computer's default e-mail program starts.

2 In the To box, type **someone@microsoft.com**.

When you send an e-mail message to someone@microsoft.com, you'll eventually get a response from Microsoft.

The appearance of the window depends on the e-mail program that you use.

The text in the first line of the attachment is automatically inserted in the Subject box. The first line of text is often the title of the document and can be an effective subject. In this case, because the title of the document is a WordArt object, Word inserted the subheading as the subject.

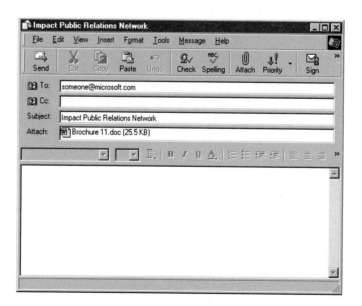

The e-mail address of the client is entered.

3 Select the text in the Subject box, and type **Impact Public Relations Brochure**.

4   Click the message area, and type **Per our discussion, here is a brochure describing the services provided by Impact Public Relations.**

> The appearance of the window depends on which e-mail program you use.

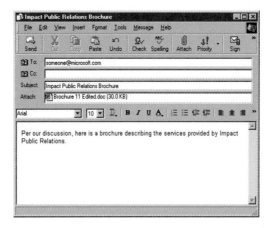

5   In the e-mail window, click the Send button.

Follow the instructions provided by your e-mail program to send the message.

Keep this file open for the next exercise.

W2000.3.3

Viewing a Document in Web Page Preview

Before you convert a Word document to a Web page (which you will do in a later exercise), you can preview how the document will look as a Web page first. This approach is useful because the formatting might change when you convert a Word file to HTML (Web page) format. You can use Web Page Preview to quickly check that your document will look the way you want prior to saving the document as a Web page. For example, if your document contains page breaks, columns, text wrapping around figures, small caps, and text effects (such as shadows) these formats do not convert to HTML format.

Web Layout view is new in Word 2000.

To preview a Word document as it will appear as a Web page, click Web Page Preview on the File menu. The Web browser starts and displays a preview of the current Word document as a Web page. You can also click the Web Layout View button to view the document as an HTML file without having to start your Web browser.

In this exercise, you preview Impact Public Relations' brochure as an HTML document in Web Page Preview and in Web Layout view.

1   On the File menu, click Web Page Preview.

The Web browser opens and displays a preview of the brochure as a Web page.

<table>
<tr><td>
You do not have to be connected to the Internet to view a document in Web Page Preview, but you must have a Web browser installed on your computer.
</td></tr>
</table>

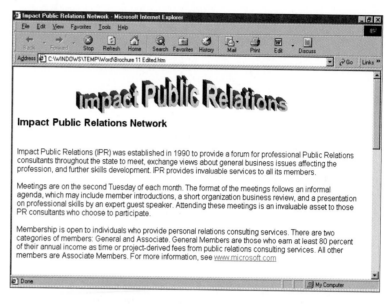

2   Scroll through the document to see if any formatting has changed.

Notice that the page border is no longer displayed and the content is no longer formatted into columns.

3   Click the Close button in the top-right corner of your Web browser.

The Web browser closes and the Word document reappears.

Web Layout View

4   Click the Web Layout View button located to the left of the horizontal scroll bar at the bottom of the screen.

Word displays the document as it would appear if it were an HTML file displayed in a Web browser.

<table>
<tr><td>
Notice that the view is different than the view in Web Page Preview.
</td></tr>
</table>

5   Scroll through the document to see what formatting has changed.

Notice that the width and length of the paragraphs are wider, the font is smaller, and you can make edits using Web Layout view.

Keep this file open for the next exercise.

W2000.4.6

Saving a Word Document as a Web Page

You can easily save any Word document as an HTML file, which can then by stored on a Web server so that other people can open the document in their Web browsers. A Web server is a computer that contains special software for receiving requests from the Internet to display Web pages. The HTML file duplicates most of the styles, format, and content of the Word document. The benefit of converting a Word document to an HTML file is that all Web browsers can interpret an HTML file; however, they cannot interpret a Word document.

Before you make changes to a document and save it as an HTML file, you should remember to save the document as a Word file. This allows you to retain changes in both the HTML document and the Word version of the document. When a Word document is converted to HTML (saved as a Web page), Word might not be able to convert some formatting to HTML. As a result, the HTML document might not look the same as the original Word document. If you saved the Word document prior to converting it to HTML, you can return to the original document and make formatting changes as necessary so that the HTML version will look more like what you intended.

In this exercise, you save the Impact Public Relations brochure as a Web page.

1   On the File menu, click Save As Web Page.

The Save As dialog box appears and the Save As Type box contains the text *Web Page*.

The text in the first line of a document is automatically inserted as the *title* for the Web page. The title is the text that is displayed in the title bar of the document or browser window and is not necessarily the same as the file name. To change the title of the Web page, click the Change Title button in the Save As dialog box. In the Set Page Title dialog box, type the title, and click OK.

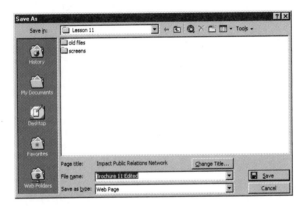

2   In the File Name box, type **Brochure11Web**.

3   Click the Save In down arrow to navigate to the Lesson11 folder.

4   Click the Save button.

The document is saved as an HTML file and is displayed in Web Layout view.

tip

If you open the Exploring window, you'll notice that a folder named Brochure11Web_files appears in addition to the HTML file. This folder has additional files that Word created after you saved the brochure as a Web page. For instance, the WordArt object from the top of the brochure was saved as a separate graphic file so that it could be viewed on the Web page. Graphics that appear on Web pages are stored in a folder so that when the Web pages are published to a Web server, the graphics appear in their intended locations on the Web pages.

Lesson Wrap-Up

In this lesson, you learned how to insert a hyperlink, how to send a Word document as an e-mail message attachment, and how to preview and save a Word document as a Web page.

If you are continuing to other lessons:

● On the File menu, click Close.
  The file closes.

If you are not continuing to other lessons:

● On the File menu, click Exit.
  The file closes and the Word program closes.

Lesson Glossary

attachment A document that is sent with an e-mail message so that recipients can open the document when they receive the message.

bookmark A link to a Web page or URL that is stored in a file. Clicking the bookmark links you to the Web page or URL.

character set The alphabetic, numeric, and special characters that are available to a particular program or feature.

e-mail Electronic mail that is sent from one computer over the Internet to a recipient's computer in another location. To send an e-mail message, you must have an e-mail program installed on your computer.

HTML (Hypertext Markup Language) A collection of styles (also called tags) that define the formatting of a Web document. HTML is a language that can be interpreted by all Web browsers.

hyperlink A line of text, a Web address, or a graphic that you click to go to a different file, a different location in the same file, or a Web page on the Internet. Text that is a hyperlink appears in a different color and is underlined.

Internet A worldwide network of thousands of computer networks, and in turn, millions of computers.

Web The term used to describe the technology that delivers text, graphics, sound, and video on the Internet.

Web address A specific string of characters that uniquely identifies a Web page on the Internet. You can use a Web address to create a hyperlink from a Word document to the Web page associated with the address. Word recognizes a string of characters as being a Web address only if the string begins with *www* or *http://*.

Web browser An application used to view Web pages and that understands HTML tags and displays file content according to the formatting specification defined in the tags.

Web pages HTML files that are stored on a Web server and viewed from within a Web browser.

Quick Quiz

1   What is the difference between Web Page Preview and Web Layout view?

2   What are two ways that you can access the Insert Hyperlink dialog box?

3   What are two types of hyperlinks in a Word document?

4   What are two ways in which you can send the information in a Word document to an e-mail recipient?

5   When you save a document as a Web page, in what format or language is the document converted?

6   What does a hyperlink in a Word document allow you to do?

7   What is a Web browser used for?

8   Why is it important to test a hyperlink after you create it?

important

In the Putting It All Together section below, you must complete Exercise 1 to continue to Exercise 2.

Putting It All Together

Exercise 1: If necessary, start Word. Open the document named Web Practice 11 in the Word Core Practice folder. At the bottom of the page, replace the text *Page 1 of 1* with a hyperlink to *www.microsoft.com*. Send the document as an e-mail message attachment to someone@microsoft.com with a short note indicating the content of the attachment. Save the document as **Web Practice 11 Edited** in the Word Core Skills folder.

Exercise 2: View the document used in Exercise 1 in Web Page Preview to verify that the formatting will be acceptable if you convert the document to a Web page. In the Word document, click one of the blank lines between the table and the line *PR Consultants Salary Survey,* and type **To view additional business statistics, click here**. Then create a hyperlink for the words *click here* to the Web address *www.microsoft.com*. Test the hyperlink. View the document in Word using Web Layout view. Save the document as a Web page using an appropriate name for an HTML file, and then close the document.

Quick Reference

Lesson 1: Getting Started with Word

To start Microsoft Word 2000

1   Click the Start button on the Windows taskbar.
2   On the Start menu, point to Programs.
3   On the Programs submenu, click Microsoft Word.

To display a ScreenTip

●   Position the mouse pointer over a button or a screen element for a few seconds.

To display a menu

●   On the menu bar, click the name of the menu.

To view an expanded menu

1   On the menu bar, click the name of the menu.
2   Click the double arrow at the bottom of the menu.
    Or
    Wait a few seconds for the expanded menu to appear on its own.

To enter text

1   Click to position the insertion point where you want to insert text.
2   Type the text.

To use Click And Type

1   In Print Layout view, position the mouse pointer where you want to insert text.
2   Double-click, and begin typing.

To save a document for the first time

Save

1   On the Standard toolbar, click the Save button.
2   Type the file name in the File Name box.
3   Click the Save In down arrow, and select a location for the file.
4   Click the Save button.

To save a document after making changes

Save

● Click the Save button.

To close a document

● On the File menu, click Close.

To create a new blank document

New Blank Document

● On the Standard toolbar, click the New Blank Document button.

To quit Word

● On the File menu, click Exit.

To display the Office Assistant

● On the Help menu, click Show The Office Assistant.

To use the Office Assistant to get help

1   On the Help menu, click Show The Office Assistant if the Office Assistant isn't already displayed.
2   Click the Office Assistant.
3   Type a question in the box.
4   Click the Search button.
5   Click one of the topics to read about it.

To hide the Office Assistant

● On the Help menu, click Hide The Office Assistant.

To turn off the Office Assistant

1   Right-click the Office Assistant, and click Options.
2   Click the Options tab.
3   Clear the Use The Office Assistant check box.
4   Click OK.

Lesson 2: Editing a Document

To open a file

Open

1   On the Standard toolbar, click the Open button.
2   Navigate to the folder where the file is stored.
3   Click the file's name.
4   Click the Open button.

To navigate through a document

● Use the mouse pointer.

     Or

Use the arrow keys.

Or

Use the scroll bars.

Or

Use the key combinations.

To scroll through text

● Use the vertical scroll bar, scroll arrows, and scroll box to move up and down.

Or

Use the horizontal scroll bar, scroll arrows, and a scroll box to move left to right.

Or

Previous Page

Use the Previous Page button to move to the beginning of the previous page.

Or

Next Page

Use the Next Page button to move to the beginning of the next page.

To insert text

1 Click to position the insertion point in the document where you want to insert the text.

2 Begin typing.

To select text

● Drag the mouse pointer over the text.

Or

Use the selection area to the left of the document.

To undo an action

Undo

● On the Standard toolbar, click the Undo button.

To restore an action

Redo

● On the Standard toolbar, click the Redo button.

To create a folder

Create New Folder

1 On the File menu, click Save As.

2 Click the Create New Folder button.

3 Type a name for the folder in the Name box.

4 Click OK.

To save a file with a different name

1 On the File menu, click Save As.

2 If necessary, navigate to the folder in which you want to store the file.

3   In the File Name box, type a name for the new copy of the file.

4   Click the Save button.

To save a file with a different format

1   On the File menu, click Save As.

2   If necessary, in the File Name box, type a new name for the document.

3   Click the Save As Type down arrow.

4   Click the file format in which you want to save the document.

5   Click Save.

Lesson 3: Using Templates and Wizards

To use the Normal template

●   On the Standard toolbar, click the New Blank Document button.

New Blank Document

To use a template other than the Normal template

1   On the File menu, click New to display the New dialog box.

2   Click the desired category tab.

3   Double-click the desired template icon.

4   Update the document as desired, and save the file.

To create a template from an existing document

1   Create or open the document on which you want to base the template.

2   On the File menu, click Save As.

3   Type a name for the template in the File Name box.

4   Click the Save As Type down arrow, and click Document Template.

5   Leave the document in the default location (the folder called Templates).

    Or

    Click the Save In down arrow, and navigate to the folder in which you want to store the template.

6   Click the Save button.

7   Modify the template as desired.

8   Save the template.

To create a template from a template

1   On the File menu, click New to display the New dialog box.

2   Click the desired category tab.

3   Double-click the template icon on which you want to base the new template.

4   Update the current template with changes that you want for the new template, and click the Save button.

5   In the File Name box, type the name of the new template.

6   Click the Save As Type down arrow, and click Document Template.

7   Click the Save button.

To start a wizard

1   On the File menu, click New.

2   Click the desired category tab.

3   Double-click the wizard icon that you want to use.

4   Follow the screen prompts, clicking Next to move from one dialog box to the next.

Or

Click the flowchart on the left side of the dialog box to skip to a specific step.

5   Click the Finish button.

6   Modify the document as desired, and save it.

Lesson 4: Formatting Text

To apply a bold attribute

1   Select the text.

Bold

2   On the Formatting toolbar, click the Bold button.

Or

Press Ctrl+B.

To apply the italics attribute

1   Select the text.

Italic

2   On the Formatting toolbar, click the Italic button.

Or

Press Ctrl+I.

To apply the underline attribute

1   Select the text.

Underline

2   On the Formatting toolbar, click the Underline button.

Or

Press Ctrl+U.

To format text

1   Select the text.

2   On the Formatting toolbar, click the Style down arrow.

Or

Click the Font down arrow.

Or

Click the Font Size down arrow.

To format text using the Font dialog box

1   Select the text.

2   On the Format menu, click Font.

3   Make selections as desired.

To align text

1   Click the paragraph that you want to align.

Or

Select all or part of the multiple paragraphs that you want to align.

2   On the Formatting toolbar, click the appropriate alignment button.

To cut or copy text

1   Select the text that you want to move or copy.

  2   On the Standard toolbar, click the Cut or Copy button.

Cut   Copy

3   Click the insertion point in the location in which the text is to appear or be duplicated.

 4   On the Standard toolbar, click the Paste button.

Paste

To paste from a file created in another program

1   Open the file and select the text or object that you want to paste into Word.

2   On the Edit menu, click Paste Special.

3   On the Paste Special dialog box, select the format that you want to insert the text or object.

4   Select Paste.

Or

Select Paste Link.

5   Click OK.

To move text using the mouse pointer

1   Select the text that you want to move or copy.

2   Position the mouse pointer over the selected text and hold down the left mouse button.

3   Drag the mouse pointer to the new location.

To paste from among multiple selections in the Office Clipboard

1   Select the text that you want to move or copy.

  2   On the Standard toolbar click the Cut or Copy button.

Cut   Copy

3   Repeat steps 1 and 2 for every selection that you want to move or copy.

4   Click where the item is to appear.

5   On the View menu, point to Toolbars, and click Clipboard.

6   On the Clipboard toolbar, click the item that you want to paste.

7   Repeat step 6 for every item that you want to paste.

To apply a style to text

1   Select the text to be formatted.

2   On the Formatting toolbar, click the Style down arrow.

3   Click the style that you want to apply.

To create a paragraph border

1   Click in the paragraph to be formatted.

Tables And Borders

2   On the Standard toolbar, click the Tables And Borders button.

3   On the Tables And Borders toolbar, click the Line Style down arrow, and click a border style.

4   Click the Border down arrow, and click the Border button to apply the border.

To add shading to a paragraph

1   Click in the paragraph to be shaded.

Tables And Borders

2   On the Standard toolbar, click the Tables And Borders button.

3   Click the Shading Color down arrow, and click a color.

To preview a document

Print Preview

●   On the Standard toolbar, click the Print Preview button.

To print a document

Print

●   On the Standard toolbar, click the Print button.

To print a document using special print settings

1   On the File menu, click Print.

2   In the Copies section, type the desired number of copies in the Number Of Copies box.

3   In the Page Range section, click Current Page to print the current page; click All to print all the pages; click Pages to print specific pages, and then type the desired page numbers in the Pages box.

4   Click OK.

To print selected text

1   Select the text that you want to print.

2   On the File menu, click Print.

3   In the Page Range section, click Selection.

4   Click OK.

Lesson 5:
Changing the Layout of a Document

To change the page margins using the Page Setup dialog box

1   On the File menu, click Page Setup.

2   If necessary, click the Page Margins tab.

3   Type the new page margin settings in the appropriate boxes.

4   Click OK.

To change page margins using the ruler

1   On the View menu, click Print Layout.

2   Position the insertion point over the page margin marker until the insertion point becomes a double-headed arrow.

3   Drag the marker to the new location.

To insert a hard page break:

1   Click to position the insertion point at the location where you want to add the break.

2   Press Ctrl+Enter.

To apply paragraph formatting:

1   Select the appropriate paragraph(s).

2   On the Format menu, click Paragraph.

3   Change the settings as necessary.

4   Click OK.

To indent a paragraph using the ruler

1   Select the paragraph.

2   Drag the First Line Indent, Hanging Indent, and the Left Indent markers to fully indent the paragraph.

Or

Drag only the First Line Indent marker only to indent the first line.

Or

Drag only the Hanging Indent marker only to create a hanging indent.

Or

Click and drag the Left Indent marker.

3   Deselect the text.

To set one tab stop:

1   On the Format menu, click Tabs.

2   Type the new tab stop in the Tab Stop Position box.

3   If desired, in the Alignment or Leader section, select the desired option.

4   Click the Set button.

5   Click OK.

To set multiple tab stops

1   On the Format menu, click Tabs.

2   In the Tab Stop Position box, type the position for the first tab stop.

3   In the Alignment section, select the desired tab alignment.

4   If desired, in the Leader section, select the desired leader option.

5   Click the Set button.

6   In the Tab Stop Position box, type the position for the second tab stop.

7   If necessary, in the Alignment or Leader sections, select the desired option.

8   Click the Set button.

9   Repeat the process for additional tab stops you want to set.

10   Click OK.

To set a tab stop using the ruler

1   Select the paragraph(s) for which you want to set the tabs.

2   Click the Tab Align button at the far left side of the ruler to specify tab alignment type.

3   Click the ruler at the location where you want the new tab.

4   Deselect the text.

To clear a tab stop

●   Drag the tab stop marker off the ruler.

To add page numbers

1   On the Insert menu, click Page Numbers.

2   Click the Position down arrow, and then select the page number position.

3   Click the Alignment down arrow, and then select the desired alignment.

4   Click OK.

To open a header or footer box

1   On the View menu, click Header And Footer.

2   Scroll to the top of a page for the header or to the bottom of a page for the footer.

To edit a header or footer

1   On the View menu, click Header And Footer.

2   Scroll to the header or footer that you want to change.

3   Click the toolbar buttons that you want to use.

4   Type or edit the text as necessary.

To change page orientation

1   On the File menu, click Page Setup.

2   If necessary, click the Paper Size tab.

3   In the Orientation section, click the Portrait or Landscape option.

4   Click OK.

Lesson 6: Using Automated Formatting

To set AutoFormat options

1   On the Tools menu, click AutoCorrect.

2   Click the AutoFormat As You Type tab.

3   In the Apply As You Type section, click the Desired settings.

4   Click OK.

To create an automatic border

1   Position the insertion point where you want to insert the border.

2   Type three dashes (—) to create a single-line border the width of the margins.

    Or

    Type three equal signs (===) to create a double-line border the width of the margins.

3   Press Enter.

To create an automatic bulleted list

1   Position the insertion point in the desired location.

2   Type * and press the Spacebar for a bulleted list.

3   Type the list data, pressing Enter after each new list item (except the last list item).

4   Press Enter twice after the last list item is entered.

To create an automatic numbered list

1   Position the insertion point in the desired location.

2   Type 1. and press the Spacebar for a numbered list.

3   Type the list data, pressing Enter after each new list item (except the last list item).

4   Press Enter twice after the last list item is entered.

To modify bulleted and numbered lists

1   Click the first item in a numbered list, or select all the items in a bulleted list.

2   On the Format menu, click Bullets And Numbering.

3   Click either the Bulleted tab or the Numbered tab on the Bullets And Numbering dialog box.

4   Click a bullet or number style.

5   If desired, click the Customize button, make changes, and then click OK.

6   Click OK.

To copy formatting using the Format Painter

1   Select the text that has the formatting you want to copy.

Or

On the Formatting toolbar (or in the Font dialog box or the Paragraph dialog box, whichever is most appropriate), click the format attributes or styles you wish to apply.

Format Painter

2   On the Standard toolbar, click the Format Painter button.

3   Select the text to be formatted and release the mouse button.

To create an AutoText entry

1   Type the text and/or insert the picture that is to be included in the AutoText entry, and then select the text and/or picture.

2   Press Alt+F3.

3   Type a name (up to 32 characters) in the Please Name Your AutoText Entry box.

4   Click OK.

To insert an AutoText entry

1   Position the insertion point where you want to insert the entry.

2   On the Insert menu, hold the mouse pointer on AutoText to open the submenu, and then click AutoText.

3   Click the desired entry in the Enter AutoText Entries Here box.

4   Click the Insert button.

Or

1   Position the insertion point where you want to insert the entry.

2   Type the name of the AutoText entry.

3   Press F3.

To create and print an envelope

1   On the Tools menu, click Envelopes And Labels, and click the Envelopes tab.

2   Enter or edit the Delivery Address.

3   Enter or edit the Return Address.

4   Insert an envelope in the printer as shown in the Feed box.

5   Click the Print button.

To create and print a label

1   On the Tools menu, click Envelopes And Labels, and click the Labels tab.

2   Enter or edit the label address.

3   To select the label type, click the Options button, click a label type in the Product Number box, and then click OK.

4   To print a full page of labels, on the Envelopes And Labels dialog box, click Full Page Of Same Label.

5   To print a single label, click the Single Label option, and type or select the row and column where you want the label to print.

6   Insert a label page in the printer.

7   Click the Print button.

Lesson 7: Using Editing and Proofing Tools

To check the spelling of an entire document

Spelling And Grammar

1   On the Standard toolbar, click the Spelling And Grammar button.

2   Click an option in the Suggestions box, and click the Change button.

Or

To ignore the word through the document, click Ignore All.

Or

To add the word to the dictionary, click Add.

3   Click OK.

To customize the spell check operations

1   On the Tools menu, click Options.

2   Click the Spelling & Grammar tab, and make selections as desired.

3   Click OK.

To turn on grammar check for a document

1   On the Tools menu, click Options.

2   Click the Spelling & Grammar tab, if necessary.

3   Click the Check Grammar With Spelling check box to turn this feature on, and click OK.

To check the grammar of a document

Spelling And Grammar

1   On the Standard toolbar, click the Spelling And Grammar button.

2   Click the Change button to make the suggested replacement displayed in the Suggestions text box.

Or

Click the Ignore button to ignore an error; click the Ignore All button to ignore the error throughout the document.

To change grammar options

1   On the Tools menu, click Options.

2   Click the Spelling & Grammar tab, if necessary.

3   Click the Writing Style down arrow and select the desired rule guidelines.

4   Click the Settings button for more control over the writing style.

5   Click OK.

To use the thesaurus

1   Right-click the word in question.

2   Point to Synonyms on the Short-cut menu.

3   Click the synonym you want to replace.

Or

1   On the Tools menu, click language and point to Thesarus.

To perform a Find operation

1   On the Edit menu, click Find.

2   To increase Find criteria and narrow the search, click the More button to display the search options.

3   In the Find What box, type the find search string.

4   Click the Find Next button until you're finished searching, or there are no more occurrences.

5   Click the Cancel button to return to the document window.

To use Go To style

1   On the Edit menu, click Go To.

2   Select Page in the Go To What list.

3   Type the desired page number in the Enter Page Number box.

4   Click the Go To button.

To perform a Replace operation

1   On the Edit menu, click Replace.

2   To increase the Find criteria and narrow the seach, click the More button to display the search options.

3   Type the search string in the Find What box.

4   Type the replacement string in the Replace With box.

5   Click the Replace button to make the replacement; click the Replace All button to make all replacements throughout the document without confirmation.

6   Click OK.

To view AutoCorrect entries

1   On the Tools menu, click AutoCorrect.

2   Click the AutoCorrect tab, if necessary.

3   Scroll through the list at the bottom of the dialog box.

To add an exception to AutoCorrect

1   On the Tools menu, click AutoCorrect.
2   Click the AutoCorrect tab, if necessary.
3   Click the Exceptions button.
4   Click the desired tab, and type the exception.
5   Click the Add button.
6   Click OK.

To highlight text

1   Select the text you want highlighted.
2   On the Formatting toolbar, click the Highlight down arrow.
3   Click a color.

Highlight

To remove highlighted text

1   Select the highlighted text.
2   On the Formatting toolbar, click the Highlight down arrow.
3   Click None.

Highlight

To insert the date and/or time

1   On the Insert menu, click Date And Time.
2   Click the desired format.
3   Click OK.

To Insert a date as a field

1   On the Insert menu, click Field.
2   Select the desired category.
3   Select the desired field name.
4   Click OK.

To insert a special character

1   On the Insert menu, click Symbol.
2   Click the Special Characters tab.
3   Select the desired character.
4   Click the Insert button.
5   Click Close.

Lesson 8: Working with Graphics

To insert a picture into a document

Print Layout View

1   If necessary, click the Print Layout View button on the status bar.
2   Click to position the insertion point where you want to insert the picture.

3   On the Insert menu, point to Picture, and click From File.

4   In the Insert Picture dialog box, click the Look In down arrow, and select the appropriate drive and folder.

5   In the file list, click the file that you want to insert.

6   Click the Insert button.

To insert a Clip Art picture into a document

Print Layout View

1   If necessary, click the Print Layout View button on the status bar.

2   Click to position the insertion point where you want to insert the picture.

3   On the Insert menu, point to Picture, and click Clip Art.

4   If necessary, in the Insert Clip Art window, click the Picture tab.

5   Click the picture category, and click the picture that you want to insert.

6   Click the Insert Clip button on the menu that appears.

To size a picture using the sizing handles

1   Select the picture.

2   Drag the left or right sizing handles to change the horizontal width of the picture.

Or

Drag the top or bottom sizing handles to change the vertical height of the picture.

Or

Drag a corner handle to simultaneously change both the horizontal and vertical dimensions.

To change the text wrap style

Text Wrapping

1   On the Picture toolbar, click the Text Wrapping button.

2   Click to position the insertion point where you want to change the text wrap.

3   Select the desired style, and click anywhere outside the picture to deselect it.

To create WordArt

Insert WordArt

1   If necessary, on the View menu, point to Toolbars, and click Drawing.

2   On the Drawing toolbar, click the Insert WordArt button.

3   Click the desired style.

4   Type the desired text, select font and size and then click Ok.

To create an AutoShape

1   On the Drawing toolbar, click the AutoShapes button to display the AutoShapes menu.

2   On the AutoShapes menu, point to the category of shape that you want to create, and click the desired shape.

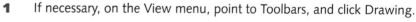

3   In the area where you want to insert the AutoShape, drag to draw the
AutoShape.

To fill a shape with color

1   Click the shape.

Fill Color

2   On the Drawing toolbar, click the Fill Color button's down arrow.

3   Click the desired fill color.

Lesson 9: Working with Columns

To create columns of equal width

1   Select the text that is to be formatted into columns. (Skip this step if
you want the entire document formatted into columns.)

Columns

2   On the Standard toolbar, click the Columns button.

3   Click the number of columns that you want, or drag the Columns menu
to the right to create more than four columns.

To create columns of unequal width using the Columns dialog box

1   Select the text to be formatted into columns.

2   On the Format menu, click Columns.

3   To create two columns of unequal width, in the Presets section, click
Left to make the left column narrower, or click Right to make the right
column narrower.

Or

To create customized columns, in the Number Of Columns box, type
the desired number of columns, clear the Equal Column Width option,
and then type the desired measurements in the Width boxes.

4   Click OK.

To adjust column widths using the Columns dialog box

1   Click the column text to be modified.

2   On the Format menu, click Columns.

3   To convert the text to two columns of unequal width, in the Presets
section, click Left to make the left column narrower, or click Right to
make the right column narrower.

Or

To customize the column widths, clear the Equal Column Width box,
and type the desired measurements in the Width boxes.

4   Click OK.

To adjust column widths using the ruler

1   Click or select the column(s) to be modified to display the ruler.

2   Position the mouse pointer on the Move Column marker.

3   Hold down the Alt key and drag the marker to adjust the column
widths.

4   When the columns are adjusted to the desired measurements, release the Alt key.

To change the spacing between columns using the Columns dialog box

1   Click the column text to be modified.

2   On the Format menu, click Columns.

3   If necessary, in the Columns dialog box, clear the Equal Column Width check box.

4   In the Spacing boxes, type the desired measurement.

5   Make adjustments to the Width boxes as desired.

6   Click OK.

To change the spacing between columns using the ruler

1   Click or select the column(s) to be modified to display the ruler.

2   On the ruler, drag the desired column marker to adjust the column spacing as desired.

To insert a manual column break using a keystroke combination

1   Move the insertion point to the location where you want to insert the break.

2   Press Ctrl+Shift+Enter.

To insert a manual column break

1   Move the insertion point to the location where you want to insert the break.

2   On the Insert menu, click Break.

3   In the Break dialog box, click the Column Break option.

4   Click OK.

To delete a manual column break

Show/Hide ¶

1   Click the Show/Hide ¶ button.

2   Position the insertion point on or to the right of the column break marker.

3   Press Delete or Backspace.

To insert a vertical line between columns

1   Click anywhere in the section that contains the columns that you want to separate with a vertical line.

2   On the Format menu, click Columns.

3   Select the Line Between check box, and click OK.

Lesson 10: Working with Tables

To insert a table using the Insert Table button

Insert Table

1   Click to position the insertion point where you want to insert the table.

2   On the Standard toolbar, click the Insert Table button.

3   On the Insert Table menu, drag the mouse pointer over the boxes and click the desired number of rows and columns.

To draw a table using the Tables And Borders button

Tables And Borders

1   On the Standard toolbar, click the Tables And Borders button.

2   Drag the mouse pointer diagonally to create the table boundaries.

3   Drag the pointer to create vertical and horizontal lines, which create the columns and rows.

4   Click the Tables And Borders button again to stop drawing.

To insert a table using the Insert Table dialog box

1   Click to position the insertion point where you want to insert the table.

2   On the Table menu, point to Insert, and click Table.

3   In the Number Of Columns box, type the number of columns that you want in the table.

4   In the Number Of Rows box, type the number of rows.

5   Click OK.

To navigate within a table

1   Click the desired cell.

2   Type the cell information

3   Press Tab to move to the next cell.

Or

Press a key combination to move to the desired location.

To select cells in a table

●   Press a key combination.

Or

Click the selection area to the left of a row.

Or

Click the top of a column.

Or

Click the bottom left corner of the cell.

To merge cells

1   Select the cells that you want to join.

2   On the Table menu, click Merge Cells.

To insert columns or rows into a table

1   Click in a cell next to where you want to insert the row or column.

2   On the Table menu, point to Insert, and click Columns To The Left, Columns To The Right, Rows Above, or Rows Below, as desired.

To delete columns or rows from a table

1   Click in the column or row that you want to delete, or select multiple rows or columns.

2   On the Table menu, point to Delete, and click Columns or Rows, depending on whether you want to delete rows or columns.

To resize an entire table

1   Position the insertion point over the table resize handle until a double-headed arrow appears.

2   Drag the handle in any direction to resize the table as desired.

To resize a column or row

1   Position the insertion point over a horizontal or vertical border anywhere in the table until a double-arrow resizing pointer appears.

2   Drag the resizing pointer in the desired direction.

To change borders in a table

Tables And Borders

1   Click anywhere in the table, and on the Standard toolbar, click the Tables And Borders button.

2   Use the toolbar buttons to select a border size and type, to draw borders, or to erase borders.

To add shading to a table

Tables And Borders

1   Select the table cells to be shaded.

2   On the Standard toolbar, click the Tables And Borders button.

3   Click the Shading Color down arrow, and click a color.

Lesson 11: Word and the Web

To create a hyperlink to a Web address

1   Type a Web address.

2   Press the Spacebar or Enter.

To create a hyperlink for a string of text

Insert Hyperlink

1   Type and select the text that you want to use as a hyperlink.

2   On the Standard toolbar, click the Insert Hyperlink button.

3   In the Type The File Or Web Page Name box, type the Web address.

4   Click OK.

To send a Word document as an attachment to an e-mail message

1   Open the document that you want to send, and then, if necessary, connect to the Internet.

2   On the File menu, point to Send To, and click Mail Recipient (As Attachment).

3   In the e-mail message window, in the To box, type the e-mail address of the recipient.

4   In the message area, type a message.

5   Click Send.

To send a Word document as the body of an e-mail message

1   Open the document that you want to send, and then, if necessary, connect to the Internet.

E-mail

2   On the Standard toolbar, click the E-mail button.

3   On the e-mail header in the To box, type the recipient's e-mail address.

4   Click Send.

To preview a Web page in the Web browser

1   Open the document that you want to preview.

2   On the File menu, click Web Page Preview.

To preview a Web page in Word

1   Open the document that you want to preview.

2   Click the Web Layout View button to the left of the horizontal scroll bar.

To save a document as a Web page

1   Save the document as a Word file.

2   On the File menu, click Save As Web Page.

3   Click Save.

Index

Special Characters

ActiveEducation and Microsoft Press

Microsoft Word 2000 Step by Step Courseware has been created by the professional trainers and writers at ActiveEducation, Inc., to the exacting standards you've come to expect from Microsoft Press. Together, we are pleased to present this training guide.

ActiveEducation creates top-quality information technology training content that teaches essential computer skills for today's workplace. ActiveEducation courses are designed to provide the most effective training available and to help people become more productive computer users. Each ActiveEducation course, including this book, undergoes rigorous quality control, instructional design, and technical review procedures to ensure that the course is instructionally and technically superior in content and approach.

ActiveEducation (*www.activeeducation.com*) courses are available in book form and on the Internet.

Microsoft Press is the book publishing division of Microsoft Corporation, the leading publisher of information about Microsoft products and services. Microsoft Press is dedicated to providing the highest quality computer books and multimedia training and reference tools that make using Microsoft software easier, more enjoyable, and more productive.

About the Authors

Core Skills

Ron Pronk is the author of more than a dozen books on computers, including *Windows 3.1 Insider* (John Wiley & Sons) and *Digital Camera Companion* (Coriolis Group Books). He is a two-time recipient of the Award of Excellence and two-time recipient of the Award of Merit from the Society for Technical Communicators and has served as an instructional design consultant for such companies as Delmar Publishing, Mitchell Press, South-Western Publishing, West Publishing, Coriolis Group Books, and National Computer Systems. He is also a certified Microsoft Word Expert.

Lori Bottom has been writing technical documentation for over 10 years. She has written HTML-Help and WinHelp systems, printed manuals, and training materials in a variety of industries, including healthcare, manufacturing, financial, and engineering design. Lori has combined hobby and career to co-author two award-winning books in the sewing industry. Formerly from California, she now lives in Vermont and enjoys the snow and the leaves of the beautiful Green Mountains. In addition to sewing, Lori enjoys skiing, hiking, and swimming.

See clearly—
now!

Here's the remarkable, *visual* way to quickly find answers about the powerfully integrated features of the Microsoft Office 2000 applications. Microsoft Press® AT A GLANCE books let you focus on particular tasks and show you, with clear, numbered steps, the easiest way to get them done right now. Put Office 2000 to work today with AT A GLANCE learning solutions, made by Microsoft.

- MICROSOFT OFFICE 2000 PROFESSIONAL AT A GLANCE
- MICROSOFT WORD 2000 AT A GLANCE
- MICROSOFT EXCEL 2000 AT A GLANCE
- MICROSOFT POWERPOINT® 2000 AT A GLANCE
- MICROSOFT ACCESS 2000 AT A GLANCE
- MICROSOFT FRONTPAGE® 2000 AT A GLANCE
- MICROSOFT PUBLISHER 2000 AT A GLANCE
- MICROSOFT OFFICE 2000 SMALL BUSINESS AT A GLANCE
- MICROSOFT PHOTODRAW™ 2000 AT A GLANCE
- MICROSOFT OUTLOOK® 2000 AT A GLANCE

Microsoft®

mspress.microsoft.com

Stay in the *running* for maximum productivity.

These are *the* answer books for business users of Microsoft Office 2000. They are packed with everything from quick, clear instructions for new users to comprehensive answers for power users—the authoritative reference to keep by your computer and use every day. The RUNNING series—learning solutions made by Microsoft.

- RUNNING MICROSOFT® EXCEL 2000
- RUNNING MICROSOFT OFFICE 2000 PREMIUM
- RUNNING MICROSOFT OFFICE 2000 PROFESSIONAL
- RUNNING MICROSOFT OFFICE 2000 SMALL BUSINESS
- RUNNING MICROSOFT WORD 2000
- RUNNING MICROSOFT POWERPOINT® 2000
- RUNNING MICROSOFT ACCESS 2000
- RUNNING MICROSOFT FRONTPAGE® 2000
- RUNNING MICROSOFT OUTLOOK® 2000

mspress.microsoft.com

up! Step

STEP BY STEP books provide quick and easy self-training—to help you learn to use the powerful word processing, spreadsheet, database, presentation, communication, and Internet components of Microsoft Office 2000—both individually and together. The easy-to-follow lessons present clear objectives and real-world business examples, with numerous screen shots and illustrations. Put Office 2000 to work today with STEP BY STEP learning solutions, made by Microsoft.

- MICROSOFT® OFFICE 2000 8-IN-1 STEP BY STEP
- MICROSOFT WORD 2000 STEP BY STEP
- MICROSOFT EXCEL 2000 STEP BY STEP
- MICROSOFT POWERPOINT® 2000 STEP BY STEP
- MICROSOFT PUBLISHER 2000 STEP BY STEP
- MICROSOFT ACCESS 2000 STEP BY STEP
- MICROSOFT FRONTPAGE® 2000 STEP BY STEP
- MICROSOFT OUTLOOK® 2000 STEP BY STEP

mspress.microsoft.com

Maximize the potential of Microsoft Office 2000—
on your PC and on the Web!

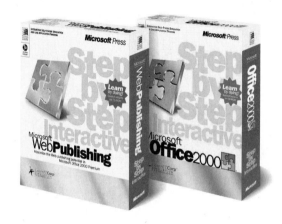

MICROSOFT OFFICE 2000 STEP BY STEP INTERACTIVE

U.S.A. **$29.99**

U.K. £20.99 [V.A.T. included]

Canada $44.99

[*Recommended*]

ISBN: 0-7356-0506-8

WEB PUBLISHING STEP BY STEP INTERACTIVE

U.S.A. **$29.99**

U.K. £20.99 [V.A.T. included]

Canada $44.99

[*Recommended*]

ISBN: 0-7356-0651-X

MICROSOFT® OFFICE 2000 STEP BY STEP INTERACTIVE and WEB PUBLISHING STEP BY STEP INTERACTIVE are the perfect multimedia learning solutions to help you get the most out of Microsoft Office 2000. MICROSOFT OFFICE 2000 STEP BY STEP INTERACTIVE shows you how to maximize the productivity potential of all the programs in the Office 2000 suite. And WEB PUBLISHING STEP BY STEP INTERACTIVE is the fast way to learn how to use all the Web publishing tools and features in Microsoft Office 2000 Premium. Build your skills quickly using real-life exercises, conceptual overviews, concrete examples, live practice, and built-in assessment tools. Get both learning systems to get productive and get on the Web fast!

mspress.microsoft.com

MICROSOFT LICENSE AGREEMENT
Book Companion CD

IMPORTANT—READ CAREFULLY: This Microsoft End-User License Agreement ("EULA") is a legal agreement between you (either an individual or an entity) and Microsoft Corporation for the Microsoft product identified above, which includes computer software and may include associated media, printed materials, and "online" or electronic documentation ("SOFTWARE PRODUCT"). Any component included within the SOFTWARE PRODUCT that is accompanied by a separate End-User License Agreement shall be governed by such agreement and not the terms set forth below. By installing, copying, or otherwise using the SOFTWARE PRODUCT, you agree to be bound by the terms of this EULA. If you do not agree to the terms of this EULA, you are not authorized to install, copy, or otherwise use the SOFTWARE PRODUCT; you may, however, return the SOFTWARE PRODUCT, along with all printed materials and other items that form a part of the Microsoft product that includes the SOFTWARE PRODUCT, to the place you obtained them for a full refund.

SOFTWARE PRODUCT LICENSE

The SOFTWARE PRODUCT is protected by United States copyright laws and international copyright treaties, as well as other intellectual property laws and treaties. The SOFTWARE PRODUCT is licensed, not sold.

1. **GRANT OF LICENSE.** This EULA grants you the following rights:

   a. **Software Product.** You may install and use one copy of the SOFTWARE PRODUCT on a single computer. The primary user of the computer on which the SOFTWARE PRODUCT is installed may make a second copy for his or her exclusive use on a portable computer.

   b. **Storage/Network Use.** You may also store or install a copy of the SOFTWARE PRODUCT on a storage device, such as a network server, used only to install or run the SOFTWARE PRODUCT on your other computers over an internal network; however, you must acquire and dedicate a license for each separate computer on which the SOFTWARE PRODUCT is installed or run from the storage device. A license for the SOFTWARE PRODUCT may not be shared or used concurrently on different computers.

   c. **License Pak.** If you have acquired this EULA in a Microsoft License Pak, you may make the number of additional copies of the computer software portion of the SOFTWARE PRODUCT authorized on the printed copy of this EULA, and you may use each copy in the manner specified above. You are also entitled to make a corresponding number of secondary copies for portable computer use as specified above.

   d. **Sample Code.** Solely with respect to portions, if any, of the SOFTWARE PRODUCT that are identified within the SOFTWARE PRODUCT as sample code (the "SAMPLE CODE"):

      i. **Use and Modification.** Microsoft grants you the right to use and modify the source code version of the SAMPLE CODE, *provided* you comply with subsection (d)(iii) below. You may not distribute the SAMPLE CODE, or any modified version of the SAMPLE CODE, in source code form.

      ii. **Redistributable Files.** Provided you comply with subsection (d)(iii) below, Microsoft grants you a nonexclusive, royalty-free right to reproduce and distribute the object code version of the SAMPLE CODE and of any modified SAMPLE CODE, other than SAMPLE CODE, or any modified version thereof, designated as not redistributable in the Readme file that forms a part of the SOFTWARE PRODUCT (the "Non-Redistributable Sample Code"). All SAMPLE CODE other than the Non-Redistributable Sample Code is collectively referred to as the "REDISTRIBUTABLES."

      iii. **Redistribution Requirements.** If you redistribute the REDISTRIBUTABLES, you agree to: (i) distribute the REDISTRIBUTABLES in object code form only in conjunction with and as a part of your software application product; (ii) not use Microsoft's name, logo, or trademarks to market your software application product; (iii) include a valid copyright notice on your software application product; (iv) indemnify, hold harmless, and defend Microsoft from and against any claims or lawsuits, including attorney's fees, that arise or result from the use or distribution of your software application product; and (v) not permit further distribution of the REDISTRIBUTABLES by your end user. Contact Microsoft for the applicable royalties due and other licensing terms for all other uses and/or distribution of the REDISTRIBUTABLES.

2. **DESCRIPTION OF OTHER RIGHTS AND LIMITATIONS.**

   - **Limitations on Reverse Engineering, Decompilation, and Disassembly.** You may not reverse engineer, decompile, or disassemble the SOFTWARE PRODUCT, except and only to the extent that such activity is expressly permitted by applicable law notwithstanding this limitation.

   - **Separation of Components.** The SOFTWARE PRODUCT is licensed as a single product. Its component parts may not be separated for use on more than one computer.

   - **Rental.** You may not rent, lease, or lend the SOFTWARE PRODUCT.

   - **Support Services.** Microsoft may, but is not obligated to, provide you with support services related to the SOFTWARE PRODUCT ("Support Services"). Use of Support Services is governed by the Microsoft policies and programs described in the user manual, in "online" documentation, and/or in other Microsoft-provided materials. Any supplemental software code provided to you as part of the Support Services shall be considered part of the SOFTWARE PRODUCT and subject to the terms and conditions of this EULA. With respect to technical information you provide to Microsoft as part of the Support Services, Microsoft may use such information for its business purposes, including for product support and development. Microsoft will not utilize such technical information in a form that personally identifies you.

   - **Software Transfer.** You may permanently transfer all of your rights under this EULA, provided you retain no copies, you transfer all of the SOFTWARE PRODUCT (including all component parts, the media and printed materials, any upgrades, this EULA, and, if applicable, the Certificate of Authenticity), **and** the recipient agrees to the terms of this EULA.

   - **Termination.** Without prejudice to any other rights, Microsoft may terminate this EULA if you fail to comply with the terms and conditions of this EULA. In such event, you must destroy all copies of the SOFTWARE PRODUCT and all of its component parts.

3. COPYRIGHT. All title and copyrights in and to the SOFTWARE PRODUCT (including but not limited to any images, photographs, animations, video, audio, music, text, SAMPLE CODE, REDISTRIBUTABLES, and "applets" incorporated into the SOFTWARE PRODUCT) and any copies of the SOFTWARE PRODUCT are owned by Microsoft or its suppliers. The SOFTWARE PRODUCT is protected by copyright laws and international treaty provisions. Therefore, you must treat the SOFTWARE PRODUCT like any other copyrighted material **except** that you may install the SOFTWARE PRODUCT on a single computer provided you keep the original solely for backup or archival purposes. You may not copy the printed materials accompanying the SOFTWARE PRODUCT.

4. U.S. GOVERNMENT RESTRICTED RIGHTS. The SOFTWARE PRODUCT and documentation are provided with RESTRICTED RIGHTS. Use, duplication, or disclosure by the Government is subject to restrictions as set forth in subparagraph (c)(1)(ii) of the Rights in Technical Data and Computer Software clause at DFARS 252.227-7013 or subparagraphs (c)(1) and (2) of the Commercial Computer Software—Restricted Rights at 48 CFR 52.227-19, as applicable. Manufacturer is Microsoft Corporation/One Microsoft Way/Redmond, WA 98052-6399.

5. EXPORT RESTRICTIONS. You agree that you will not export or re-export the SOFTWARE PRODUCT, any part thereof, or any process or service that is the direct product of the SOFTWARE PRODUCT (the foregoing collectively referred to as the "Restricted Components"), to any country, person, entity, or end user subject to U.S. export restrictions. You specifically agree not to export or re-export any of the Restricted Components (i) to any country to which the U.S. has embargoed or restricted the export of goods or services, which currently include, but are not necessarily limited to, Cuba, Iran, Iraq, Libya, North Korea, Sudan, and Syria, or to any national of any such country, wherever located, who intends to transmit or transport the Restricted Components back to such country; (ii) to any end user who you know or have reason to know will utilize the Restricted Components in the design, development, or production of nuclear, chemical, or biological weapons; or (iii) to any end user who has been prohibited from participating in U.S. export transactions by any federal agency of the U.S. government. You warrant and represent that neither the BXA nor any other U.S. federal agency has suspended, revoked, or denied your export privileges.

DISCLAIMER OF WARRANTY

NO WARRANTIES OR CONDITIONS. MICROSOFT EXPRESSLY DISCLAIMS ANY WARRANTY OR CONDITION FOR THE SOFT-WARE PRODUCT. THE SOFTWARE PRODUCT AND ANY RELATED DOCUMENTATION ARE PROVIDED "AS IS" WITHOUT WARRANTY OR CONDITION OF ANY KIND, EITHER EXPRESS OR IMPLIED, INCLUDING, WITHOUT LIMITATION, THE IMPLIED WARRANTIES OF MERCHANTABILITY, FITNESS FOR A PARTICULAR PURPOSE, OR NONINFRINGEMENT. THE ENTIRE RISK ARISING OUT OF USE OR PERFORMANCE OF THE SOFTWARE PRODUCT REMAINS WITH YOU.

LIMITATION OF LIABILITY. TO THE MAXIMUM EXTENT PERMITTED BY APPLICABLE LAW, IN NO EVENT SHALL MICROSOFT OR ITS SUPPLIERS BE LIABLE FOR ANY SPECIAL, INCIDENTAL, INDIRECT, OR CONSEQUENTIAL DAMAGES WHATSOEVER (INCLUDING, WITHOUT LIMITATION, DAMAGES FOR LOSS OF BUSINESS PROFITS, BUSINESS INTERRUPTION, LOSS OF BUSINESS INFORMATION, OR ANY OTHER PECUNIARY LOSS) ARISING OUT OF THE USE OF OR INABILITY TO USE THE SOFTWARE PRODUCT OR THE PROVISION OF OR FAILURE TO PROVIDE SUPPORT SERVICES, EVEN IF MICROSOFT HAS BEEN ADVISED OF THE POSSIBILITY OF SUCH DAMAGES. IN ANY CASE, MICROSOFT'S ENTIRE LIABILITY UNDER ANY PROVISION OF THIS EULA SHALL BE LIMITED TO THE GREATER OF THE AMOUNT ACTUALLY PAID BY YOU FOR THE SOFTWARE PRODUCT OR US$5.00; PROVIDED, HOWEVER, IF YOU HAVE ENTERED INTO A MICROSOFT SUPPORT SERVICES AGREEMENT, MICROSOFT'S ENTIRE LIABILITY REGARDING SUPPORT SERVICES SHALL BE GOVERNED BY THE TERMS OF THAT AGREE-MENT. BECAUSE SOME STATES AND JURISDICTIONS DO NOT ALLOW THE EXCLUSION OR LIMITATION OF LIABILITY, THE ABOVE LIMITATION MAY NOT APPLY TO YOU.

MISCELLANEOUS

This EULA is governed by the laws of the State of Washington USA, except and only to the extent that applicable law mandates governing law of a different jurisdiction.

Should you have any questions concerning this EULA, or if you desire to contact Microsoft for any reason, please contact the Microsoft subsidi-ary serving your country, or write: Microsoft Sales Information Center/One Microsoft Way/Redmond, WA 98052-6399.

Proof of Purchase

0-7356-0699-

Do not send this card with your registration.
Use this card as proof of purchase if participating in a promotion or rebate offer on *Microsoft® Word 2000 Step by Step Courseware Core Skills Student Guide*.
Card must be used in conjunction with other proof(s) of payment such as your dated sales receipt—see offer details.

Microsoft® Word 2000 Step by Step Courseware Core Skills Student Guide

WHERE DID YOU PURCHASE THIS PRODUCT?

CUSTOMER NAME

Microsoft®

mspress.microsoft.com

Microsoft Press, PO Box 97017, Redmond, WA 98073-9830

OWNER REGISTRATION CARD

Register Today!

0-7356-0699-4

Return the bottom portion of this card to register today.

Microsoft® Word 2000 Step by Step Courseware Core Skills Student Guide

FIRST NAME | MIDDLE INITIAL | LAST NAME

INSTITUTION OR COMPANY NAME

ADDRESS

CITY | STATE | ZIP

E-MAIL ADDRESS | ( ) PHONE NUMBER

U.S. and Canada addresses only. Fill in information above and mail postage-free.
Please mail only the bottom half of this page.

For information about Microsoft Press®
products, visit our Web site at
mspress.microsoft.com